Alien Zone

Alien Zone

Cultural Theory and Contemporary Science Fiction Cinema

Edited by
ANNETTE KUHN

VERSO
London · New York

First published by Verso 1990
This collection © Annette Kuhn 1990
Fifth impression 1998

Verso
UK: 6 Meard Street, London W1V 3 HR
USA: 180 Varick Street, New York, NY 10014-4606

Verso is the imprint of New Left Books

British Library Cataloguing in Publication Data

Alien zone : cultural theory and contemporary science
    fiction cinema.
    1. Cinema films: Science fictions films – Encyclopaedias
    1. Kuhn, Annette, *1945-*
791.43'09'0915

ISBN 0-86091-278-7
ISBN 0-86091-993-5 pbk

Library of Congress in Cataloging-in-Publication Data

Alien zone : cultural theory and contemporary science fiction cinema /
    edited by Annette Kuhn.
        p.   cm.
    ISBN 0-86091-278-7. – ISBN 0-86091-993-5 (pbk.)
    1. Science fiction films-History and criticism. I. Kuhn,
Annette.
PN1995.9.S26A818   1990
791.43'656-dc20

Printed in Finland by Werner Söderström Osakeyhtiö
Typeset in Times by Leaper & Gard Ltd, Bristol, England

Contents

Acknowledgements

The editor and publishers wish to thank copyright holders of material previously published elsewhere for their permission to reprint the following items in the present volume.

'Visions of the Future in Science Fiction Films from 1970 to 1982' was previously published under the title 'Don't Look Where We're Going: Visions of the Future in Science Fiction Films, 1970–82' in *Science Fiction Studies*, vol. 10, no. 1 (1983); and in *Shadows of the Magic Lamp*, edited by George E. Slusser and Eric S. Rabkin, Southern Illinois University Press, 1985. It is reprinted by permission of the author and *Science Fiction Studies*, copyright © 1982 by H. Bruce Franklin.

'The Alien Messiah' is excerpted from 'The Alien Messiah in Recent Science Fiction Films', *Journal of Popular Film and TV*, vol. 14, no. 4 (1987) by permission of the Helen Dwight Reid Educational Foundation; published by Heldref Publications, 4000 Albemarle St N.W., Washington DC 20016, copyright © 1987.

'Commodity Futures' was originally published in *Science Fiction Studies*, vol. 14, no. 3 (1987) under the title 'Commodity Futures: Corporate State and Personal Style in Three Science Fiction Movies'. 'Making Culture Into Nature' was originally published in *Science Fiction Studies*, vol. 7, no. 3 (1980) under the title 'Making Culture Into Nature: Or Who Put the "Special" Into "Special Effects"?'. 'Feminism and Anxiety in *Alien*' was originally published as part of 'Symposium on *Alien*' in *Science Fiction Studies*, vol. 7, no. 3 (1980). All three articles appear in this volume by permission of *Science Fiction Studies*.

'Technophobia' is reprinted from *Camera Politica: Politics and Ideology of the Contemporary Hollywood Film*, by Michael Ryan and Douglas Kellner, Indiana University Press, 1988, with permission of Indiana University Press.

'Feminism, Humanism and Science in *Alien*' was first published in

October, no. 13 (1980) under the title '"Son of a Bitch": Feminism, Humanism and Science in *Alien*', and is reprinted here by kind permission of James H. Kavanagh.

'Primal Conditions and Conventions: the Genre of Science Fiction' is a shortened version of 'Primal Conditions and Conventions: the Genres of Comedy and Science Fiction', originally published in *Film/Psychology Review*, vol. 4, no. 1 (1980).

'The Virginity of Astronauts: Sex and the Science Fiction Film' is a shortened version of a chapter of the same title in *Shadows of the Magic Lamp*, edited by George E. Slusser and Eric S. Rabkin, Southern Illinois University Press, 1985, and appears in this volume by kind permission of Vivian Sobchack.

'Time Travel, Primal Scene and the Critical Dystopia' is a slightly shortened version of an article published under the same title in *Camera Obscura*, no. 15 (1986), and is reprinted by kind permission of Constance Penley.

'*Alien* and the Monstrous-Feminine' is excerpted from 'Horror and the Monstrous-Feminine: an Imaginary Abjection', *Screen*, vol. 27, no. 1 (1986). 'Gynesis, Postmodernism and the Science Fiction Horror Film' is excerpted from 'From Here to Modernity: Feminism and Post-modernism', *Screen*, vol. 28, no. 2 (1987). Both items are reprinted by permission of *Screen* and Barbara Creed.

'The Doubles of Fantasy and the Space of Desire' is reprinted from *Film Criticism*, vol. 7, no. 1 (1982) with permission of *Film Criticism*.

'Cataract Surgery: Cinema in the Year 2000' was originally published in *Cahiers du cinéma*, no. 386 (1986) under the title 'L'operation de la cataracte', and appears in English translation by permission of *Cahiers du cinéma*.

'Ramble City: Postmodernism and *Blade Runner*' is reprinted from *October*, no. 41 (1987) by permission of MIT Press, Cambridge, Massachusetts, copyright © 1987 by the Massachusetts Institute of Technology and October Magazine Ltd.

The articles '"You've Got To Be Fucking Kidding!" Knowledge, Belief and Judgement in Science Fiction', 'Who Programs You? The Science Fiction of the Spectacle', and 'Feminist Futures: A Generic Study' were written especially for this volume. Thanks are due to authors Steve Neale, Scott Bukatman and Anne Cranny-Francis.

Stills are from films distributed by Twentieth Century Fox (*Alien*), Columbia (*Close Encounters of the Third Kind*), Palace Pictures (*Videodrome*), Warner Bros (*Blade Runner*), and the Smithsonian Institution's National Air and Space Museum (*The Dream Is Alive*); they are supplied courtesy of the National Film Archive.

Cultural Theory and Science Fiction Cinema

Annette Kuhn

Science fiction cinema has an immense popular following. Newly released blockbusters attract huge audiences, and older films are revived again and again – in the large cinema chains during school holidays, as cult classics in art houses and on television. There are numerous sci-fi fanzines; entire journals are devoted to showing and explaining the special effects technologies behind images of space flight, extraterrestrial worlds, and alien monsters; and publishers produce a steady stream of coffee-table books filled with glossy colour stills from science fiction films. And yet science fiction cinema has never received the degree of critical and theoretical attention devoted to other film genres – or indeed to science fiction literature. Is this yet another manifestation of an elitism which regards popular media and genres as beneath serious critical attention?

One of the problems here must be the very difficulty of arriving at a critical definition of science fiction cinema as a genre, even if it is readily recognizable in practice. This is true to some extent of all film genres, a fact which, for reasons which should become clear, has been regarded as a serious methodological drawback to genre criticism. But as a genre, science fiction also has reasons of its own for being hard to pin down. For one thing, it overlaps with other types of films, notably horror and fantasy; and efforts to draw lines of demarcation between science fiction and its neighbouring genres have proved on the whole unsatisfactory: though perhaps more interesting, and probably more important, than what a film genre *is* is the question of what, in cultural terms, it *does* – its 'cultural instrumentality'.

In considering the cultural instrumentality of science fiction film, it is essential to bear in mind that we are talking precisely about fiction –

about stories and the telling of stories, narratives and narration. But we are talking about cinema, too: science fiction cinema tells its stories through this medium as against any of the others in which science fictions have been narrated – novels, comic books, radio, television even. It is through these two terms – narrative and cinema – and their interrelation, that a consideration of the cultural instrumentality of science fiction as a film genre may usefully be approached. Before addressing the specific generic qualities of science fiction, though, some broader consideration of the ways in which the notion of genre has itself been understood and put to use as a critical category within film theory is in order.

The history of the concept of genre, first of all in literary criticism and then in its application to a study of cinema, is well documented elsewhere.[1] It is important to note, though, that genre criticism in cinema has had a history and an impulse which sets it apart somewhat from literary genre studies. Its origins (usually dated to the late 1950s) lie in a populist reaction to the perceived elitism of a film criticism which stressed authorship – the genius or the creativity of one individual, usually male, and usually the director – as the key to understanding films. By contrast with this approach, the notion of genre, applied to cinema, could highlight the industrial and collective nature of the medium as well as its qualities as popular art or mass entertainment. It could also bring the cinema audience into the critical equation, because genre films can be understood in terms of expectations: expectations on the part of audiences that films will provide the security of generic conventions whilst promising the pleasure, and limiting the risk, of the new, the unexpected: a kind of contract between the film industry and cinema audiences, perhaps. Genre criticism within film theory, then, was motivated originally by a populist impulse, and had a sociological edge, qualities lacking in many literary approaches to the genre. Through all the vicissitudes of genre criticism within film theory, these two qualities – populism and social concern – have, in one form or another, remained.

Film genre criticism has enjoyed several ups and suffered a good many downs. Its theoretical trajectory, echoing changes of focus within film theory more generally, describes a move away from sociology and towards psychoanalysis as the dominant explanatory model. But this would imply a more even and less contradictory passage than has actually taken place. In particular, genre criticism has been vitiated from the start by an uneasy relationship between *genre* on the one hand – broad theories of how genre works in cinema, and *genres* on the other – studies of individual film genres: the western, the gangster film, film noir, and so on. The former could readily adopt the lofty, but by the same token rather abstract, sociological view that genre operates as the key term in a relationship between film industry, film texts and audiences. The latter, on the other hand, focussing more closely on the formal organization of film texts, has been dogged by problems of methodology, notably by apriorism, an 'empiricist dilemma' facing every attempt to define and delimit specific film genres. In 1973, sociologist Andrew Tudor summed up the difficulty thus:

> we are caught in a circle which first requires that the films are isolated, for which purpose a criterion [for defining a genre] is necessary, but the criterion is, in turn, meant to emerge from the empirically established common characteristics of the films.[2]

Although this dilemma was never really resolved, studies of individual film genres nevertheless did proceed, at first via descriptions of shared surface conventions of plot and iconography across groupings of film texts defined in advance as belonging to a particular genre. This emphasis on surface conventions was then challenged by structuralist-style analyses, modelled on anthropologist Claude Lévi-Strauss's work on myth, of underlying codes or structural oppositions governing all films belonging to a genre. But studies of genre, and to a certain extent also of genres, soon fell into a decline – which has been attributed to the influence of semiotics, psychoanalysis and latterly feminism on developments in film theory. Certainly, genre virtually disappeared from the critical agenda as film theory increasingly preoccupied itself either with close readings of individual films or with the production across the whole of cinema of certain forms of pleasure. By the late 1970s, genre, situated between the film text and what was now termed the cinematic apparatus, had dropped from view.

In 1980, however, Steve Neale made an attempt to revive genre criticism, shifting its theoretical grounding to take account of the very developments in film theory which had brought about its eclipse. To a concern – informed by current developments in film theory – with meaning, or signification, and with the ways in which spectators are addressed and subjectivities formed in their interactions with film texts, Neale added a post-Althusserian consideration of the relationship between cinema and its social and economic conditions of existence:

> What is required is a set of concepts with which the pressure of genre can begin to be located: in terms of the relations of subjectivity involved; in terms of the structures and practices both of the cinematic institution as a whole and of that sector known variously as 'Hollywood' or as 'the commercial cinema'; and in terms of the determinants and effects of each of these within and across the social formation and its component areas.[3]

This approach would allow cinema to be considered in its totality as a social practice; and genre and genres to be understood as components of this totality, the cinematic apparatus: 'systems of orientations, expectations and conventions that circulate between industry, text and subject'.[4]

One of the benefits of this model of genre was that it situated the spectator's active enjoyment of a film within the whole 'machine' of cinema. If genres occupied the gap between text and cinematic apparatus, the relation between all three could now be theorized. Neale's programme, accommodating as it did a variety of instances or levels – and also the possibility of contradiction between these component parts of the apparatus – offered a potentially dynamic, fluid and processual model of genre and genres. This model remains exploratory and programmatic, however: references to particular film genres are brief and serve mainly as illustrations of a more general argument. Unfortunately, the model for the study of film genre set out by Neale was not taken up or developed, and the field of genre criticism has lain virtually uncultivated for almost a decade.

One consequence of the uneven development of genre criticism has been its almost haphazard treatment of different film genres: critical approaches have varied enormously, and some genres have received a great deal more attention than others. Must it be concluded from this that theoretical and methodological approaches taken to the study of film genres have been governed by the distinctive characteristics of various genres? Or is it perhaps the case that particular genres were singled out for study in the degree to which they appeared to accord with critical methods currently available – or in fashion?

As a number of writers have pointed out, genre criticism of the late 1960s and early 1970s preoccupied itself almost exclusively with two genres: the gangster movie and the western.[5] Writings on gangster films, stressing their visual, iconographic features, represented an early step towards criticism of film as film, of cinema as a medium in its own right. Critical work on the western – another traditionally male genre, with its mythic, sometimes biblical, sometimes Oedipal, themes – seemed readily to accommodate itself to a 'deep structures' approach. Other genres which have subsequently received critical attention – film noir, the musical, the Hollywood melodrama and its subgenres – have done so under the pressure of developments in feminist film theory rather than in genre criticism.[6] Such studies have consequently addressed themselves to issues central to the former rather than the latter – questions like female narrative agency, woman as spectacle, female spectatorship – advancing genre criticism only incidentally, if at all.

Genre criticism, then, appears to have been led by broader developments in film theory rather than by any concern to understand, say, the cultural instrumentalities of genre or genres. Aside from a consequent unevenness of approach across studies of those film genres which have actually come under scrutiny, others have suffered serious critical and theoretical neglect. The forgotten genres include groups of films popularly recognized as genres, presenting high profiles as marketing categories within and outside the film industry, and in some cases enjoying significant grassroots followings. Comedy, science fiction and (perhaps decreasingly) horror stand out especially as film genres with high popular, but relatively low critical, profiles.[7]

Science fiction cinema has certainly not entirely bypassed critical attention; but such work as exists is a long way from constituting a coherent body of genre criticism. There have, of course, been a number of readings of individual films belonging to the genre: but these are precisely textual analyses, and are not as a rule offered as contributions to genre criticism. Attempts at more broadly based cultural commentary on science fiction cinema have been few and far between. If science fiction cinema as a *genre* has been neglected, however, there has lately been an upsurge of interest in certain science fiction *films*. This seems to be due largely to the appearance, in the past ten years or so, of a handful of films which have caught the attention of film theorists and cultural critics. However, this interest has so far not extended to systematic generic analyses of science fiction cinema. This state of affairs is undoubtedly connected with the low fortunes of the concept of genre within film theory: genre is at present frankly unfashionable. In these circumstances, any attempt to define science fiction as a film genre calls for a piecing together of fragments from a critical literature on science fiction films which has rarely addressed science fiction cinema as a genre.[8]

Writers on literary science fiction, who are less shy than film theorists about discussing science fiction as a genre, draw attention to a set of oft-repeated themes in science fiction stories. These include the conflict between science and technology on the one hand and human nature on the other, and themes of spatial and temporal displacement. The recurrence across such themes of particular accoutrements of science fictional worlds – unfamiliar technologies, futuristic devices, and so on – has also been noted. Themes and accoutrements – the latter in the shape of iconographic motifs of spaceships, robots, computers and the like – may readily be extended to a consideration of science fiction cinema.[9] Some critics writing about literary science fiction suggest that stance, or viewpoint, on the themes of science fiction stories may also be regarded as a generic indicator.[10] Science fiction might, then, usefully be defined in

terms of its narrative viewpoints as well as its thematics and icono-
graphies: *is* science fiction associated with particular modes of
narration? But it becomes questionable at this point to extend literary
definitions to cinema without also taking into account film 'language',
cinema's specific qualities as a narrative medium. Might it, for example,
be less readily said of science fiction as a cinematic – as against a literary
– genre that it proposes estrangement or uncertainty through narrative
viewpoint?

Despite the difficulties, though, literary definitions of science fiction
can offer a useful starting point for thinking about science fiction as a
film genre. In particular, they suggest that key features of the genre
might be its construction of particular types of fictional worlds and
narrative themes, and its enactment of certain narrative viewpoints and
modes of address. Attention to aspects of narration can be specified in
relation to film by considering how, by means of its own 'language', the
medium of cinema organizes the telling of science fiction stories. In
other words, science fiction cinema is usefully looked at in terms not
merely of narrative themes and viewpoints, but also – and perhaps more
significantly – of the cinematic image; at the levels of iconography and
mise-en-scène, certainly, but also – and especially – in terms of film's
own 'language', its 'specifically cinematic codes'.

Indeed, the most obvious difference between science fiction as literature and science fiction as film lies in the latter's mobilization of the
visible, the spectacle. If cinema is one among a number of narrative
media, it also has its own language, its own codes, through which it
makes meaning and tells stories. These codes derive from cinema's
capacity to *show* the fictional worlds of the narratives it creates, literally
putting them on display for spectators to look at. The peculiar qualities
of cinematic storytelling hinge crucially on the very visibility of the film
image, and on the fact that 'reading' a film necessarily involves looking
at it. In 'classical' cinema, narration and visibility are so closely inter-
twined that to the casual observer they will usually appear inseparable:
sound, image and story are welded together, and it takes a work of
deconstruction to pull them apart in order to trace the processes through
which films produce their meanings.[11]

If such codes of visibility operate in some way or other in all of classical cinema, they are likely to be inflected in specific ways in different
film genres, science fiction included. For example, many science fiction
films create particular kinds of fictional worlds, worlds which present
themselves as other, or outside everyday reality – deep space, the inner
geography of spacecraft, the contours of alien planets. At the same time,
these worlds are quite 'readable' for the spectator, for they are
constructed through science fiction's iconographic conventions. The

image merely *signifies* unfamiliarity through familiar sets of codes: strangeness is not as a rule proposed in the film's narrative viewpoint. The story is understandable and pleasurable, and its fictional world plausible in its own terms. At the same time, codes of visibility may at moments exceed narrative requirements: but this too is subsumable to generic conventions. Thus in particular ways in science fiction cinema, spectacle can become an end in itself: spectacular visual effects and sounds temporarily interrupt the flow of the narrative, inviting the spectator to contemplate, with awe and wonder, the vastness of deep space or the technological miracles of future societies.

While there has been little, if indeed any, systematic analytical consideration of the generic features of science fiction cinema, critical writing on science fiction films does tend to assume certain shared understandings about the genre. Such assumptions also mark the rare, and always brief, references to science fiction film to be found in works of genre criticism. While these assumptions remain unelaborated, certain regularities in the generic characteristics attributed to science fiction films do emerge from the critical literature. Perhaps the most commonly adduced, and most theoretically elaborated, of these relate to narrativity. A preoccupation with the sorts of stories told in science fiction films sometimes extends to a concern with how these stories are told. The critical literature ranges across questions such as surface features of plot and characterization, narrative structures and underlying themes, narrative viewpoint and enunciation.

Less common, but relatively highly theorized, are discussions of science fiction cinema which focus on its iconography and its cinematic 'language'. Cinematic codes specific to science fiction as against other film genres are seen to be at work especially in special effects of sound and vision. It is its association with these effects, or so the argument goes, that makes science fiction the most cinematic of all film genres. This is not only because, for the best effect, science fiction films must be seen and heard in cinema auditoria; but also because the technology of cinematic illusion displays the state of its own art in science fiction films. Since the films themselves are often about new or imagined future technologies, this must be a perfect example of the medium fitting, if not exactly being, the message.

Lastly, widespread but largely untheorized, is an assumption that science fiction films operate within a network of meanings (and indeed actions) which extends beyond the films themselves. This assumption is at stake, for example, in arguments that science fiction films have certain 'effects' in society, or that they evoke particular behavioural or emotional responses in those who see them. Such views range from a strong, but usually untheorized, appeal to conventional wisdom about

the effects films have on people's behaviour (though such 'effects' arguments are rare in discussions of science fiction films, being more
characteristic of commentary on horror and pornography), through to
more overtly theoretical arguments concerning the ways in which
cinema, film genres and film texts express, enact and produce ideologies.
These arguments in turn raise questions about the relationship between
cultural practices and the 'real world', between films or film genres and
society. Critics wary of the distinction between representation and
reality which underlies these arguments may argue instead that science
fiction films participate in intertexts – in broader systems of cultural
meaning.

If the critical literature on science fiction cinema has on the whole not
addressed itself directly to questions of genre, the essays collected in this
volume will necessarily reflect such a state of affairs, demonstrating the
current state of critical theory in relation to science fiction cinema. But
they might also signal some ways in which gaps could be filled and new
directions taken in future work on this genre. The essays have been
selected and organized not merely – nor even especially – to be 'representative' of some larger body of work; though they do highlight –
purposefully – the varied critical approaches which have been taken to
science fiction cinema, illustrating the well-developed areas as well as
exposing relatively unexplored terrain. This anthology, like any other,
must be more than the sum of its parts: for example, if the question of
genre is addressed explicitly in only a few of the individual contributions, the collection as a whole should provide some sense of how
contemporary science fiction cinema draws on, reworks and transforms
some of the conventions of this old-established popular film genre.

In the critical literature, generic transformations have been charted
most consistently at the levels of narrative theme and viewpoint; and
certainly several new *themes* are referred to in writings on recent science
fiction cinema. For example, the genre's long-standing preoccupation
with narratives involving masculine mastery over nature and creation
currently manifests itself, as some critics have noted, in stories involving
the 'birthing' of human substitutes by corporations rather than by the
Frankenstein/mad scientist villains of earlier films (*Alien* (1979); *Blade
Runner* (1982)). The old science fiction opposition of human and non-
human is also transformed when boundaries between the one and the
other become blurred, and the human body itself is constituted as other
or as potentially monstrous (*The Thing* (1982); *The Fly* (1986)): it is no
longer assumed that human beings are superior to humanoid machines
or alien creatures. To this extent, the human technologies which create
humanoids and discover and investigate alien creatures are revealed as

dreadfully flawed (*The Terminator* (1984)): in such circumstances aliens, far from menacing humankind, may hold out a promise of redemption (*Close Encounters of the Third Kind* (1977)). Other familiar themes taken up and reworked in recent science fiction films include the structure and organization of future and other societies: power in these fictional worlds is typically constituted as invisible but all-pervasive, institutional rather than personal, corporate rather than governmental (*Alien*; *Aliens* (1986)).[12]

It is perhaps worth reiterating that these points emerge not from genre criticism as such but from a body of textual analysis – readings of individual science fiction films which, taken collectively, might shed some light on the genre as a whole. But these textual readings do not always address the specifically cinematic qualities of the genre with the sophistication with which they handle questions of theme and narration. However, it might be asked, do cinematic codes of visibility and developments in special effects and in sound and colour technologies connect with thematic transformations of the genre? How do narrative and spectacle, in their transformation and their interrelation, intersect with the cultural instrumentalities of science fiction cinema? How, in other words, do changes in the textual conventions of the genre relate to broader sociocultural contexts?

These questions necessarily move us beyond film texts and genres, into the sphere of discourses and practices at work beyond cinema itself, but in which films and genres participate. Films and genres, it should be noted, are always products – commodities of a very particular sort, perhaps, but nonetheless embodying use value in the cultural sphere as well as exchange value in the economic. By comparison with textual analysis, however, critical and theoretical work on the links between science fiction cinema and various other institutions, powers, discourses or practices remains underdeveloped. In this area, there is a good deal of assumption and generalization and little systematic research and analysis; such work as does exist is more often than not a by-product of attention to something else. Readings of individual science fiction films provoke questions about connections between films, genres, spectators and other social practices – about their cultural instrumentalities, in other words. At the same time, textual analysis as a method is by its nature inadequately equipped to cope with extratextual questions – which consequently remain unanswered.

The organization of the material included in this collection has been governed by this absence, in that each contribution is categorized according to the cultural instrumentalities of films and genre implicit in its argument. This is strategic, in that it necessarily brings to the fore the neglected issue of cultural instrumentality. Highlighting cultural instrumentality

in this way cuts across the collective grain of the contributions – all
the better to expose this and other areas of critical neglect, and thus
to signal directions for future work in the field. If this sounds negative, it
is certainly not intended to be so: on the contrary. This strategy of classification foregrounds, in a positive manner, the interdependence of, and
the flow and exchange between, the varied theories and methods which
have been brought to bear on critical work on contemporary science
fiction films. Arrangement according to the methods themselves would,
by setting them apart from each other, fail to do justice to the richness
and productivity of these exchanges. In any case, it is not always easy in
practice to say that this or that piece of writing belongs exclusively to
this or that critical or theoretical tendency: nor, again, is this a bad thing.
The potential of science fiction film criticism may well lie in its very
unevenness, in the very contradictory manner in which it has evolved.

The cultural instrumentalities identified as the basis for organizing the
essays in this volume are fivefold. First of all, there is a notion that the
overt contents of science fiction films are *reflections* of social trends and
attitudes of the time, mirroring the preoccupations of the historical
moment in which the films were made. In this reflectionist model, films
are treated as, in a sense, sociological evidence. Secondly, there is the
idea that science fiction films relate to the social order through the
mediation of *ideologies*, society's representations of itself in and for itself
– that films speak, enact, even produce certain ideologies, which cannot
always be read directly off films' surface contents. Third is the view that
films voice cultural *repressions* in 'unconscious' textual processes which,
like the dreams, associations and bodily symptoms of psychoanalytic
patients, require interpretation in order to reveal the meanings hidden in
them. A fourth cultural instrumentality concerns what science fiction
films do to and for their *spectators* – the sorts of pleasures they evoke
and the fantasies they activate. Finally, there is the view that science
fiction films are actively involved in a whole network of *intertexts*, of
cultural meanings and social discourses. The five parts into which this
collection is divided correspond to these instrumentalities, each of which
is explored more fully in its own section introduction.

A key point emerging from this process of classification is that
cultural instrumentality and critical methodology are not necessarily
coterminous: one method or approach may straddle two or more types
of instrumentality, and vice versa. The essays included in this volume
represent a wide range of tendencies within film theory and critical
theory: sociological criticism, Marxism, semiotics, structuralism, psychoanalysis, deconstruction, feminism. Some of them combine approaches –
marrying feminism with Marxism, Marxism with sociology, feminism
with psychoanalysis, and so on. Many are methodologically pragmatic,

seizing on whichever approaches will best shed light on the object at hand. It becomes clear, too, that attention to science fiction films may allow critics to address themselves to a wide range of issues of social and cultural concern. If the focus of critical attention tends to be science fiction *films* as against science fiction *cinema*, questions about the latter – and about its cultural instrumentalities – are inevitably raised.

The range of critical approaches represented here also illustrates the extent to which film texts may be open to different readings, by critics as much as by audiences. This appears to be especially true of those contemporary science fiction films which have attracted extraordinary amounts of critical commentary and analysis. *Alien* and *Blade Runner* are perhaps the principal cases in point here; and indeed it might well be the case that these two films – *Alien* in particular – are responsible for the upsurge of interest in science fiction cinema among film theorists and cultural critics. In fact, many would maintain that *Alien*, released in 1979, was in the vanguard of a renaissance in the genre. Accordingly, the 'contemporary' in 'contemporary science fiction cinema' refers in this context approximately to the period from the late 1970s to the present.

The debate about *Alien* and *Blade Runner* that runs through a number of the essays here illustrates the enormous fascination these two films have held for critics and theorists. The variety of approaches taken to them is in itself highly revealing, pointing to issues that reach far beyond the actual films, or even the genre to which they belong. What is the relationship between different types of cultural theory? Between cultural theory and film practices? Between film practices and society? Contemporary science fiction cinema raises questions that range back and forth, from film texts to spectators to social formations. It is time for these questions to be addressed.

Notes

1. On genre and cinema see, for example, Edward Buscombe, 'The Idea of Genre in the American Cinema' in Barry K. Grant, ed., *Film Genre: Theory and Criticism*, Metuchen, NJ: Scarecrow Press 1977; Paul Willemen, 'Presentation' in Stephen Neale, *Genre*, London: British Film Institute 1980; Christine Gledhill, 'Genre' in Pam Cook, ed., *The Cinema Book*, London: British Film Institute 1985.

2. Andrew Tudor, 'Genre' in Grant.

3. Neale, p. 17.

4. Ibid., p. 19.

5. For examples of this work, see Colin McArthur, *Underworld USA*, London: Secker and Warburg 1972; Jim Kitses, *Horizons West*, London: Secker and Warburg 1969; Will Wright, *Sixguns and Society: A Structural Study of the Western*, Berkeley: University of California Press 1975.

6. See E. Ann Kaplan, ed., *Women in Film Noir*, London: British Film Institute 1978; Rick Altman, ed., *Genre: The Musical*, London: Routledge & Kegan Paul 1981;

Christine Gledhill, ed., *Home Is Where the Heart Is: Studies in Melodrama and the Woman's Film*, London: British Film Institute 1987.

7. On the horror film, which has the highest critical profile of the 'neglected' genres, see Robin Wood, 'Return of the Repressed', *Film Comment*, July–August 1978; Robin Wood, 'Neglected Nightmares', *Film Comment*, March–April 1980; Linda Williams, 'When the Woman Looks' in Mary Anne Doane, Patricia Mellencamp and Linda Williams, eds, *Re-Vision: Essays in Feminist Film Criticism*, Los Angeles: American Film Institute 1984; *Screen* Body Horror issue, vol. 27, no. 1, 1986. On comedy, see Steve Neale and Frank Krutnik, *Comedy in Film and Television*, London: Routledge, forthcoming. Genre studies of the 1970s (see, for example, the essays in Grant) rarely mention horror, comedy or science fiction. The overview of genre and genres in Cook includes discussion of the western, melodrama, the gangster film, film noir, the horror film and the musical.

8. Vivian Sobchack is rare among film theorists in having produced a sustained body of work on science fiction cinema. See, for example, *Screening Space: The American Science Fiction Film*, 2nd edn, New York: Ungar 1988.

9. On science fiction cinema's iconographic aspects, see ibid., chapter 2.

10. See, for example, Louis James, '"Science Fiction" and the "Literary Mind"' in David Punter, ed., *Introduction to Contemporary Cultural Studies*, London: Longman 1986; Darko Suvin, 'Narrative Logic, Ideological Domination, and the Range of Science Fiction: A Hypothesis with a Historical Test', *Science Fiction Studies*, vol. 9, no. 1, 1982, p. 4. Tzvetan Todorov, *The Fantastic: A Structural Approach to a Literary Genre*, Ithaca, NY: Cornell University Press 1975, is also suggestive in this context.

11. For discussions on narration and visibility in classical cinema, see David Bordwell and Kristin Thompson, *Film Art: An Introduction*, Reading, MA: Addison-Wesley 1979, chapter 3; Annette Kuhn, 'History of Narrative Codes' in Cook; John Ellis, *Visible Fictions*, London: Routledge & Kegan Paul 1982.

12. Some of these themes are discussed in J.P. Telotte, 'Human Artifice and the Science Fiction Film', *Film Quarterly*, vol. 36, no. 3, 1983; Annette Kuhn, 'Humanity and Otherness in Recent Science Fiction Films', Power Foundation lecture, University of Sydney, November 1988.

PART I

Reflections

It is widely believed that social concerns and trends are reflected in mass media such as film and television, and that popular cultural forms can in consequence be regarded as a gauge of social attitudes and social change. Feminist film critics, for example, have looked at how women have been portrayed in cinema at various periods – their roles, the kinds of stories they figure in – linking differences over time with changes in real women's fortunes, their power and status in society. Cinematic representations of war, the family, crime and masculinity have been subjected to similar scrutiny. Genre films are usually included in surveys of this kind, despite the fact that genres work very much in terms of their own conventions of theme, plot, narration, iconography, and so forth. In many respects, genre films refer more obviously to each other than to the social world. On the other hand, these films' very formulaic and self-referential qualities may be regarded as providing opportunities for social comment which cultural forms with greater claims to actuality rarely enjoy. Genre, as well as being a portmanteau, can be an umbrella.

Nowhere is this clearer than with science fiction, among whose principal generic features must be the spatial and temporal distance from the here and now of the fictional worlds it creates. 'Few things reveal so sharply as science fiction the wishes, hopes, fears, inner stresses and tensions of an era, or define its limitations with such exactness,' said H.L. Gold, editor of *Galaxy Science Fiction.*[1] Gold was referring to science fiction literature, but his sentiments can readily be extended to film. It is virtually inevitable, critics contend, that films which appeal to our imaginings of future or alternative worlds will, intentionally or otherwise, also address contemporary concerns. 'Most science fiction films tend to disguise, and thereby reveal more schematically, the social or

15

psychological preoccupations of the moment,' wrote Gerald Mead and Sam Appelbaum in a review of *Westworld*, a science fiction film released in 1973.[2] The disguise referred to here is the genre itself, the very codes and conventions which assert that a science fiction film is nothing more than fantasy. But under the cloak of fantasy, issues of actuality may be addressed all the more directly. In this reflectionist criticism, the issues dealt with in films resolve themselves into two types, already hinted at in Mead and Appelbaum's statement: films are seen either as mirroring attitudes, trends and changes in society (social preoccupations), or as expressing the collective psyche of an era (social psychological preoccupations).

The reflectionist model – whether sociological or social psychological in tendency – assumes that representation and the 'real world' are distinct from one another, and that the former is subordinate to the latter: films are always precisely *reflections* of things going on outside them. Films' reflection of the real is often seen as unmediated, direct or transparent: the assumption is that social trends and attitudes in a sense produce films, which can then be read as evidence of these trends and attitudes. The sociological view, for example, holds that different sorts of fictional worlds and narratives can be observed in science fiction films of various periods, and that such variations, being indicative of the problems and issues of the society in which the films were produced and originally consumed, have as much to do with events in the 'real world' as with any transformations within the genre itself: or rather, perhaps, that generic transformations themselves mirror changes at the level of the social.

For example, it is widely held that 1950s Hollywood science fiction cinema, with its pervasive but invisible and undetectable aliens menacing the human world in films like *Invasion of the Body Snatchers* (1956) and *The Thing from Another World* (1951), was 'really' about the Cold War, reflecting the hysterical fears of a communist takeover by the 'enemy within' that swept the US in those years.[3] And it has been suggested of science fiction films of the early and middle 1970s that, in dealing with basically terrestrial issues such as overpopulation, pollution and ecology (*Silent Running* (1972), *Soylent Green* (1973) and *Logan's Run* (1976)), they express a variant of US isolationism.[4]

H. Bruce Franklin, looking at more than fifty science fiction films released between the years 1970 and 1982, here brings the sociological argument close to the present, addressing amongst others films which were in the vanguard of the late 1970s renaissance of the genre. His conclusion is that the 'visions of the future' in the films he discusses are deeply pessimistic, and that the dystopias of contemporary science fiction 'mirror the profound social decay we are experiencing'.

Overviews like Franklin's are the outcome of attention to surface elements of the content – usually plot and characterization – of large numbers of films made over a particular period of time. The sociological approach embodied in such wide-ranging surveys may shade off into a second version of reflectionist criticism, a more idiographic social psychological view. Here discussion focuses less on social structures and more on collective consciousness – mental states shared across a culture at a particular historical moment, usually bound in some manner to events in the social world. Thus, for instance, Susan Sontag could characterize the science fiction cinema of a certain period as reflecting people's fears and anxieties about the dehumanizing qualities of contemporary society.[5] In this social psychological model, methods of analysis tend to be scaled down somewhat by comparison with the survey approach adopted by exponents of the sociological view, arguments here being based more often than not on readings of quite small numbers of films. For example, looking at just two films – *Close Encounters of the Third Kind* (1977) and *E.T.* (1982) – critics have attributed their success at the box office to their articulation of widely held longings for a return to moral certainties, in these instances in the form of the traditional values of small-community life.[6]

Hugh Ruppersberg also adopts this kind of social psychological approach and methodology, in his essay 'The Alien Messiah'; advancing the view that a number of recent science fiction films – he looks in some detail at four or five, including *Close Encounters* and *E.T.* – voice the despair of individuals unable to find meaning in the modern world. These two films, Ruppersberg argues, are wish fulfilments, in the sense that their narrative resolutions proffer the possibility of redemption for a 'fallen' humankind – through the messianic agency of benevolent alien creatures. In the final instance, though, perhaps these films' messages are not entirely hopeful, says Ruppersberg: for what they imply is that human beings are impotent, incapable of dealing with their own problems – in need, literally, of a *deus ex machina* to save them. This is ultimately reactionary: the films are 'escapist fantasies grounded in patterns of the past instead of the possibilities of the future'. It appears to be the view of a majority of critics of a reflectionist persuasion that contemporary science fiction is either pessimistic or regressively optimistic about the future – and therefore about the present.

Thomas B. Byers, in his essay on corporatism and personal style in three recent science fiction films, is equally gloomy: but unlike either Franklin or Ruppersberg, he suggests that popular science fiction cinema, while reflecting a dreadful contemporary reality, can at least be critical of that reality. *Alien* (1979), *Blade Runner* (1982) and *Star Trek II: The Wrath of Khan* (1982) all explore the relationship between high-tech corporate capitalism and individual styles and behaviours, says Byers, but the future worlds they propose are merely extrapolations of current trends. In this sense the films are engaged in a debate about present-day society. Byers takes the view that *Star Trek II* is reactionary, because its resolution proposes a style of adjustment to a mega-corporate world which involves reaffirmation of traditional, white, male, bourgeois values: an assertion, once more, of past certainties in the face of an uncertain present. But if *Alien* and *Blade Runner* also propose worlds in which social relations are seriously awry, they also, contends Byers, offer some sort of criticism of – though no solution to – this state of affairs. In this sense at least, these two films may be regarded as more 'progressive' than *Star Trek II*.

Byers's argument, suggesting that science fiction cinema can at once reflect and critique the current social order, imports a potential for contradiction into a generally reflectionist analysis. This, together with the implication that films can be either reactionary or progressive; and that this is culturally important because films shape, as well as reflect, the ways we think about the world, brings Byers's approach close to those taken in the ideological readings of science fiction cinema which appear in Part II.

Notes

1. Quoted by Kingsley Amis, *New Maps of Hell*, London: Gollancz 1961, p. 64.

2. Gerald Mead and Sam Appelbaum, '*Westworld*: Fantasy and Exploitation', *Jump Cut*, no. 7, 1975.

3. See, for example, Peter Biskind, *Seeing is Believing: How Hollywood Taught Us to Stop Worrying and Love the Fifties*, New York: Pantheon Books 1983, chapter 3.

4. Joan F. Dean, 'Between *2001* and *Star Wars*', *Journal of Popular Film and Television*, vol. 7, no. 1, 1978.

5. Susan Sontag, 'The Imagination of Disaster' in *Against Interpretation*, London: Eyre and Spottiswoode 1966.

6. Robert Entman and Francie Seymour, 'Close Encounters with the Third Reich', *Jump Cut*, no. 18, 1978; Marina Heung, 'Why E.T. Must Go Home: The New Family in American Cinema', *Journal of Popular Film and Television*, vol. 11, no. 2, 1983; Tony Williams, 'Close Encounters of the Authoritarian Kind', *Wide Angle*, vol. 5, no. 4, 1983.

1

Visions of the Future in Science Fiction Films from 1970 to 1982

H. Bruce Franklin

By the end of the 1960s, it seemed that we were experiencing the most profound crisis in human history. Although our species now possessed the science and technology potentially allowing us to shape the future of the planet according to human needs and desires, we faced these forces as alien powers – which we ourselves had created – slipping out of our control and threatening to wipe us off the planet. America itself was being torn apart by the Vietnam war, with its destruction not only of Indochina but also of our own economy, social cohesion, and illusions about our history and destiny. Amidst a planet in revolution, America's leaders, equipped with pushbuttons to annihilate civilization, seemed ignorant of the past and oblivious to the future. It was no wonder that SF was now a central organ of Anglo-American imagination, pumping its content into many cultural forms.

The apocalyptic imagination had already burst forth into film with images of catastrophe in all shapes – from the very likely possibility of thermonuclear holocaust to absurd projections of the human race being overcome by even the most harmless life forms. By the late 1960s, visions of decay and doom had become the normal Anglo-American cinematic view of our possible future, whether in the over-exposed sterile whiteness of George Lucas's *THX 1138* (1969) or the shattered Statue of Liberty sprawled across the end of the aptly named *Planet of the Apes* (1968). Our only hope for salvation seemed to lie outside ourselves, perhaps with the godlike aliens who might remould someone to rescue us from the killer apes wearing the uniforms of US generals in *2001* (1968).

In 1972, I attempted to comprehend this doomsday imagination and

concluded that it was an expression of a decaying empire, whose
economic and social relations were inexorably disintegrating.[1] At that
time, this hypothesis was somewhat speculative, for the decay of the
empire was far less evident than today, and the doomsday visions of the
future tended to imagine external or sudden causes for their cata-
strophes.

The immediate future of the 1960s is now our immediate past. As we
know, the 1970s and early 1980s has been a period of unending and
deepening social and economic crisis, and visions of the future projected
in Anglo-American SF films during this period have been overwhelmingly pessimistic. No longer limited to displaced symbols of
cultural anxiety, many of these films openly proclaim that their dismal
futures are extrapolations of tendencies perceived in present society.
With a cultural lag typical of the film industry, New Wave literary SF of
the 1960s begins to shape movies a decade or so later. The gloom
becomes so conventional that old-fashioned cotton-candy optimism is
passed off as audacious cultural innovation.

Selecting one's own examples always makes it easy to defend cultural
generalizations. Rather than selecting arbitrarily, I shall adopt a more
scientific procedure, briefly surveying the entire body of films set in the
future and released since 1970; then I shall take a close look at all the
films offering coherent views of some future period released after 1980
and prior to the writing of this essay. This exploration will not include
films set in a past time even if their surface is quite futuristic (such as
Battlestar Galactica or the *Star Wars* epic) nor films set in a present
which does not transform into a distinct 'future' even though extraordinary events occur (*Twilight's Last Gleaming, Close Encounters of
the Third Kind, E.T.: The Extraterrestrial*, John Carpenter's 1982 remake
of *The Thing*, and so on. To comprehend the cultural significance of these
films and of their central images, it will be helpful first to leap back in
time to recall the dominant images of the future in very early SF films.

The first great archetypal image of the future projected in the early SF
film is THE WONDER CITY OF THE FUTURE. One thinks immediately of *Metropolis* (1926), where the wonder city is part of a dialectic, consuming the
lives of the impoverished masses toiling in its foundations deep in the
earth. The dialectic itself was buried in 1930 by Hollywood, which spent
a quarter of a million Depression dollars to create, in the ill-starred
blockbuster SF musical *Just Imagine*, its own WONDER CITY OF
THE FUTURE: the magnificent futuristic New York of 1980. In 1936,
Things to Come displayed THE WONDER CITY OF THE FUTURE as the creation
of the technological elite. 'The Wings Over the World', whose vast
airships and space vehicle form the second received archetype, THE

MARVELLOUS FLYING MACHINE. These early archetypes – THE WONDER CITY OF THE FUTURE and THE MARVELLOUS FLYING MACHINE – undergo revealing transformations in the visions of the future projected by SF movies released in the 1970s and early 1980s.

According to my count – and I have no doubt missed a few – fifty-two Anglo-American SF movies set wholly or in part in some distinctly future time were released for general distribution from 1970 through early summer 1982.

Only three of these show anything resembling the triumph of progressive technology projected in *Things to Come* (unless one counts *Heart Beeps*, a 1981 farce about robots in love). These three are aimed at a mainly juvenile audience, as though we adults, who really know better, think this cotton candy is best left for children. Walt Disney Productions presented *The Black Hole*, where the human environment consists of nothing but MARVELLOUS FLYING MACHINES. *Star Trek: The Motion Picture* gives a very brief glimpse, in a clumsy backdrop, of THE WONDER CITY OF THE FUTURE and *Star Trek: The Wrath of Khan* shows an elegant futuristic room in Captain Kirk's house overlooking San Francisco Bay; but of course most of these two cinematic offshoots of the TV series are also set, like *The Black Hole*, far, far from Earth in MARVELLOUS FLYING MACHINES. These are the optimistic visions among the fifty-two. Their optimism can be maintained only by making the MARVELLOUS FLYING MACHINE become virtually the entire inhabited universe. The dazzling adventures of the spacers seem to have no relevance whatsoever to the economic and social life of the rest of our species. In stark contrast to this escapism, the 'adult' films, as we shall see, tend to show space travel as a means for the hideous monopolistic society on Earth to loot and devastate other parts of the universe.

Equally rare are the old 1950s images of aliens coming to threaten the future of our species. I can think of only two, both released in 1978. As in the original 1950s alien invader movie, the aliens in the remake of *Invasion of the Body Snatchers* are primarily metaphors for forces already present and shaping the future. No longer representing the communists, the pods are now, as many have noted, indistinguishable from the mods they replace. Altogether vanished are the middle-American, small-town virtues whose imminent demise constitutes the nightmare of the original. That other 1978 release, *The End of the World,* is virtually a parody of 1950s alien invader movies. In fact it ends with the vicious aliens not only destroying the Earth but forcing the last human survivors – our hero and heroine, the converse of Adam and Eve – to watch the whole show on TV, where we actually see footage from previous disaster movies, with earthquakes, volcanoes, fires, floods, and so on.

We get a similar show in *The Late Great Planet Earth* (1979), where the ponderous narration of Orson Welles accompanies images of the destruction of the world by earthquakes, tornadoes, floods, and killer bees as part of 'Nature's growing offensive' culminating in 'the Juniper Effect of 1982'. But one should note that all this mess is actually caused somehow by various forms of human behaviour, including terrorism, pollution, nuclear war, communism, fascism, DNA research, religious sects and gurus, the European Common Market, Red China, Red Russia, and Black Africa.

Movies set in the present do continue to marshal more or less successful forays against us by such monsters as worms, bugs, bees, sharks, a giant gorilla, and so on, as in *Squirm, The Swarm, The Bees, Empire of the Ants, Bug,* the *Jaws* films, and the remake of *King Kong.* But none of those fifty-two films of the future shows other life forms from Earth affecting the course of human history, except for the four sequels to *The Planet of the Apes: Beneath the Planet of the Apes* (1970), *Escape from the Planet of the Apes* (1971), *Conquest of the Planet of the Apes* (1972), and *Battle for the Planet of the Apes* (1973). The remaining films display catastrophic or very nasty futures caused directly by human behaviour or human creations.

In *Colossus, The Forbin Project* (1970), the war computers of the US and the USSR link up to rule the planet. In *No Blade of Grass* (1970), pollution has devastated the environment. Biological warfare destroys most of the human race in *The Omega Man* (1971), while it is poison gas that kills everybody over the age of twenty-five in Roger Corman's *Gas-s-s! Or, It Became Necessary to Destroy the World in Order to Save It* (1970); an echo of the assertion by the US officer who ordered the annihilation of the Vietnamese village of Ben Tre, 'It was necessary to destroy the town in order to save it'. A post-holocaust future is the setting for the X-rated *Glen and Randa* (1971), *The Ultimate Warrior* (1975), *A Boy and His Dog* (1975), *Damnation Alley* (1977), and *Logan's Run* (1976), which begins with a roll-up stating that the scene is after the catastrophe caused by overpopulation *and* pollution *and* thermonuclear war. In *Z.P.G.* (1972) and *Soylent Green* (1973), over-population has helped spawn evil governments, in the former one that bans births, in the latter one that feeds its citizens with green crackers made out of the corpses of fellow citizens.

Not one of these fifty-two movies shows a functioning democracy in the future. Many display future societies ruled by some form of con-spiracy, monopoly, or totalitarian apparatus. *THX 1138* (1969) shows a conformistic police state in which one of the most terrifying images is an enlargement of the police who were then beating up anti-Vietnam-War demonstrators. *Ice* (1970) focusses on underground revolutionaries fighting back against a police state extrapolated from the same social scene of the late 1960s. The technocratic order extolled in the 1936 *Things To Come* has become the nemesis in these movies as well as in *A Clockwork Orange* (1971), where those who impose order are presented as even more frightening than the terrifying disorder they attempt to suppress. Other varieties of our dreadful political future appear in *Sleeper* (1973), *Zardoz* (1974), *The Man Who Fell To Earth* (1976), *Capricorn One* (1978) – of course really a thinly veiled picture of the present –, *Alien* (1979), *Saturn 3* (1980), and the four more recent movies, which we will explore more closely, *Escape from New York* (1981), *Outland* (1981), *The Last Chase* (1981), and *Parasite* (1982).

A little subgenre of this type appears in the form of future worlds where the most interesting remaining normal human activity is some kind of sport or amusement, usually deadly, as in *Westworld* (1973), *Rollerball* and *Death Race 2000* (both 1975), *Futureworld* (1976), and *Deathsport* (1978).

In the 1970s and 1980s, the fundamental contradictions of US society have become visibly blatant in its cities, where high above the pot-holed streets, sleazy porno districts, decayed public transport, dilapidated small businesses, cockroach-infested housing, violence, and squalor have soared vestiges of that old visionary SF WONDER CITY OF THE FUTURE in the form of banks and corporate headquarters in glittering futuristic skyscrapers. It's no surprise that THE WONDER CITY OF THE FUTURE rarely appears any longer in the cinematic visions of tomorrow, except occasionally as some kind of domed world of illusory pleasures, as in *Logan's Run* or *Futureworld.* Instead, the cities of the present have been reduced to rubble through which our poor descendants have their last pathetic adventures. Fragments of our decayed world are almost a cliché: the ruins of New York are strewn from the *Apes* movies through *The Ultimate Warrior* to the first episode of *Heavy Metal* (1981) and *Escape from New York*, featuring the rat-infested subways, the crumbled pillars of the Stock Exchange, and the New York Public Library as the site of a creaky primitive oil well. The political centre of America now appears as the ivy-covered ruins of the Capitol in *Logan's Run*, while middle America is anything from a series of abandoned towns inhabited by monstrous mutants in *Damnation Alley* to the underground all-American nightmare of Topeka in *A Boy and his Dog.*

When THE MARVELLOUS FLYING MACHINE makes an appearance, it is usually as a harbinger not of progress but of terror. It may be a vehicle bringing either some threatening alien life-form – as in *The Andromeda Strain* (1971) or *Alien*; or assassins sent by human powers – as in *Outland*; or some hideous human invention – as in *Saturn 3*. In

Zardoz, THE MARVELLOUS FLYING MACHINE is no longer either a sleek aerodynamic beauty or an intricate functional maze of machinery but a grotesque mask presiding over the subjugation and programmed killing of the effete survivors on Earth. In *Dark Star* (1974), the purpose of THE MARVELLOUS FLYING MACHINE is to annihilate stars that are deemed inconvenient. In *Silent Running* (1972), it is the final repository of Earth's remaining vegetation: when the heartless technocratic authorities on Earth order the jettisoning of this cargo, we are supposed to applaud the response of the introspective captain (Bruce Dern), who murders the crew and embarks with his plants and robots on a lonely quest into deep space. In *Capricorn One,* manned space travel has degenerated into a hoax, and the US government is out to kill off its phony spacemen so they can't reveal that THE MARVELLOUS FLYING MACHINE hasn't really gone anywhere. In *The Last Chase,* the last remaining flying machine is a decrepit ancient T-38 piloted by an alcoholic Burgess Meredith in a suicide attack on one of the last vestiges of technological 'progress', an automated laser gun. In a world living under the incessant threat of thermonuclear doomsday, movies might find it difficult to project the kind of salvation from war envisioned by *Things to Come,* with its technocratic elite forming a beneficent 'Wings Over the World'.

Of the four more recent movies displaying the future, *The Last Chase* is probably the worst example of cinematic art, in both form and content. Nevertheless, as a cultural symptom of the early 1980s, it is well worth our attention.

Sometime in the 1980s, a mysterious plague had wiped out most of the population. Simultaneously, oil had either run out or was somehow shut off. (Though released in 1981, *The Last Chase* has tell-tale signs of being made somewhat earlier, back perhaps in 1979 when we didn't know about the global glut in oil as we were waiting in lines at the gas station.) The implication is that 'They' – the all-powerful bureaucrats in Washington – had shut off the oil and maybe even released some biological agent to wipe out droves of people. Why? Because 'They' believe that society must be static and stationary. Their *bête noire* is the private automobile, which allows the individual to be mobile and free. We can tell that these rulers are evil because they are committed to public transport, solar power, pacifism, and a calm, regulated life in a few cities under their total control.

The scene is now twenty years later – that is, in the twenty-first century. Franklin Hart (Lee Majors), a former racing car driver, has buried his red Porsche under his garage. He works in what seems THE WONDER CITY OF THE FUTURE, actually a sinister anti-utopia with efficient public transport, soaring futuristic buildings, and streets empty except for bicycles and sparse groups of pedestrians. Technology is concentrated in the computer and communications network which is used for total surveillance and bureaucratic omnipotence. Majors is about to be arrested for social deviance because his lectures to schoolchildren have been hinting that things were better in the past. *The Last Chase* projects the opposite of Wells's vision of the technocratic WONDER CITY OF THE FUTURE in *Things to Come*: the technocrats are now the bad guys and the good guys are the reactionaries. (Even the plague that helps pave the way for the rule of the technocrats seems to be a reversed image from *Things to Come*.)

Enter the boy genius – a bespectacled misfit who has been jamming the state's jam-proof communications network with a transmitter he's thrown together out of spare parts. Hart, who has lost his own son in the plague, finds a new son in the boy genius. Together, they take off across the country in Hart's racing car in search of freedom in the far West, which has been beaming subversive messages on Radio Free California.

The state gets Captain Williams (Burgess Meredith), the unappreciated jet ace of both the Korean War and the Vietnam War, now a kite-flying dipsomaniac, to give chase in that last MARVELLOUS FLYING MACHINE, the old T-38 armed with machine guns – and napalm. The setting for this epic conflict is the North American continent.

At this point, *The Last Chase* becomes a road movie, very similar in its mythic configuration to *Damnation Alley*. In each film, a tiny group of heroic survivors, beset by dangers on all sides, drives across a ruined America in search of some place where the good old past still lives. The transcontinental road ends in each movie with the quest completed as our heroes drive into a recreation of the mythic small town of the past. The small town community in *Damnation Alley* is Albany, New York: in *The Last Chase* it is some unnamed town in Free California. Both scenes are identical, with a band of citizens from the good old American small town community strung out along the road as a cheering welcoming committee. This quest for the mythic middle-American past is the exact opposite of the vision in *A Boy and his Dog*, where it is the values of middle America itself that have launched the devastation, and where the red-white-and-blue Mom-and-apple-pie underground town of Topeka is the demonic centre of the hell it has created.

In *The Last Chase*, the private automobile in its most gas-guzzling avatar – the roaring Porsche – symbolizes the opposition to bureaucracy, the state, conformism, solar power, public transport, ecology, anti-war movements, and other equally sinister parts of progress. The grizzled super-male and the boy genius heading ever-westward in the last private car incarnate an ironic twist of the first great formative myth of popular SF.

In late nineteenth-century America, the most popular and influential form of culture was not the movies or television but the dime novel. Probably the very first SF dime novel was Edward Sylvester Ellis's *The Steam Man of the Prairies*, which appeared in 1865, at the exact moment of the triumph of industrial capitalism in America. The hero, typical of the SF dime novel, is a lone genius in the form of a teenaged boy: Johnny Brainerd, a fifteen-year-old dwarfed, hunchbacked lad whose father has died. Johnny's masterpiece among his many inventions is a ten-foot-tall robot driven by an internal steam engine, capable of speeding along at sixty miles an hour while drawing a four-passenger carriage, also designed and built by Johnny all by himself. Johnny *Brain*erd, with his hand-crafted sixty-miles-per-hour horseless carriage, foreshadows the figure of Henry Ford and those swarms of horseless carriages which, together with their manufacturers, have transformed our environment. His machine is the progenitor of the long line that will end with Franklin *Hart*'s red Porsche.

Having created his wonderful machine, Johnny receives a brand new father in the person of a grizzled old hunter, trapper, and goldminer from the West. Together they pack the steam man into a crate and take him out West, to exploit the old man-of-action's fabulous gold strike and to kill off hordes of 'treacherous' 'redskin' 'savages'. This father and son who together, without benefit of women, will breed the future of America are now replaced by the father and son driving alone to a past that never existed but whose myth may be capable of destroying us all. Indeed, there are some internal hints that *The Last Chase* might originally have been intended to assist the campaign of another questor after that mythic past, who came from California to capture the White House.

Outland also seeks to recreate the past, but in quite a different form. Space is the New Frontier, a notion popularized by Robert A. Heinlein and politicized by John F. Kennedy, and the movie is a space version of *High Noon*. *Outland* is set in the not-too-distant future on Io, one of Jupiter's moons, in a mining colony belonging to the now familiar gigantic monopolistic Company. The newly arrived Marshall (Sean Connery) pits his lonely existential heroism against the omnipresent depravity and greed personified by the ruthless General Manager (Peter Boyle), ironically named Shepphard, who has been speeding up the workers with an amphetamine that slowly destroys their minds. (As in *9 to 5*, it is middle management that takes the rap for the worst crimes of the corporations.)

The Marshall finds himself deserted by everybody but the hardbitten burnt-out Company doctor with a cynical exterior and a heart of pure cornmush (brilliantly played by Frances Sternhagen). Writer and director Peter Hyams, who also made *Capricorn One*, gives a revealing reason for having changed the doctor's role from a man to a woman: 'After the first draft of the script, I decided it was absurd for a picture set in the future to be unpopulated by women'.[2] What this reveals is made even more blatant by a widely syndicated film critic (Richard Freedman) whose review calls the doctor 'the satellite nurse'.

The entire colony of tough workers is too cowardly to defend itself, so soon the Marshall finds himself being stalked by the Manager's hired killers, whose arrival time on THE MARVELLOUS FLYING MACHINE is marked by the camera cutting frequently to a digital clock, reminding us that we are indeed watching a futuristic version of *High Noon*, that classic western appearing in – and about – the 1950s. In *High Noon*, however, Gary Cooper is making the frontier safe for the advance of the cowardly burghers who represent capitalist civilization. In *Outland* the gunslinging embodiment of law and order is merely keeping things from getting any worse in this hellish labour colony: he is just draining a little pus from one of the abscesses of decaying interplanetary monopoly capitalism.

Outland is actually two different movies. One is a somewhat illogical but mildly entertaining recreation of the western form of the myth of the lone hero – the lone lawman, the lone ranger. (Unlike Tonto, however, his non-white subordinate turns out to be a coward who joins the bad guys.) What we have here is a broken fragment of a myth, a shard, floating around like other fragments in a disintegrating world. (*Battle Beyond the Stars*, a minor 1980 masterpiece by Roger Corman, embodies this in Cowboy, a lonely raygun slinger from Earth recruited to defend a distant planet of pacifists against evil alien imperialists.)

The other movie in *Outland* is, in all senses of the term, a *set* of images. The mining colony is an overwhelming image of alienation. The workers labour in conditions that combine the claustrophobic dangers of deep South African gold mines, the treacherous isolation of offshore or North Slope oil rigs, and the entrapment of a modern prison. A three-dimensional chase through their quarters takes us through what seem endless stacks of cages, as though Borges's 'The Library of Babel' had been used as a blueprint by the Company in designing a warehouse for its workers. Early in the movie, we see the consequences of venturing outside this entirely artificial alien environment into the even more alien natural surroundings: a worker, his mind consumed by the drug that has made him speed up his production, wanders outside the pressurized world without his space suit and explodes (not that this would happen in reality).

The two movies come to a rather unsatisfactory juncture when the chase culminates in the climactic shootout. Both Sean Connery and the two assassins are rather improbably armed with weapons out of the nineteenth century – shotguns – a heavy-handed reminder that we're witnessing a western set in space, the mythic past projected into an imagined future. A shotgun blows a hole in the wall separating the interior artificial world, with its alienated labour, from the exterior world, with its deadly emptiness. But the gaping hole between the pressurized interior world and the airless exterior world merely serves as a convenience of the adventure plot, disposing of one of the nasty gunmen. *Outland* ends up as uninterested in the workers and their predicament as they seem to be in the plot.

Outland's vision of the giant monopoly and its slave-like workers is certainly never reduced to the absurdity of the end of *Metropolis*, where the dictator at the head of the monopoly shakes hands with the spokesman of his workers and agrees to reform the system. Nor does *Outland* project the outlandish notion central to *Things to Come*, that the technocrats will save all the rest of us – stupid sheep that we are – from ourselves and from the vicious predators we mindlessly obey. But the limits of *Outland*'s imagination become clear when we compare it with Heinlein's remarkably similar story 'Logic of Empire', which appeared in 1941, forty years earlier. Unlike *Outland*, 'Logic of Empire' sees the slave labour colonies on Venus as products of a particular economic system located within history and being changed by the processes of history. Heinlein's story shows the consciousness of both the capitalists and the workers determined by the conditions of their class existence, but for the workers this means not the stupefying cowardice projected in *Outland* but the beginnings of resistance and rebellion. Hollywood seems, for whatever reason, unwilling or unable to handle such a theme. Perhaps the closest we have is one of the true masterpieces of the genre, *Alien*, in which it is the workers and the women who understand the true situation, and learn what to do about it, far better than their stereotypical ultra-competent super-male commander, who unwittingly serves the most fiendish designs of the monopolistic Company.

The first vision of the future projected in 1982 has to be seen through glasses that are not only rose-coloured but also polarized. It is the 3D thriller *Parasite*, brazenly set just a decade ahead in 1992. America is now a virtual wasteland under the unofficial tyranny and open terror of the 'Merchants'. As one character explains: 'You can't tell the Government and the Merchants apart any more; they work for each other'. The economy has collapsed, and paper money is worthless; regular gas costs $29.98 a gallon, payable in gold or silver; practically no food is available except for old canned goods as such rare luxuries as packets of sugar or instant coffee; the landscape is strewn with abandoned cars and houses; some mysterious 'atomic shit' has rained down on New York City, sending survivors fleeing into remote small towns.

As in *Outland*, work has been reduced to blatant slave labour, but here the 'work camps' run by the Merchants are established not on a moon of Jupiter but in the suburbs of America. The significance of this is spelled out. Witnessing an especially gruesome death of a friend, one escapee from these work camps laments: 'It's just like the suburbs all over again – you can't care for anybody'.

Parasite combines that first great myth emerging out of industrial capitalism – Frankenstein – with that now all-too-familiar myth of small-town America. The scientist, Dr Paul Dean, author of the weighty tome *The Pathology of Parasites*, has created, on special orders from the state, a brand new super-parasite, capable of either eating people up from inside or growing to enormous size by grabbing them from outside and sucking out all their blood. This parasite, potentially capable of boundless reproduction, bears a striking resemblance to the creature in *Alien*, which may help explain why the Merchants, like the Company in *Alien*, are so eager to get it into profitable operation.

Dr Dean realizes the sinister alienation of his scientific labour, rebels against the state, and destroys all but two of his creatures: one growing inside him, another he needs for experiments to figure out how to kill the one inside. He manages to escape with his books, laboratory apparatus, and the two creatures to the little town of Joshua, 'Population 64, Altitude 1100'. There he is befriended by a black bartender recently escaped from New York and a young woman who grows lemon trees in her little Edenic garden so that she can offer fresh lemonade as a nice healthy old-fashioned alternative to the unrelieved diet of leftover canned goods. Dr Dean and his new friends are abused by a hot-rod gang of young bullies and their molls and hunted down by the Merchants, embodied by a thin-lipped crewcut blond in a dark three-piece suit, careening around in a futuristic car, and armed with a death-ray gun in his black-gloved hand.

The little adventure has a happy ending: Dr Dean discovers the means to kill the parasite within; the other parasite and the Merchant are consumed in flames: even the hot-rod gangsters turn out to be decent young people, just driven to bad attitudes and behaviour by their environment. However, as usual in these recent visions of the future, although the good people win their little adventure against over-whelming odds, both their heroism and their victory are essentially irrelevant. Typical of the heroes of these movies, they overcome some especially horrible excrescence of their society without even trying to deal with the fundamental evil, which remains omnipotent and unassailable.

The despair of *Outland* and *Parasite* looks like bubbling optimism alongside the bleak landscape of *Escape from New York*, directed and partly written by John Carpenter, who in 1974 had made *Dark Star*, one of a handful of truly original SF films. The time is 1997. America is a thinly-concealed fascist society in a chronic state of war, escalating crime, and social decay.

The President is on his way to a summit meeting with the Soviets, arranged as a last desperate attempt to avert thermonuclear war while preserving US power. An underground revolutionary organization hijacks his plane; it crashes into Manhattan, which had been sealed off in the 1980s, turned into a prison colony, and left to the anarchy of its inmates, who are patrolled by the killer helicopters of the United States Police Force, garrisoned, appropriately enough, at the Statue of Liberty. THE WONDER CITY OF THE FUTURE is now society's garbage dump, a pile of rubble and human rot prefiguring worse things to come. THE MARVELLOUS FLYING MACHINE is now represented by the smouldering wreck of Air Force One, being looted by New York's raggedy criminals, the helicopters of the police state, and, in a fitting comedown, a glider which lands on the abandoned World Trade Center in a final attempt to save the President and the world – or at least keep it safe for American democracy.

As in *The Last Chase, Outland*, and *Parasite*, the plot centres on the adventure of a lone hero fighting, along with a helper or two, against near-impossible odds and overwhelming forces. As usual, he will win his minor victory in a hopeless world. Heroes challenge evil empires and change history only in such escapist times and places as the setting of the *Star Wars* epic: 'Long ago, and in a galaxy far, far away . . .'.

The lone hero of *Escape from New York* is Snake Plissken (Kurt Russell), once the Special Forces hero of the Siberia Campaign, now a notorious bank robber. The US Police have implanted an explosive, which only they can deactivate, in Snake's neck, giving him only twenty-four hours to rescue the President from the apparent arch-villain, the Duke of New York, played by Isaac Hayes and driving around, as a racist caricature of black aspirations, in a limousine bedecked with crystal chandeliers. Sporting a sinister patch and limp, and aided by a resourceful veteran cab driver (just like the cabbie in the first episode of *Heavy Metal*, who also manoeuvres craftily through the crime-infested rubble of the future New York), Snake slithers on his mission through the collapsing concrete jungle of Manhattan (actually photographed mainly in St Louis).

At the end, Snake delivers the President, but temporarily withholds the secret tape that the President is about to broadcast to the Soviet leaders. Then he watches with disgust as the President, in a power-mad frenzy, sprays the Duke with submachine-gun fire. Snake's face cagily records the nihilistic message symbolized by this scene, he hands over a tape, and we listen as the President broadcasts what he proclaims as his final proposal to the Soviets – the pop-music tape Snake has just given him. Apparently nothing now stands in the way of the final apocalypse for this rotten world of the very near future.[3]

If archaeologists can infer something of the character of a society from a few shards, certainly visions of the future created by large groups of highly skilled people armed with advanced technology, financed by millions of dollars, on behalf of giant corporations, intended to make handsome profits by enticing the cost of expensive tickets from masses of consumers, must reveal something about the character of our own society. Of course they mirror the profound social decay we are experiencing. Obviously some of them are also meant as warnings.

We must be cautious in making inferences from these despairing visions of the future. After all, more optimistic products have come out of Hollywood, including the current resident of the White House. It's by no means clear that all this pessimism sells well to the public. And certainly there is more to American culture than its movie industry. After all, we do have video games. But perhaps these visions are the appropriate imaginative projections of a society that is destroying its own cities to finance its 'defence' against alleged external enemies, a society that has borrowed over a thousand billion dollars from the future in order to construct the marvellous weapons that may guarantee that there won't be any future humans to collect the debts.

Given the military, economic, and political hegemony of the US in much of the world, these cultural projections are also profoundly frightening. The only future that seems unimaginable in Hollywood is a better one. With no better vision of the future than these to offer, the US may possibly succeed in forcing the rest of the world into one of the kinds of future Hollywood can imagine. Perhaps these movies are then best seen as warnings – whether or not intended – not to follow the leadership of a society that either doesn't know where it's going or sees its own future as hopeless.

Notes

1. H. Bruce Franklin, 'Chic Bleak in Fantasy Fiction', *Saturday Review: The Arts*, 15 July 1972.
2. *New York Times*, 26 May 1981.
3. This essay was written before the release of *Blade Runner* (1982), a film which exemplifies many of the points in this essay. *Blade Runner* is discussed in the present volume by Thomas B. Byers, Michael Ryan and Douglas Kellner, J.P. Telotte, and Guiliana Bruno.

2

The Alien Messiah

Hugh Ruppersberg

The alien messiah has been such a pervasive figure in science fiction films of the last twenty years as to mark some sort of cultural phenomenon. Its modern origins extend at least back to the 1951 film *The Day the Earth Stood Still,* where an alien visitor warns the inhabitants of Earth to eschew war and violence or suffer destruction. This film followed by seven years the explosion of the first atomic bomb and appeared during the early days of 1950s Cold War nuclear paranoia. It reflected a general public concern over the same historical circumstances that have influenced more recent science fiction films: the fear that civilization has run amok and is about to destroy itself, the individual's consequent despair and sense of unimportance, the inability to find coherent meaning in the modern world. The alien messiah serves to resolve these problems, at least imaginatively, to replace despair with hope and purpose, to provide resolution in a world where solution seems impossible. A wave of popular mysticism in the middle and late 1960s, followed by an outright religious revival in the 1970s and 1980s, has been at least a secondary influence on the theme's recent prominence.[1]

Science fiction cinema often assumes a rather confused attitude toward science and technology. On the one hand, it views them as redemptive forces that can lift humanity out of the muck and mire of its own biological imperfections. On the other, it sees them as potentially destructive forces, inimical to humanity. What small hope there is, here on earth or elsewhere, lies in the human imagination and heart.

A number of films produced in the last twenty years, and especially in the last decade, look beyond the human for salvation. They invoke a messiah figure, an overtly or covertly religious personage, whose numinous, supra-human qualities offer solace and inspiration to a humanity threatened by technology and the banality of modern life. Ironically, these films do not hesitate to use that technology, both in the stories they tell and the special effects that make them popular. They are, finally, reactionary in their rejection of science and their advocacy of the supernatural, although several of them appear intentionally to confuse the genuinely messianic with extremely advanced technology. The messiah figure's presence in films that at first seem to deify technology thus constitutes quite a paradox.

The alien messiah's appearance usually occurs in two stages. The first establishes the vulnerability and weakness of the human characters. In *The Last Starfighter* (1984), *Star Wars* (1976), and *Close Encounters of the Third Kind* (1977), the protagonists feel trapped in a meaningless, trivial existence. In *The Fight of the Navigator* (1986) a young boy feels beleaguered by his parents and his spoiled younger brother. In *Cocoon* (1985) the central human characters are old men approaching death. In *E.T.* (1982) a young boy is upset over his parents' collapsed marriage. In *Starman* (1984) a young woman grieves for her dead husband. In *2010* (1984) civilization is threatened by nuclear war.

The second stage brings an alien force that rescues the human characters from the threatening circumstances they suffer. Inevitably, in the first stage human existence is circumscribed by closure. Inevitably, in the second stage closure gives way to openness. Meaningless lives find meaning. Old men are granted immortality. A boy gains a friend. A grief-stricken woman is consoled. Nuclear war is avoided.

The term messiah seems appropriate here not only because of what the alien figure does but also because he hails from a culture whose superior technology makes him appear 'divine' to earthly mortals. Less frequently, the messiah figure acts out a role previously prepared for him, as with the messiah in *Dune* (1984), based on the Frank Herbert novels. The three *Star Wars* films revolve around a similar messianism, apparently influenced by the *Dune* novels and by a fusion of conventional Christianity, Zen Buddhism, Arthurian romance, and 1970s self-help narcissism.[2] Although the messianic theme lent these films a governing mythology (mainly the first and second films, the third more or less abandoning mythic pretensions entirely), the primary emphasis falls on action and character. In these films, of course, the messiah figure is not alien but human, although from an advanced culture on a planet other than earth. The struggle of good and evil never develops beyond an amorphously defined abstraction, a vagueness reflected in the essential philosophic vacuity of the trilogy. Yet only one or two of the films I have in mind here ever transcend the vacuity to begin with.

Underlying the motif of the alien messiah is the mythos of the

Christian messiah, begotten by the divine Jehovah on a mortal woman, sent to redeem a sin-ridden humanity and to offer immortality. Several recent films have made bald use of this myth. In *Starman* the messiah figure is an alien who crash-lands on the Earth. In *The Terminator* (1984) he is a human from a post-nuclear war future. In both films, these characters beget a child on an earthly woman. In each case the consequent male child is destined to be of great service to the human race. In *The Terminator* he will lead the battle against robots who seek to destroy all human life. In *Starman* he will become a teacher who imparts the alien wisdom encoded in his genes. Oddly, the films present *two* messiah figures. In effect, the first messiah acts as Jehovah, impregnating the Virgin with the second messiah, the divine son. The alien of *Starman* reinforces his messianic identity by restoring the woman to life when she is accidentally killed by pursuing government agents.

Behind the Christian mythic pattern loom other mythic presences. Greek and Roman mythology is rife with accounts of young women molested and impregnated by assorted male deities, usually Zeus (less often Apollo, Pluto, or a lesser god), who appears in a variety of forms, as a shower of golden coins, for example, or a bull. The Psyche myth is another analogue. World mythologies offer many such tales. But these classical sources are not so accessible to the popular mind as Christian myth, which gives the messiah figure in these films the power and attraction it possesses. In whatever form, the messiah is an expression of transcendence, from the first stage of vulnerability and closure to the second stage of transcendence and openness. And it is the desire of popular audiences for transcendence that these films seek to satisfy.

The alien's messianic identity points directly to a fundamental assumption of these films: that alien visitors would be not only benign but benevolent, and sublimely so. Indeed, hostile aliens appear only rarely. (This is a striking contrast to films of the 1950s and 1960s, which usually portrayed the alien as an enemy. *War of the Worlds* (1953) is a case in point.)

In Stephen Spielberg's *Close Encounters* aliens seek out disgruntled and depressed middle-class humans and announce their intention to pay Earth a visit. Their reasons for doing so are unclear. What use might we be to them? To the poor humans singled out, they seem inescapably godlike. It is worth noting what Mr Kurtz, in Joseph Conrad's *Heart of Darkness*, wrote in his diary about missionaries and natives in the African jungle: 'We [the white Europeans] ... must necessarily appear to them in the nature of supernatural beings – we approach them with the might as of a deity.... By the simple exercise of our will we can exert a power for good practically unbounded'.[3]

Although the aliens' desire to do good is usually clear enough, none

of the films suggests whether any aliens ever suffered Kurtz's disillusion-
ment, or met his fate (*The Explorers* (1985) does show their corruption
by earthly materialism, and a similar thing occurs in Nicolas Roeg's *The
Man Who Fell to Earth* (1976)). Kurtz, of course, wants to redeem and
civilize the depraved jungle. Most of these films share his naiveté. They
rest on the premise that advanced technology breeds not only miracu-
lous wonders but moral redemption as well. The aliens of *Cocoon* and
Close Encounters and even *2001* show no sign of corruption or natural
imperfection or original sin. (The first two *Superman* films even make
fun of how good and innocent the title character really is.)[4] Moreover,
they often employ their sophistication to warn earthlings against the
danger of not using their own technology with sufficient care. This is the
overt theme of *2010* and an implied theme in *2001* and *Close Encounters.*

We find also in *Close Encounters* a close association between technological sophistication and religious exaltation. The aliens are exalted by
their own technological sophistication. They behave as exalted beings.
They appear exalted to earthly humans because of that sophistication.
Technology has redeemed them from original sin, made them godlike,
sent them to us with the best of intentions. In *Close Encounters* they
seem quite eager to play the messianic role. And as if to underscore their
mission, they choose to carry up into space a man who has lost his
family and job struggling to prove that he actually saw them. He is a
man searching for meaning, for a faith, which the aliens provide by
carrying him aloft.

The final image of ascension is clearly meant to be inspirational. But
why? Is the idea that there are other beings in the universe besides
ourselves inspirational? Are we to be moved that the man finally found
the meaning he so longed for? What are we to make of the jewel-like
alien ship, revolving in the evening sky, credits reeling past? Are we, like
Ezekiel, to take it as proof of a benevolent God's existence, of reason
for faith and hope? And if so, haven't we been duped by a very vivid but
very imagined and fabricated version of alien visitation cloaked in the
unctuous veil of holiness?[5]

Spielberg's *E.T.: The Extraterrestrial* carries the deception a step
further: the benevolent alien personalized in a cute, lovable space
creature. Stranded on Earth, he becomes friends with a confused and
lonely boy who feels misunderstood by everyone. Moreover, although
the alien creature belongs to a superior alien culture, he is neither aloof,
superior, nor mysterious. In fact, he is just like the boy – confused and
lonely. He acts out his messianic role by relieving the boy's confusion
and giving him a sense of worth. He does this through friendship more
than anything else. He also heals wounds, revivifies dead flowers, and

levitates fruit and bicycles. Moreover, when he begins trying to contact his own species, and when scientists begin to hunt him, he gives the boy a purpose: to help his friend return home and to protect him from the scientists.

As occasionally happens with alien messiahs (it happens in *The Last Starfighter*), the creature dies and is then resurrected, a focus of the film's inspirational theme.[6] When E.T. boards his space ship to ascend into the heavens, he touches the grieving boy on the forehead and says, 'I'll be right here', meaning that his memory will remain in the boy's heart and mind in future years, a source of faith and comfort. As the ship rises, it leaves a rainbow in its wake, the symbol of divine blessing and protection. Again we find the image of the good-hearted, kind, loving alien, the cosmic incarnation of Christian myth and doctrine.[7] The film succeeds by stimulating religious emotions in camouflaged form and by its vision of a cosmos where the individual has a cosy and secure place.

Although the alien messiah is usually a benevolent, anthropomorphic being intent on doing good, darker incarnations do occur. In *The Day the Earth Stood Still* the robot Gort serves as a policeman to the people who created it. He uses his ultimate power to maintain peace, law, and order, his owner assures us, and to destroy those who turn to violence. Yet we are also told that he is capable of destroying the Earth, which he would not hesitate to do if he found it necessary. Given developments of the last thirty-five years, this film's faith in technology is grimly touching.

In *The Terminator*, much more reflective of contemporary attitudes toward technology, just such a 'race' of robots has taken over the Earth, ravaged by nuclear war, and is determined to wipe out the human species. They are prevented by one man and his band of rebels. To destroy him, the robots build a time machine and send an android back to the past, assigned to kill the leader's mother, preventing his conception. Played effortlessly by Arnold Schwarzenegger, the rapacious android destroys everything in his path, including a police station and forty policemen. He is a 'negative' messiah, an irresistible force intent not on goodness to the human race but on its destruction. Similar examples occur in such films as *War of the Worlds*, *Invasion of the Body Snatchers* (1956, 1978), *Alien* (1979), and *Aliens* (1986).

Usually, although not always, some human agent arises to defeat them. In *The Terminator*, as we have seen, that force comes as a positive messiah, sent by the future rebels to protect their leader's mother. He succeeds, in the process becoming the woman's lover, and thus the father of the infant whose existence he was sent to ensure. When he is killed, the woman drives off alone into the Mexican desert to await the holocaust and give birth to the messiah who will redeem the humans from the robots. As in *Starman*, faint reverberations of Christian myth inform this film, especially its second half. The android is evil; the woman and her lover from the future are good. They battle for the fate of an unborn, even unconceived child who will redeem humanity – once again, camouflaged religious impulses and patterns.

The alien messiah's frequent presence in recent science fiction films propels us toward certain conclusions. The first is that contemporary movie audiences and film writers suffer from a terminal sense of inadequacy and insecurity and a parallel fatalistic certainty that the problems of our contemporary world are insurmountable, incapable of solution. The second is that these films suggest that the only satisfactory way of addressing the world's problems is imaginative appeal to superhuman agencies, that is, highly advanced aliens eager to do good, or the deities of traditional religion. Humanity itself is impotent, incompetent. The third is that science fiction films of the 1970s and 1980s serve the same function as the biblical epics of the 1950s and 1960s. What exactly is the difference between *King of Kings* (1961) and *Close Encounters*, between *The Robe* (1953) and *E.T.*? Except for details of setting and character, there is no difference. The earlier films were more honest, or perhaps less subtle, in their illumination of religious doctrine. If these latter ones are not so open, at least they are better films.

Paradoxically, they invoke the messiah, that overtly or covertly religious personage who renders irrelevant the technological marvels that all the special effects highlight and which science fiction itself in some sense is supposed to concern. Ultimately, they reflect reactionary, defeatist attitudes in their makers and their audiences. If they do not reject science and technology, they at least ignore it. If they regard the future with hope and wonder, they simultaneously discourage the hope that humankind will be more capable in the future of handling the problems that confront it today. Entertaining as they are, these films are escapist fantasies grounded in the patterns of the past instead of the possibilities of the future.

Notes

1. Janice Hocker Rushing in '*E.T.* as Rhetorical Transcendence', *Quarterly Journal of Speech*, vol. 71, no. 2, 1985, asserts that 'It may be that space fiction or fantasy is the most important contemporary genre for presenting and responding to the rhetorical exigency of fragmentation' (p. 200). Bonnie Brain, in 'Saviors and Scientists: Extraterrestrials in Recent Science Fiction Films', *Et Cetera: A Review of General Semantics*, vol. 40, no. 2, 1983, likewise associates these films with prevailing concerns of their audiences and finds

them specifically religious in tone: 'Not surprisingly, the human reaction – and the audience response – [aliens] inspire borders on reverence' (p. 219).

2. Leonard M. Scigaj, in 'Bettelheim, Castaneda, and Zen: The Powers behind the
Force in *Star Wars*', *Extrapolation*, vol. 22, no. 3, 1981, discusses the influence in the
films of Zen Buddhism and the writings of Carlos Castaneda.

3. Joseph Conrad, *Heart of Darkness*, New York: W.W. Norton & Co 1971, p. 51.

4. Superman is obviously an alien messiah figure, too, although he was more a product
of the 1930s than of the 1970s or 1980s. The first film emphasizes Superman's messianic
character. His father explains that he has sent his 'only son' to do service to the people of
Earth. Superman performs miracles, raises Lois Lane from the dead, and more or less dedi-
cates himself to good deeds.

5. See also Tony Williams, 'Close Encounters of the Authoritarian Kind', *Wide Angle*,
vol. 5, no. 4, 1983.

6. Resurrections occur in one form or another in *The Day the Earth Stood Still*, *Superman*, *Cocoon*, *Star Trek III: The Search for Spock*, *Starman*, *Star Wars*, *The Last Starfighter*, *E.T.* and *2010*.

7. In this sense Janice Hocker Rushing calls *E.T.* 'a significant experiment in the
rhetoric of mythic transcendence' (p. 200). On *E.T.*, see also Andrew Gordon, '*E.T.* as
Fairy Tale', *Science Fiction Studies*, vol. 10, no. 3, 1983.

3

Commodity Futures

Thomas B. Byers

Visions of the future that extrapolate contemporary trends to envision their possible consequences have long been part of cultural and political discourse and debate. Three notably successful movies of recent years – Ridley Scott's *Alien* (1979) and *Blade Runner* (1982), and Nicholas Meyer's *Star Trek II: The Wrath of Khan* (1982) – together offer an interesting example of such visionary debate. It is significant that all three appeared during the explosion of popular interest in computers, high-tech industry, and genetic engineering, and that the latter two were in production during the political elevation of Ronald Reagan and the rise of young urban professionals as a highly visible force in patterns of culture and consumption. But the link among them is not merely temporal; it is also thematic. All three specifically explore the relationship between high-tech corporate capitalism on the one hand, and individual modes and styles of personal behaviour on the other.[1] Interestingly enough, they express a good deal of agreement concerning the *nature* of the infrastructure's demands and influences on the individual, but Scott and Meyer – or, more properly, Scott and the whole *Star Trek* team – are diametrically opposed in their *evaluation* of these demands and influences. All three films suggest an inevitable conflict between human feelings and bonds on the one hand, and duty to the socioeconomic structure on the other. *Alien* and *Blade Runner* warn us against a capitalist future gone wrong, where such feelings and bonds are so severely truncated that a quite literal dehumanization has become perhaps the gravest danger. In a surprisingly direct contrast, *Star Trek II* smiles on a future whose challenges are met by a reaffirmation of the traditional values, and in particular the repressed and withholding interpersonal style, of the white male bourgeoisie.

Alien spins one of the most terrifying of SF's many ecological cautionary tales. The crew of the *Nostromo* work for a corporation whose stated (if at first secret) orders make all other considerations secondary to the delivery of an alien life-form that, as one character suggests, may prove to be an asset for the weapons division. For the corporation, all life is commodity, and the crew members are expendable. Hence the latter are victims at once of the corporation's greed and of an incomprehensible, sinister, and overwhelmingly powerful natural creature that in a sense wreaks vengeance for its disturbance by the human beings. Indeed, by their transformation of nature into commodity, human beings have become the true aliens.[2]

As for the monster itself, Jeff Gould points out that it is 'implacably hostile' and 'in all respects a superior product of competitive evolution ... [it] resembles nothing so much as that other superorganism, itself victor in an evolutionary struggle: the multinational (soon to be interstellar) corporation. In the system of the narrative, the Alien is the double . . . of the Company'.[3] The creature is, in fact, an embodiment of nature as perceived by corporate capitalism, and by an evolutionary science whose emphasis on competition is a manifestation of capitalist ideology. As such it is, as we will see later, in some horrible sense the nature that the crew of the *Nostromo* in general deserve.

But the creature is not the only antagonist, nor the most direct sign of the corporation's evil, present on the ship. It is covertly aided by the science officer, Ash, until, in one of the movie's most shocking scenes, he is decapitated and thus revealed to be a stunningly complex and life-like robot. If the creature is an other that turns out to be less different from the crew than at first appears, the robot is one that at first appears to be one of them. The relation of corporate technocracy to personal behaviour is raised most explicitly by his very indistinguishability. All along, Ash has been at once the most disagreeable character and the one most loyal to the corporation. Significantly, however, until this point he has seemed to differ from the others only in degree, not at all in kind. *All* of the crew are children of technology; at the beginning they emerge, dressed in diaper-like wrappings, from the suspended animation units that are the frozen womb of the ship's computer, whose name is 'Mother'. All, including the protagonist and sole survivor, Ripley, are technocrats, and their behavioural style is efficient but, as Harvey R. Greenberg points out, 'impersonal, tense, slightly abrasive. There is hardly a trace of empathy.... [Moreover,] it is strongly suggested that the source of the *Nostromo*'s impoverished relatedness lies in an overweening lust for gain, a life-denying greediness that extends from the highest levels of *Alien* world to root itself within the individual psyche'.[4] The crew's ordeals and (with one exception) their deaths result in large part from the fact that they cannot tell Ash from themselves until it is too late. But one reason they cannot do so is that they have chosen, out of the same greed that motivated his creators, to be like him.

Moreover, once the crew members have made such a choice, the problem of recognizing the machine in their midst is compounded by the fact that they now find themselves in circumstances where the key traits necessary for success, or even survival, are self-control and cool competence. Ripley endures in part because she is amply gifted with these (in contrast to the other female crew member, Lambert, who is slaughtered when she freezes with fear). Audience identification with Ripley is strong, partly because her situation is so desperate. But she is excellently adapted to her spaceship environment and her coldness, especially unusual for a Hollywood-style heroine, is part of her adaptation.

Both her unwillingness to act on emotion and her own dedication to company policy emerge most strongly in contrast with Ash's only moment of apparent emotion or altruism. This comes when he violates policy by opening the quarantine door to admit the explorers Dallas, Lambert, and Kane, together with the creature, which has attached itself to Kane's face. Though Ash seems to act out of sympathy for Kane, we find later that he has in fact been motivated only by the company's top priority, the safe return of the alien. But most interesting here is the fact that, given their present situation, the crew *must*, for the sake of their very survival, do as Ripley does, and follow procedures that leave no room for emotion or for sympathy with the individual. The irony, of course, is that this is precisely the sort of behaviour both honoured and manifested by a corporation that finally cares about its workers not at all. Thus its robot agent admires the horrible alien for what he calls 'its purity', a structural perfection matched only by its hostility, and geared solely for survival, unclouded by conscience or delusions of morality.

Of course, the film's own values finally contradict Ash's.[5] Not only is his behaviour (or more precisely that of the corporate force behind him) clearly evil, but the deaths of the crew members may be seen symbolically in terms of a system of moral retribution. Kane, who dies first, is the most eager raider of nature, and as such the clearest embodiment of the imperialist attitude towards the other. He volunteers for the exploratory mission; and it is he who looks around most curiously and aggressively, who finds the alien, and who triggers its hostile life by his prying at its egg. For this latter act, he earns a name homonymous with that of the first murderer. Dallas, the captain, dies because, in ceding authority about the alien to the sinister Ash (against Ripley's advice), he too blindly accepts company policy and thus fails to protect his colleagues adequately. At first glance this seems to suggest a contradiction, for

Ripley was right when she tried to follow policy. But the difference is that in her case policy intersects with human needs, and indeed turns out not to be consonant with the company's true but concealed interest in the situation; that interest is finally being protected by Ash when he violates the stated policy. As for Dallas, he acts more or less mechanically, with no individual assessment of the situation at all; he simply does what he has been told to do. If Kane actively embodies the values of venture capitalism and imperialism, Dallas follows the system's orders. Here, as at Nuremburg, his type is found guilty.

Brett and Parker, the crew's working class, clearly hold the least allegiance to the corporation. But they do buy into its values, for their primary concern is their own economic gain. Brett is the less helpful and more overtly selfish of the two, and hence he gets his first. Lambert's problem is a little different; she is so weakened by fear for her own life that she lacks competence and fails to help Parker, and her weakness is finally fatal. There is, by the way, a dig at the predominantly white male power structure in the fact that the minority character (Parker, who is black) and the women (Lambert, Ripley) live the longest.

In moral terms, Ripley survives, despite her coldness, for two major reasons. First, she is the most group-oriented (or least totally self-absorbed) character; she sounds genuinely concerned when she tells Dallas to be careful, and after his death insists to the others that 'we have to stick together'. Indeed, though her decision not to open the quarantine door seems heartless, it is motivated in part by a sense of the collective good, and is vindicated later. Second, Ripley does show some altruism, and some connection to a not-totally-alien nature, when she risks her life to save the cat, Jonesey. Note also that when she is on the escape ship and thinks she has blown up the alien, she holds and strokes the cat, and says comfortingly, 'All right, it's nice to see you too'. And when she finally does triumph, her last line is: 'Let's go home, Jonesey'.

Yet even though Ripley avoids total amorality and iciness (and thereby earns a name only one letter different from the director's as well as an escape from death), her case, too, is part of the cautionary tale. She too must suffer horrible tribulations for her vocational choice. For, again, what she has chosen is a situation in which the most valued and even necessary traits are also the ones that serve to make human beings essentially indistinguishable from the corporation's literal, and malevolently controlled, robots.

It is just this indistinguishability that lies at the heart of *Blade Runner*.[6] Here the giant Tyrell Corporation's most advanced products are utterly lifelike 'replicants', produced by genetic engineers. They are stronger than, and at least as intelligent as, their creators. Moreover, they are so advanced that they have developed a serious flaw: they have the capacity, over an extended period of time, to develop human emotions, and when they do so they can become uncontrollable. So they have been given a failsafe mechanism – a 'life'-span of only four years, after which they self-destruct. In addition, the newest models have been supplied with built-in memories of their fictitious childhoods, as a kind of cushion against the emotions, so that they may be controlled more easily. But even these devices haven't been enough, and hence replicants have been outlawed on Earth since some of them rebelled and killed several people off-planet. Emotion may lead to revolution. Indeed, the replicants are now such a threat that units of special police/executioners – blade runners – have been formed on Earth to 'retire' (kill) them on sight.

Social attitudes towards the replicants are racist: a police captain refers to them as 'skin-jobs', and the protagonist, a blade runner named Deckard, tells us that this is the equivalent of 'nigger' in our own time. Moreover, as in racist societies generally, a great deal of emphasis is put on the making of ever finer distinctions between the dominant group and those believed to be inferior. And this emphasis results from the increasing difficulty of sustaining any clear or justifiable distinction between master and slave.

The difference is blurred most obviously by the increasingly human traits of the replicants. Indeed, with the addition of the memories, and of snapshots purporting to document them, at least one replicant, Rachael, is herself unaware that she is not human. Deckard finds this fact somewhat disturbing and perhaps cruel. But when he asks Mr Tyrell, the corporate head who is the film's most unmitigated villain, how Rachael can not know what she is, he really explains *why*, not how. 'Commerce,' he says with a gleam of satisfaction, and then: 'More human than human is our motto'.

All of this ends up posing a problem for Deckard that goes far beyond the difficulty of making sure he's discovered the proper figures to 'retire'. He cannot be certain that he himself is not a replicant. This uncertainty is made explicit when Rachael asks him if he has ever taken the test by which replicants are identified. Her question arises because of a pattern similar to the one we saw in *Alien*. For Deckard to do his unpleasant job, and thus to remain a cop rather than one of the 'little people' (a potential victim of the power structure),[7] he must be emotionless. He has been the best of blade runners, but at the expense of, among other things, his marriage: he says that his ex-wife called him 'sushi', which he translates as 'cold fish'. To fulfil his social function, a function necessitated by and executed in the service of corporate interests, he must have precisely the qualities that Ash values in the alien or that the society of *Blade Runner* values in replicants. He must be strong, intelligent, competent, and above all without qualm, fear, or any other human emotional response.

Now, however, he has tried to quit because he has 'had a bellyful of killing' (he rejects the euphemism 'retirement'). In other words, he has begun to see the replicants as human, and to get squeamish. Later he tells us: 'Replicants weren't supposed to have feelings. Neither were blade runners. What the hell was happening to me?' Immediately after he explains that the replicants have a special attachment to their photographs (because they need them to shore up their 'memories'), we see Deckard himself deep in contemplation over his own collection of old photos. More is suggested in these details than a mere growth in sympathy for the replicants. Deckard's development of feelings parallels their own, and is just as inappropriate to his social role. If he *is* human, human beings and their artificial doubles are fast converging.

Hence in the climactic scene, the ironies proliferate around the taunting question that Roy Batty, the most fearsome of the replicants, poses to Deckard as Roy stalks him. The question is 'Aren't you the good man?' First of all, Deckard cannot say whether he is a man of any sort. Second, being a good man seems in this society to mean being a good killer, inhumane and affectless. Third, at the crucial moment it is Roy who acts humanely, sparing and even saving his victim, out of a love of life. And these ironies are further compounded by the tribute paid to Deckard after his violent mission is completed: 'You've done a man's job'. Ultimately, his developing feelings for Rachael force Deckard to flee the society, to enter a natural wilderness as he plunges into an existential commitment to a life – and especially an emotional life – with her. The Tyrell Corporation's society has no place for such a 'natural' life.

Of course, the movie ends with the affirmation of Deckard's commitment. But it also leaves us with the nagging fear that he may be a replicant, and hence doomed. We tend to assume that he is human, but we cannot be certain. And even if he is taken to be a replicant, the film's cautionary point is simply reinforced, for the society portrayed is one that has become so cold that the robots are more human than the human beings. Indeed, the overall effect of the tale is to indicate that in such a society the identifying characteristics of humanity (at least in the sense of humaneness) would be so drained away as to deconstruct more or less thoroughly the traditional human/robot (humane/inhumane, feeling/ unfeeling) opposition. What SF has traditionally taken to be a difference *between* the human and the robotic would then emerge more clearly as a difference *within* the human. That this is in fact already the true locus of the opposition was the explicitly stated position of the late Philip K. Dick, the author of the novel (*Do Androids Dream of Electric Sheep?*) on which *Blade Runner* is based:

There is amongst us something that is a bi-pedal humanoid, morphologically identical to the human being but which is not human.... *Within our species* is a bifurcation, a dichotomy between the truly human and that which mimics the truly human.[8]

As others have pointed out, *Blade Runner*, like *Alien*, finally retreats from the implications of its radical critique into filmic clichés and individualist solutions.[9] Created within the Hollywood style in terms of both genre and cinematography, and aiming at an audience that is both identified and managed by the Hollywood system of production and distribution, the films are bound, consciously or not, by formidable constraints. Nonetheless, both of them do offer such a radical critique, in more ways than one. Their strongest common element in this regard is their insistence on the dehumanization necessary for human survival in a world dominated by mega-corporations. Human relationships to the robotic villain of *Alien*'s glossy high-tech spaceship, and to the more complex but equally fearsome replicants of *Blade Runner*'s futuristic film noir vision of urban decay, function to raise this issue in powerful terms.

In many regards, what *Alien* and *Blade Runner* criticize, *Star Trek II: The Wrath of Kahn* mythicizes and justifies by presenting an entirely different vision of the capitalist future. Since, unlike the works already discussed, this movie does not focus its exploration of the relationship between the economic infrastructure and the behaviour of individuals on the doubling motif, and since this particular episode in the ongoing *Star Trek* saga has received relatively little critical attention, it is necessary to consider it somewhat more broadly here. What such a consideration ultimately will show is that *Star Trek II* largely affirms, with some variations, not only the personal styles that *Alien* and *Blade Runner* question, but also the bourgeois patriarchal structures of power and values that give rise to these ways of behaving. Where conformity to the demands of these structures is dehumanizing and dangerous in Scott's films, it is seen as both necessary and proper in *Star Trek II*.

Typically enough for a bourgeois myth, *Star Trek II* seldom overtly discusses economic arrangements. It prefers instead to emphasize the military half of the military-industrial complex. However, its very silence on economics, when coupled with its support of contemporary middle-class notions, suggests that there is no major economic difference between its world and our own, and thus implicitly supports the present status quo. The starship, after all, is the *Enterprise.* What *is* different in this future, however, is the total erasure of any systemic racial, national, class, or gender conflict. The good characters include a black captain

(Terrell), an Asian (Sulu), a Russian (Chekhov), and a woman (Saavik). All of these have been successfully assimilated; all admire and (when not mentally controlled by the villain) work loyally for Kirk, the white male supreme. The black even commits suicide rather than betray him (the contrast between this group's allegiances and those of the crew of the *Nostromo* is instructive). As for class differences, there aren't any; the only hierarchy is a meritocratic one of rank and experience.

Though the Klingons get passing mention, they are simply a faceless evil force. The only true villain is the mad, overweening egotist, Khan. His extreme personality places him outside the social order. For one thing, he's too intellectual – and eccentric – to be 'one of us' (as we are represented by the crew of the *Enterprise*), for he reads Shakespeare and even quotes Melville. More importantly, he's finally brought down by blind, tumultuous *passion* for vengeance: Kirk has inadvertently caused Khan's wife's death, but Chekhov sets the record straight by telling Khan that Kirk was 'only doing his duty'. Thus Khan lacks or rejects the technocratic values of moderation, self-control, obedience to authority, and objectivity. Consequently, he is a 'bad father', who leads his band of disaffected youth to their deaths. If the example of the Ahab he quotes was a caution against transcendentalism, Khan himself is an exemplary caution against the emotionalist and non-conformist spirit of the 1960s, which revived that earlier movement. As for his young followers, they are clearly space-hippies in their hairstyles and clothes, and are thus opposed to Kirk's clean-cut, uniformed 'children' (his word) whom he commands on a 'training mission' that becomes a rite of passage. The uniformity that is in *Alien* a sign of dehumanization is here a sign of proper allegiance.

Moreover, Khan's people are not only hippies, but terrorists; they seek to weaken the power structure by attacks on innocent third parties. In a world where there are no political problems, however, their violent actions are as emptied of historical justification as their hip appearance; such actions only serve the leader's desire for personal revenge, the desire of an idiosyncratic, warped, and malevolent mind. The question of whether, and when, terrorism is politically or historically justified is evaded in favour of a mythification that implies that things are really all much easier than that: terrorists are simply Khans, selfishly aggrieved loonies who refuse to accept our wonderful world and the happiness it offers uniformly to all, regardless of race, colour, national origin, or gender.

Of course, this view of terrorism is precisely what we would expect of such a Hollywood product; it is nearly as conventional as the 'bomber-crew' ethnic pattern. But in this movie the common Hollywood myth that all the world's problems stem from personal villainy is also part of a larger pattern that works uncommonly hard to resolve the 'generation gap' of the 1960s in favour of the patriarchy's vision of the 'good father'. Thus the movie includes two other major lines of conflict. The first concerns Kirk – Captain America, in more than one important sense – against his own ageing and the demands of a culture that would subtly emasculate him by installing him as teacher and bureaucrat rather than violent, heroic man of action. Here the movie does suggest some criticism of the homogenizing tendencies of the liberal technocracy. But it is clearly a critique from the right, not the left. For Kirk (unlike his crew) is envisioned along entrepreneurial lines in terms of personal style (though not in terms of actual economic niche). Though he both accepts and serves the Establishment's ultimate interests and values, he quarrels with its notion of means. He can be more effective if he is freer to operate – if he is able, for instance, to act on the intuition that is clearly part of his character.[10] In his particular case (though by no means in general), a somewhat more *laissez-faire* attitude on the part of the power structure would be more productive.

The second, related conflict is between Kirk and domesticity, as embodied in his former lover and in the son he fathered but deserted for the larger role of protecting society. It's no accident that the latter two are civilians working on a government grant; they are part of the mistaken liberal establishment. The son, David, has developed a hatred for Kirk and all he stands for. When Khan tries to steal the funded research – the life-giving Genesis Project – the son all too easily believes Kirk is stealing it for the military, and thereby breaking the government's promise. David has pacifist tendencies, and his pacifism seems to be both a consequence of his having been raised by his mother, without a properly virile, violent role-model, and a kind of reaction-formation. He reacts both against the father he really 'is a lot like' (as his mother says) and against his Oedipal hostility towards that figure. Thus it comes as only a mild surprise when at one point his psychic defences fail and he goes for Kirk with a knife. The knife is something of an anachronism in this movie's world, but its Freudian resonances make it the only fitting weapon for this scene. And it comes as no surprise at all when the father easily disarms the son. However, the attack does divert Kirk just long enough to allow some agents of Khan to get the drop on him. David's adolescent rebellion helps place Dad in a much more serious crisis, just as rightists claimed the youth rebellion of the 1960s threatened to distract and thereby weaken America vis-à-vis its external enemies.

Naturally, this family conflict is resolved towards the end. After Khan has been defeated, David comes to Kirk who, knowing the boy's previous hatred, tries to dodge the encounter. But what David forces him to hear is music to his ears: 'I was wrong about you, and I'm sorry.

I'm proud to be your son'. Then in one of those rare moments of an emotion Kirk generally withholds, the two embrace. Fathers all over the theatre should be cheering at this point, for Kirk and all he stands for – patriarchal white America, the sex-role division that approves the father's non-participation in the work of child-rearing, and the benign violence of proper authority – have been vindicated. Kirk's choice to absent himself from personal relationships, his repression of eros and empathy for the sake of duty to a larger socio-economic structure, is here seen not as Ridley Scott would see it – as a sign of alienation or dehumanization – but as a mark of altruism. Despite the son's earlier feelings, the father's love has not really been withheld; rather, it has been expressed in protection for his family and for the society. If anyone has really suffered here, it has not been the single-parent mother (whose job it was to rear the child anyway), not the immature lad, but the father who has given up so much – who has even risked giving up their love – for their sake. Of course an even remotely feminist analysis exposes how self-serving this position is for the father; and the movie itself (un-wittingly, I think) signals the duplicity involved in it, by showing how much Kirk enjoys the world of work to which he has supposedly sacri-ficed himself.

In order further to grasp the movie's view specifically of emotion, and of proper masculine behaviour, we must consider the treatment of Mr Spock. Though rendered quite differently, he is *Star Trek*'s equivalent of *Alien*'s robot in that he is supposedly emotionless and absolutely logical.[11] However, since to make him a robot would, by the SF code, be clearly pejorative, he is an alien instead. Nonetheless, he is Kirk's best friend (while he also serves to make Kirk more human by contrast). And as Spock dies in *Star Trek II*, we find once again that even he is not really emotionless. Like Kirk, he must have feelings in order to be good. But they must be concealed except in the most compelling circum-stances, and then they must be drastically understated, and expressed only to another man in male camaraderie. In this movie, as often in white male middle-class America, we are to hide our cake and eat it too, as gestures of feeling become the more poignant for their rarity. This essentially anal attitude is precisely fitted to the man's role in capitalist society. On one level, it keeps him subdued and under control, and prevents feelings from interfering with duty. On another, it is a manifest-ation of the supremely bourgeois Calvinist ideology that makes emotion the equivalent of other commodified values; one is to have it and hoard it, but not to use it or show it ostentatiously.

Finally, *Star Trek II* represents the apotheosis of the rational, emotionally restrained man. Spock dies that others may live, and there is a clear implication, at the end, of his impending resurrection in *Star*

Trek III: The Search for Spock. Thus themes and myths converge with box-office necessity. Moreover, not only is the rational man Christ-like, but in a brash reversal of cinematic codes, he is identified with nature as positive value; at the end, in his black capsule/coffin, Spock lies on the new, fecund planet Genesis, awaiting his own return to life.

It would be easy to make too much of all this. *Star Trek II*, like *Alien* and *Blade Runner*, is intended primarily as entertainment, not propaganda. Certainly it is more a reflection and reinforcement than an active shaper of current values. Nonetheless, it does seem to affirm the very sorts of social arrangements and trends that *Alien* and *Blade Runner* find so threatening. That it does so with considerable wit simply makes careful 'reading' of it more important (and thus helps keep critics in business, too). In any case, all these movies demonstrate once again how actively popular art in general, and especially SF, may engage in cultural debate, and hence may demand a response that recognizes and evaluates the messages they carry. In this particular case, as all three movies see a specific kind of value system and personal style as emerging from large-scale corporate capitalism, they encourage us to pose certain crucial questions. If we choose to try to maintain our current social and economic arrangements (and if they aren't changed for us), will we become Ripleys or Kirks, Spocks or Ashes? Will we be able to tell the difference? Or will we choose not to find out?

Notes

1. For a broader overview of recent futuristic movies in their cultural context, see H. Bruce Franklin, 'Visions of the Future in Science Fiction Films from 1970 to 1982' in this volume.

2. A further ironic application of the title to the crew themselves is suggested by Kenneth Jurkiewitz's description of them, in 'Technology in the Void: Politics and Science in Four Contemporary Space Movies', *New Orleans Review*, vol. 9, no. 1, 1982, as 'classically alienated laborers' (p. 17). See also Judith Newton, 'Feminism and Anxiety in *Alien*' in this volume.

3. Jeff Gould, 'The Destruction of the Social by the Organic in *Alien*' in Charles Elkins, ed., 'Symposium on *Alien*', *Science Fiction Studies*, vol. 7, no. 3, 1980, p. 283.

4. Harvey R. Greenberg, 'The Fractures of Desire: Psychoanalytic Notes on *Alien* and the Contemporary "Cruel" Horror Film', *The Psychoanalytical Review*, vol. 70, no. 2, 1983, p. 260.

5. For a dialogue on the ideological complexity and confusion of *Alien*, see Elkins, ed., and Greenberg.

6. See J.P. Telotte, 'The Doubles of Fantasy and the Space of Desire' in this volume; J.P. Telotte, 'Human Artifice and the Science Fiction Film', *Film Quarterly*, vol. 36, no. 3, 1983; Leonard G. Heldreth, 'The Cutting Edges of *Blade Runner*', presented at the Popular Culture Association Symposium, Toronto, March 1984.

7. In *Blade Runner*, as in Fritz Lang's *Metropolis* (1926), class structure is vividly reflected in the city's physical levels. Here, however, the lower classes are not underground, but on the surface, while the upper classes are far above, detached from Earth and from the

ecological wreckage they have made of it. See Yves Chevrier, '*Blade Runner*; or, the Sociology of Anticipation', *Science Fiction Studies*, vol. 11, no. 1, 1984, p. 52.

8. Philip Strick, 'The Age of the Replicant', *Sight and Sound*, vol. 51, no. 3, 1982. p. 172 (emphasis added).

9. Chevrier, p. 57; Douglas Kellner, Flo Leibowitz and Michael Ryan, '*Blade Runner*: A Diagnostic Critique', *Jump Cut*, no. 29, 1984, p. 8.

10. Jane Elizabeth Ellington and Joseph W. Critelli, 'Analysis of a Modern Myth: The *Star Trek* Series', *Extrapolation*, vol. 24, no. 3, 1982, pp. 244, 247.

11. For a similar comparison of Spock with *Alien*'s Ash, see Jurkiewitz. For a study of the patriarchal structures of the 'Star Trek' television series, see Anne Cranny-Francis, 'Sexuality and Sex-Role Stereotyping in "Star Trek"', *Science Fiction Studies*. vol. 12, no. 3, 1984.

PART II

Ideologies

The basic premises of reflectionist criticism are that the 'real world' pre-exists and determines representation, and that representation portrays the real world in unmediated fashion. However, other views exist about representation and the real which, while not questioning the actual distinction, would nevertheless take issue with the view that the relationship between its two terms is one of unilinear determination.[1] In critical theory, this position is expressed in certain kinds of attitudes towards the instrumentality of cultural productions; in particular the view that representations may have effects of their own, can themselves impinge upon the realm of the social.

For example, the real-representation relation can be regarded as dialectical – interactive and potentially contradictory – rather than simply reflective. Such a view implies that representation possesses some degree of autonomy, and can thus be active in the production of the 'real', as well as vice versa. This has implications for our understanding of the nature of meaning, of how processes of signification work in representations. If representations are no longer seen as simply mirroring the real, then the production of meaning can be regarded as an *activity*, and representations understood as systems of meaning. If meanings are produced, then the questions for cultural theory must be: How are they produced, and with what consequences? What, in cultural terms, does signification do?

In producing meanings, representations may in effect shape our understanding of the world we live in. This is a process of ideology, which in one of its several definitions is understood precisely as a society's representations of itself in and for itself, and the ways in which people both live out and produce these representations. In a divided

53

society, of course, ideologies can be heterogeneous and meanings contested – and indeed ideology is commonly associated with power or hegemony, which suggests that meaning is never neutral, but always caught up in relations of power. At the same time, though, ideology works to conceal this fact from us. If meaning presents itself as already there, immanent and not constructed, then representation in a way invites us to adopt a reflectionist stance. Ideology, in consequence, rarely proclaims itself as such, but is invisible, *naturalized*. Unravelling the work of ideology calls first of all for it to be denaturalized.

Films are representations of a particular kind – they have their own semiotic processes, their own ways of making meaning. Cinema's part in the production and circulation of ideologies thus involves its own signifying practices, central among which must be the capacity of the film image to present itself as uncoded, a direct record of the real. Ideology, in this view, is grounded not only in social relations – of class, power and so on – but also in signification. It has been argued, for example, that genre films refer to each other – to the codes and conventions through which particular generic meanings are produced across a body of film texts – as much as to any social/historical actuality outside the films.[2] If ideology is grounded in signification, then ideologies and their activity can be brought to light by looking at film texts. But, given their capacity for self-concealment, ideologies cannot as a rule be uncovered by means of an empiricist approach, one which attends to the immediately observable; it will usually be necessary to dig deeper, to seek out subtexts and underlying meanings.

For this reason, ideological readings of films – analyses of film texts and genres directed at revealing their ideological work – have tended to adopt structuralist rather than empiricist approaches to method. Structuralism assumes both that texts are constructs – that textual meanings are made, not already there; and also that while signification processes may not be immediately observable, they can be discovered through a process of deconstruction. The underlying ideological operations of a film text or a group of texts are exposed by means of symptomatic readings, which attend to what is not there – the gaps, the silences, the 'structuring absences' – as much as to what is.[3]

Ideological criticism is usually tendentious – which is to say, it is motivated by an explicit political impulse. It aims to lay bare, and so make available for comment and critique, the relations of power of which ideologies are part. This interventionist approach to criticism has been closely associated with oppositional political stances such as Marxism and feminism, and especially with versions of these influenced by the ideas of the philosopher Louis Althusser, whose revisionist approach to Marxist thought emphasized its structuralist aspects. Althusser advanced the view that ideology can have its own effects, independently of other elements of the social formation, and thus that interventions in the sphere of ideology – including, presumably, ideological film criticism – can be political in their own right. The four essays in this section, which are concerned with the ideological operations of recent science fiction films, are influenced in varying degrees by Marxism, feminism, or Althusserianism. They all suggest that these films – under the cover of entertainment – are actively involved in 'interpellating' their audiences (see also Part IV), placing us within a framework of ideology; and in shaping our views of the world – but in ways that may not be apparent at first glance.

Michael Ryan and Douglas Kellner take up an issue already raised in some of the essays in Part I: representations of technology in science fiction films. Much of their essay is devoted to a reading of the ideological figuration of technology in Ridley Scott's *Blade Runner* (1982) – a film which, they contend, distances itself from the 'conservative technophobia' of earlier science fiction films like *THX 1138* (1970) and *Logan's Run* (1976).The implication is that a deconstructive analysis of science fiction films permits a more positive evaluation of technology than is common in more reflectionist approaches, which – as has been noted – tend towards the apocalyptic. In contending that *Blade Runner* can be read as a 'progressive' science fiction film, Ryan and Kellner echo Thomas B. Byers's conclusion (see Part I) about this same film. This suggests that the cultural instrumentalities implicit in reflectionist and ideological approaches to science fiction cinema may, at their boundaries, shade off into one another.

Michael Stern's essay, 'Making Culture into Nature', distances itself somewhat further from reflectionism, proclaiming itself a structuralist project of denaturalization – in this instance of the ideological work of special effects in science fiction films and other media productions. Special effects, says Stern, 'accomplish the political work of legitimizing current structures of domination': their ideological work forms part of society's structures of power, all the more effective because they present themselves as magical – and thus outside history and beyond the reach of human intervention.

The analysis of *Alien* (1979) by James H. Kavanagh, emphasizing 'the film's ... internally overdetermined and contradictory construction', is explicitly Althusserian. *Alien*'s ideological work, in this reading, centres on the split between science and humanism, and – even if riven with contradictions – the film, says Kavanagh, in the end asserts a triumphant rebirth of humanism. Kavanagh's contention is that all of *Alien*'s contradictions revolve around the science/humanism problematic, leaving the image of the 'strong woman' in the figure of the film's hero, Ripley (Sigourney Weaver) more internally consistent. *Alien*, Kavanagh concludes, is unproblematically progressive from a feminist standpoint. Judith Newton, however, takes issue with this. In her Marxist-feminist reading of the film, she advances the argument that it is simultaneously utopian and repressive. It is utopian in suggesting that individual action – notably on Ripley's part – can resolve problems that are fundamentally social and economic in origin; and that women can redress the horrors of capitalism's public sphere – but only on an individual level. It is repressive, she says, in its displacement of masculine fears of female sexuality and castrating femininity onto the monstrously female, and phallic, alien. *Alien*'s stance in relation to feminism is equally, and perhaps more overtly, compromised, says Newton, by Ripley's resumption of traditionally feminine qualities (nurturance, vulnerability) in the film's closing sequences. The ideological work of the film is in the end to voice, and to produce, anxieties about feminism as a collective and potentially radical force.

These two contributions to the debate about *Alien* illustrate the range of approaches that can be brought to ideological readings of films, and also perhaps suggest the extent to which this particular film is open to a variety of interpretations – part of its fascination, no doubt. They also highlight the primarily text-based character of ideological criticism, though this is by no means inherent in the method itself. Michael Stern's essay is witness that ideological criticism can be brought to bear at least on groupings of film texts – such as genres, science fiction included. But Stern's analysis is exceptional. Surprisingly, perhaps, there appears to have been little, if any, critical work directed at the cultural instrumentality of ideology across the genre as a whole.[4]

Taken in sum, the essays in this section demonstrate that ideological analysis always refers back to some notion or other of society, the social order, or social/historical actuality. If this form of criticism is based on the premise that meaning production has its own logics, it always assumes as well that meanings are in some way grounded in the social, the 'real': in this sense ideological criticism is basically materialist. At the same time, as has been noted, much of it is text-based: thus to the extent that it takes individual films as its starting point, ideological criticism is a type of textual analysis. Other types of textual analysis, however, root themselves in rather different conceptualizations of the real-representation relation. The textual analyses in Part III, for example, are premised not on a notion of signification as socially grounded so much as on an impulse to explore the connections between meanings in film texts and processes of the human unconscious.

Notes

1. For a discussion of this issue, see Terry Lovell, *Pictures of Reality*, London: British Film Institute 1980.

2. Christine Gledhill, 'Genre' in Pam Cook, ed., *The Cinema Book*, London: British Film Institute 1985.

3. For a fuller discussion of ideological criticism, see Annette Kuhn, *Women's Pictures: Feminism and Cinema*, London: Routledge & Kegan Paul 1982, chapters 4 and 5.

4. For a critique of this state of affairs, see Pam Annas, 'Science Fiction Film Criticism in the US', *Science Fiction Studies*, vol. 7, no. 3, 1980.

4

Technophobia

Michael Ryan and Douglas Kellner

Science fiction films concerning fears of machines or of technology usually negatively affirm such social values as freedom, individualism, and the family. In 1970s films, technology was frequently a metaphor for everything that threatened 'natural' social arrangements, and conservative values associated with nature were generally mobilized as antidotes to that threat. But technophobic films are also the site where the metaphor of nature which sustains those values can be most saliently deconstructed. From a conservative perspective, technology represents artifice as opposed to nature, the mechanical as opposed to the spontaneous, the regulated as opposed to the free, an equalizer as opposed to a promoter of individual distinction, equality triumphant as opposed to liberty, democratic levelling as opposed to hierarchy derived from individual superiority. Most important for the conservative individualist critique, it represents modernity, the triumph of radical change over traditional social institutions. Those institutions are legitimated by being endowed with the aura of nature, and technology represents the possibility that nature might be reconstructable, not the bedrock of unchanging authority that conservative discourse requires. Indeed, as the figure for artificial construction, technology represents the possibility that such discursive figures as 'nature' (and the ideal of free immediacy it connotes) might merely be constructs, artificial devices, metaphors designed to legitimate inequality by positing a false ground of authority for unjust social institutions.

The significance of technology thus exceeds simple questions of mechanics. It is usually a crucial ideological figure. Indeed, as the possibility of reconstructing institutions conservatives declare to be part of nature, technology represents everything that threatens the grounding of conservative social authority and everything that ideology is designed to neutralize. It should not be surprising, then, that this era should witness the development of a strain of films that portray technology negatively, usually from a conservative perspective.

The technophobic theme is most visible in the early 1970s in George Lucas's *THX 1138* (1970), a quest narrative set in a cybernetic society where all of life is regulated by the state. Individuals are forced to take drugs to regulate sexual desires; thoughts and individual action are monitored by electronic surveillance devices. A sense of mass, collectivist conformity is connoted by shaved heads, the assigning of numbers instead of names, and starkly lit white environments. The lack of differentiation between individuals is suggested by the limitless quality of space; everything lacks boundaries, from the self to the city. The libertarian basis of the film's value system cuts both ways politically – liberally, in that recorded messages allude to the McCarthyite repression of dissidents; and conservatively, in that they also refer negatively to socialism ('Blessings of the State, blessings of the masses. We are created in the image of the masses, by the masses, for the masses'). Against undifferentiated totalitarianism, the film valorizes the differentiated individual. THX flees the cybernetic society, and the last image depicts his emergence into freedom and nature. His liberation is associated with a bright orange sun that strikingly isolates him as he emerges. The bright sun is a metaphor for individual freedom, for the departure from a world of contrivance and artifice into nature. The sun literally singularizes THX by giving him a distinguishing boundary. He is no longer one of the intersubstitutable mass. In addition, the sense the image imparts is of something literal, the thing itself, nature in its pure presence. Indeed, nature is supposed to be just that, something outside contrivance, artifice, technology, and the sort of substitution which rhetorical figures (the very opposite of what is literal) usually connote. The grounding of the ideology of liberty in nature is tantamount to grounding it in literality, since literality implies things as they are, unadulterated by the sort of artificial intersubstitution of people which prevails in the egalitarian city. Visual style connotes political attitudes, and given a choice between the deep white frieze of equality and the warm orange glow of liberty, one suspects what people are likely to choose.

The rhetorical strategy of many technophobic films, therefore, is to establish a strong opposition between terms (liberty vs equality) that does not permit any intermediation. The elimination of the middle ground is an essential operation of this ideology. A major mid-seventies film that executes this strategy is *Logan's Run* (1976), in which a policeman named Logan is induced into fleeing a cybernetic city by a young female rebel against the city's totalitarian regime. The representation of

the city evokes all the negative traits in the conservative vision assigned
to the figure of technology – the destruction of the family, the inter-
changeability of sexual partners so that feeling is destroyed by rationality, enforced mass conformity that places the collective before the
individual and effaces individual differences in an egalitarian levelling,
the power of state control over the freedom to choose, and so on. The
city is a mid-seventies liberal pleasure dome where one can summon
sexual partners at the touch of a button, or periodically receive a new
identity. Population size is regulated, and no one has parents. This lack
of self-identity is associated with hedonism and collectivity. Logan and
the woman rebel get caught up in an orgy at one point, and the colours
suggest hell. When the two are separated (divorced, one might say, to
emphasize the ideological motif), they almost lose their identities in the
teeming crowd. In such a sexually permissive, hedonistic world, clearly
no social hierarchy or subjective boundary can be established or
maintained. Collectivity is thus associated with a loss of self-identity and
a lack of sexual discipline that breaks family bonds.

One of the first things that Logan says upon emerging into nature is,
'We're free'. In nature one knows who one's mother and father are,
whereas in the city of collectivism and sexual hedonism no one knows
his/her parents. Thus one can only be an individual, a self, within a
society of monogamous marriage, in which sexuality primarily serves the
'natural' function of reproduction rather than pleasure. In the film's
conservative ideology, the restoration of the traditional family, the
preservation of individualism, and the curtailing of nonreproductive
sexuality seem to be interdependent, and they all depend on the
rejection of everything technology represents – mediation, equality,
intersubstitutability, and so on. In this vision one catches a glimpse of
the actual ingredients of the emerging conservative movement whose
values the film transcodes.

Outside the technological city, the rebels discover nature as well as
supposedly natural institutions like patriarchy and political republican-
ism. The woman ceases to be an equal of the man, a structure of
equivalence generated in the city by representations, primarily wide-
angle long shots of crowds, that place everyone on the same plane in the
same frame and imply their equality. In nature, she assumes a subordinate position, both socially and within the camera frame as they sit by a
crude campfire. Close-ups connote an unmediated spontaneity of 'natural' feeling, a literality of social structure uncontaminated by liberal revision. This is the real thing once again, not a technical substitute or an
artificial contrivance. One senses why empiricism is often the best
recourse of ideology. At the level of empirical literality, equivalences
cannot be established of the sort that thrive in the technological city,

where the possibility of infinite copies annuls individual differences. At the level of social literality, everything is radically individuated, incapable of comparison. Appropriately, then, Logan kills his police partner, who has followed the rebels out of the city. He is a double or copy who is Logan's functional equal, and his death individuates Logan, who renounces his identity as a cybernetic functionary precisely because his intersubstitutability means he has no identity as such. The death occurs at the moment in the narrative when the rebels have come to Washington and rediscovered the United States's republican political system. With it, they rediscover the predominance of liberty over equality, the individual over the collective.

The peculiar twist of this ideal of liberty, therefore, is that it is a social theory that rejects the social (being other than oneself, mediated by social relation, a copy or technological robot). The choice of nature, as an alternative to technological collectivity, is thus appropriate, since nature is what is entirely nonsocial. What conservatives ultimately want is a ground of authority that will make inequalities that are in fact socially constructed seem natural. This is tantamount to saying that such instituted inequalities must seem to embody the literal truth of nature, things as they are and should always be. For this reason, the strategy of ontologizing, of making technology and technological constructs seem as if they possess a being or essence in themselves, independent of context and use, is crucial to the conservative ideological undertaking. Technology must seem to be intrinsically evil, and this is so if the natural alternatives to technological society – the family and the individual especially – are to seem inherently good, ontologically grounded in themselves and not subject to figural comparison or connection to something outside them that might possibly serve as a substitute or equivalent. What is literal cannot be transported, as in metaphor, out of itself and made to stand for something else. Thus, technology represents a threat not only to self-presence in the sense of individual freedom in the conservative frame, but also to presence as the criterion of the ontological ground, the nature and the literality that anchor conservative social institutions.

A deconstructive analysis would point out that what is posited in this ideology as an ontological and literal cause that gives rise to social institutions – as well as to derivative, secondary, and unauthorized deviations of the original intent of nature through technological simulation and figural substitutions – is in fact an effect of those very things. The nature of ideology is the product of technology; literality is an effect of rhetoric. One notices this as those moments when nature and the literal are shown forth in films like *THX* and *Logan*. Nature takes on meaning as such within the films only as the other of urban technology. Its immediacy is mediated by that against which it is posed, just as the individual is necessarily mediated by society. Moreover, the supposed literal ground of social institutions is the effect of the metaphoric comparison of those institutions to nature. In order to call them natural, one has to engage in precisely the sort of metaphoric or figural comparison, the sort of rhetorical 'technology' that is supposedly excluded by that ascription. It is a case of innocence by association, and as a result, those institutions are guilty of being something they must claim not to be, that is, rhetorical constructs, mere technology. Thus a deconstructive reading points out the extent to which representation plays a constitutive role in the making of social institutions, because the metaphors and representations that construct the ideal images of such institutions are also models for social action.

The ideological character of the conservative technophobia films stands in greater relief when they are compared to more liberal or radical films that depict technology not as in itself, by nature, or ontologically evil, but as being subject to changes in meaning according to context and use. For example, the figure of technology is given socially critical political inflections in *Silent Running* (1971), which opposes nature and individual freedom to corporate misuse of technology in an ecological vein, representing the corporation as putting profit before the preservation of the environment. In *Star Trek* (1979) a human actually mates with an astral body born of a space probe, proving that humans and machines can get along more intimately than conservatives ever imagine. And in *Brainstorm* (1983), the story of a technological invention that can be used either for war or peace, the family is shown falling apart, then mending with the help of the invention. Through this narrative motif the family is depicted as a constructed institution, itself an invention reliant more on negotiation than on naturally given laws.

Perhaps the most significant film in regard to an alternative representation of technology that takes issue with the ideology deployed in conservative technophobia films is *Blade Runner* (1982), directed by Ridley Scott. The film, based on a novel by Philip K. Dick, concerns four androids ('replicants') who revolt against their 'maker', the Tyrell Corporation. A policeman, Deckard (Harrison Ford), is assigned to 'retire' them. Deckard falls in love with Rachael (Sean Young), one of Tyrell's most advanced replicants. With Rachael's help, he manages to kill three of the rebels and fights a final battle with the fourth, Roy (Rutger Hauer), who allows Deckard to live because he himself is about to die. At the end, a fellow policeman allows Deckard and Rachael to escape from the city and flee to nature. The film offers a mediation between technology and human values. 'Replicants are like any other machine. They can be a benefit or a hazard,' Deckard says. And the film concludes with a happy marriage of humans and machines.

Blade Runner deconstructs certain ideological oppositions at work in more conservative technology films. The marrying of human and replicant undercuts the posing of nature as an opposite to a negative technological civilization. The film also deconstructs the conservative romantic opposition of reason and feeling. In the film, reason is represented by analytic machines that dissect human and objective reality. The police detect replicants with analytic instruments that observe emotional reactions in the eye. When Deckard analyses the photograph of a room, he breaks down the reality into small parts until he captures what he seeks. The analytic gaze is thus represented as an instrument of power. Posed against this power is feeling. But the film suggests that feeling is not the polar opposite of reason. Rather, feeling, especially in the replicants, is the product of technology. And these machine humans are shown to be in many ways more 'human' than their makers. Analytic rationality is depicted as irrational and anti-human when used instrumentally in a policed, exploitative society, but it is also the instrument for constructing a more communal ethic. Thus, the film deconstructs the oppositions – human/technology, reason/feeling, culture/nature – that underwrite the conservative fear of technology by refusing to privilege one pole of the dichotomy over another and by leaving their meaning undecidable.

Blade Runner also calls attention to the oppressive core of capitalism and advocates revolt against exploitation. The Tyrell Corporation invents replicants in order to have a more pliable labour force, and the film depicts how capitalism turns humans into machines, a motif that recalls Lang's *Metropolis*. Indeed, German Expressionist features are evident throughout. The bright pink and red colours of the huge electric billboards contrast with the dark underworld of the streets, and this contrast highlights the discrepancy between the realm of leisure consumption and the underclass realm of urban poverty and labour in capitalism. In addition, the neo-Mayan architecture of the corporate buildings suggests human sacrifice for the capitalist god, and Tyrell is indeed depicted as something of a divine patriarch.

Although the film contains several sexist moments (Deckard more or less rapes Rachael), it can also be read as depicting the construction of female subjectivity under patriarchy as something pliant and submissive as well as threatening and 'castratory'. (The female replicants are sex functionaries as well as killers.) Similarly, the flight to romance and to nature at the end of the film gives rise to at least a double reading. Romance is escape to an empathetic interior realm from the external realm of public callousness in a capitalist society. Although it promotes personalization and atomization, the final flight also creates a space of autonomy and compassion which can be the basis for collective and egalitarian social arrangements. If the film privileges privatism, it may be because in US society of the time, it was possible to locate humane values only in the private sphere.

The film implies that even the supposedly grounding, ontologically authoritative, categories of conservatism like the individual, nature, the family, and sentiment are indeterminate. They have alternative political inflections that revalorize their meaning according to pragmatic criteria of context and use. It is important, then, that unlike the conservative films that end with a move toward (cinematic as well as ideological) literality that supposedly reduces constructed social institutions to a natural or ontological ground of meaning, this film ends in a way that foregrounds the construction of alternative meanings from the literal through the figural or rhetorical techniques of substitution and equivalence, especially the equivalence of human life and technology (of Rachael the machine and Deckard the human at the end, for example). Figurality is foregrounded through juxtapositions that are not justified by the literal logic of the narrative. For example, Roy suddenly carries a white dove that soon becomes a symbol of charity and forgiveness. He himself in fact becomes a figure for Christ as he lowers his head and dies. The dove he releases flies up into a blue sky that also appears out of nowhere for the first time in the film, for no literal reason. The figural or rhetorical quality of these images is thus underscored by their narratively illogical emergence. The same is true of the origami doll the other detective leaves for Deckard as he and Rachael flee; it signals that the detective allows them to escape and becomes a figure for charity. And the wry, ironic comments Deckard makes at the end about his new relationship with the android woman foreground a figural doubleness or undecidability of meaning.

All of these figures place literality in abeyance, and they underscore the fact that the metaphors conservatives employ to create a sense of a natural or literal ground are irredeemably figural. Indeed, the reconstituted family at the end is working on such a high level of constructedness and figurality, an open-ended relationship between a human and a machine, that it could never touch ground with any literal authority of a sort that the closing images of nature might have conveyed in a conservative or ideological film. What rhetoric, like technology, opens is the possibility of an ungrounded play with social institutions, simulating them, substituting for them, reconstructing them, removing them from any ground of literal meaning that would hold them responsible to its authority. Perhaps this is why technology is such an object of fear in conservative science fiction films of the current era. It is a metaphor for a possibility of reconstruction that would put the stability of conservative social institutions in question.

But the longing for literality and nature in conservative technophobic films might also be indicative of an antinomy of conservatism in the modern world. As conservative economic values became ascendent, increasingly technical criteria of efficiency came to be dominant. In addition, conservative economic development emphasizes the displacement of excessively costly human labour by machines. The increasingly technical sophistication of the economic world and the shift away from industrialized manufacturing to tertiary sector 'information age' production creates a hypermodernization that is at odds with the traditionalist impulse in conservatism, the desire that old forms and institutions be preserved. Yet the new technologies make possible alternative institutions and lifestyles, as well as the reconstruction of the social world. Perhaps this accounts for the desire for a more literal, natural world in conservative films. It is a reaction to the world they themselves help create through an ideal of efficient economic development. One antinomy of conservatism is that it requires technology for its economic programme, yet it fears technological modernity on a social and cultural plane. This can be read as a sign of the dilemma conservatives faced in the 1980s. In control of political and economic life, they could not gain power in the private realm of social values that on the whole continued to be more liberal.

Although in the mid eighties there was a marked decline in the number of conservative technophobic films, those fearful of technology do not give up easily, as might be suggested by a film like *The Terminator* (1984), in which androids continue to look and act like Arnold Schwarzenegger. Indeed, the film is about a punitive robot that just won't give up. It keeps coming on, not having seen *Blade Runner*, unaware that it is supposed to forgive and forget.

5

Making Culture into Nature

Michael Stern

Kubrick's *2001: A Space Odyssey* won the 1968 Academy Award For Special Visual Effects, but was not even nominated for make-up and costuming. This was surprising, given one of the film's most striking achievements: the extraordinarily convincing simian protomen with whose alien-prompted discovery of technology it begins. The unofficial explanation (plausible in the light of the attention and awards lavished on far inferior work in *Planet of the Apes*) was that the Academy members did not realize that Kubrick's hominids were actors, not monkeys.

This story suggests a great deal about the nature of special effects, their role in SF films and television programmes, and SF's role as the designated cultural showplace for special effects. I will try to connect SF as a discourse featuring special effects to other forms of mass communications, especially advertising and news, which have their own version of special effects. This involves the problem of 'textuality' – the idea of a 'text' as a form of practice which has been the focus of recent poststructuralist criticism.

It is possible to explore the distinction between the sorts of special effects which call attention to their 'specialness' – their status as artefacts – and those which seek to hide it. The hundreds of Japanese 'monster' movies and TV shows produced since the 1950s are examples of the former in regard to their repeated spectacles of what are clearly puppets, stuffed animals, or costumed stuntmen trampling toy block cities, model cars, and papier-mâché scenery. The explicit conventionality of these effects serves (to extend Susan Sontag's argument in 'The Imagination of Disaster'[1]) both to invoke and to contain the Japanese national experience of destruction, culminating in nuclear holocaust, at the hands of a superior technology in World War II. These films deliberately miniaturize this devastation, making it comic and unreal. A film like *Star Wars*, in contrast, celebrates the technology of destruction from the point of view of those used to employing it as victors. Hence the film's special effects are 'realistic': great pains are taken to create the illusion of giant starships in flight, in combat and so on.[2] This naturalization of artifice re-enacts the ideology of the film as a whole in its celebration of the scope and role of war, weapons, and large-scale technology in daily life. In the 1970s, the two sorts of films exemplified by the *Godzilla/Star Wars* polarity have begun to converge. The Japanese now make movies and kiddie shows with 'good' monsters, in United Nations-like coalitions, taking on extraterrestrial bad guys, smog creatures, and the Syndicate. This suggests Japan's renascent confidence in large-scale violence being under rational control, and used for acceptable ends.

Analyses of this sort, however, beg a more fundamental question about how special effects accomplish the political work of legitimizing current structures of domination. This is the question suggested by Hollywood's professional response to *2001*. Kubrick's peers were awed by, and highly appreciative of, his pioneering use of front-screen projection, slow-motion filming of model spaceships, and simulation of weightlessness; but they failed even to notice the sort of artifice involving make-up and costuming. The question, put simply is: What makes an effect 'special'? Everything in a film is an 'effect' – something fabricated, made. No shots compose or photograph themselves. The camera constructs a visual field rather than simply recording what is 'out there' in front of it, and locations are no less producers' artefacts than sound stages. Every frame of every film is a product of human labour and intention, however unanticipated the image produced may be. Why are some of the many kinds of effects which constitute a film fore-grounded by film makers and audiences as 'special', and others left in the background as ordinary, natural, unworthy of attention?

Another way of asking this question – what are the formal features of texts, and where do they come from? – puts it into the context of recent conflicts between schools of literary and social theory and criticism. By formal features, I mean the stuff in books and movies that is there to be interpreted: characters, themes, symbols, settings, chapters, stanzas, rhymes, tone, acting, frames, camera angles – the traditional vocabulary of literary and cinematic content.

In literary criticism, there has been telling dialogue between affective stylistics (whose best known exponent is Stanley Fish[3]) and structuralism and poststructuralism. For Fish, the formal features of texts – those ordinarily taken to be its irreducible elements, and preceding any critical act by the reader whatsoever – are in fact constituted by readers in a dialogue with a text which is governed by a tacit sense of context. Different formal features are generated by different ways of reading, which are themselves constituted by the assumptions of different communities of readers which change over time. Doctrines like authorial intention and appeals to the objective meanings of words are seen as the retroactive positing of origins which effaces from consciousness the awareness of its own constituting power.

Affective stylistics counters the structuralist negation of consciousness – the notion that texts are assembled out of pre-existing atoms of meaning by bricoleurs rummaging through the dustbin of the already-narrated, and are decoded by receivers who respond in rule-governed ways to the stimuli of context-free units of significance. It also counters the poststructuralist idealization of consciousness, which involves the notion that texts may be liberated from the bourgeois reification of referential meaning in order to play freely, signify endlessly, and that the word itself may be discarded as a formal feature (since it too is a fetishized commodity) in favour of anagrams and other recodings or 'graphemes'.

This conflict over the origin and nature of textual features has analogues in other disciplines: philosophy and linguistics (speech act theory vs psycholinguistics); artificial intelligence research (tacit knowledge as the ground for orderly but non-rule-like behaviour vs formalized rules as the ground for formalizable behaviour) and (what is most relevant for my argument here) sociology (ethnomethodology's account of facts as the practical accomplishments of actors with competing political ends vs academic sociology's version of facts as natural objects encountered by actors with varyingly accurate and responsible perceptions of them). The question of where the formal features of texts come from is a version of the question of where the formal features of the social world come from, and vice versa.

The intersection between ways of reading the text and ways of reading the world is where Fish's work is weakest, however. Where ways of reading texts come from, how they change, how they are connected to the social construction of reality-as-text, and above all whose interests they serve – these are questions Fish does not raise. For him, the larger explanatory context for the production of textual meaning is that of academic literary criticism and the logic of professional advancement in university English departments (that careers are best made by adopting a deviant way of reading is on the way to becoming, if not an orthodoxy, at least a co-optable heresy). Fish's suggestive work on reading as the production of formal textual features can be extended, however, to SF film and its social context.

In SF film, the special effects which its consumers' way of seeing foregrounds as formal features – recognizes as 'special' – are ones that enact the possibilities, delights, and terrors of glamorous new technologies: space flights, death rays, matter transmitters, cloning, living on the moon or at the bottom of the Pacific, socializing or fighting with aliens, being raped by a computer, and so on. A double effacement is at work in this way of seeing. The actual film maker's technology which makes these effects possible is lost to view, concealed, or ignored. And all of the other effects which make up the film are transformed from cultural artefacts into natural objects.

The simultaneous movement of foregrounding some features (special effects) while backgrounding others (effects not recognized as special) corresponds to the structure and role of other forms of discourse in advanced capitalist society. News is one example. News is taken to be what is not routine, a departure from the ordinary. Journalism, therefore (as Alvin Gouldner has suggested), tacitly divides the world into the seen-but-unnoticed regularities of daily existence and the news, which is seen, noticed, and commented upon as a departure from those regularities.[4] News both focuses and defocalizes attention simultaneously. It premises a social reality unworthy of attention as the ground against which the figure of the newsworthy appears. Furthermore, by defining news as a neutral record of events which happen in a world 'out there', the journalist's professional creed covers up the process of selection by which a tiny proportion of noticed happenings is deemed all the news fit to print. Like other commodities, news is fetishized: seen as an autonomous set of objects or processes rather than as the product of human labour and intention.

From an ethnomethodological perspective, news is produced by actors trying to impose their standards of importance and relevance on others, buttressed by the tacit assumption that these standards are universal ones. Rather than reflecting some independently existing external world empirically investigated, however, news is the trace of the way a specific social group constitutes an intelligible – and hence manageable – world in the first place. These practices, in turn, must be grounded in the structures of the organizations to which journalists and their sources belong. Daily and weekly news organizations must fill a given space on time to stay in business, which makes them dependent on routine – and almost always official – channels of information. Editors assign reporters to do stories or cover events which they must assume *in advance* will generate 'news', in order to be certain their pages or allotted time period will be filled up on deadline. News, therefore, is defined by reporters and editors before it 'happens', it is generated by the record-keeping activities of journalists and exists because it is reported, not reported because it already exists. News is a social product, a constructed reality, and newsmaking – the routinization and packaging of the predictably unexpected – is political work which constitutes social reality in ways which serve the interests of hegemonic elites.[5] For example, the rhetoric of unmasking used to announce scandals in the Western media simultaneously masks the interests of those who leak scandalous information and the reasons why the press chooses to co-operate with them (or with some of them – all leaks are not reported, and scandals can be known to journalists for years before they are publicized). More generally, the assumption that underlies the very possibility of scandal is that ordinary, everyday economic and political activity is 'normal', unproblematic, unworthy of attention. This assumption inhibits, if it does not altogether repress, awarenesss that this 'order' is both suspect and open to change.

SF films and TV shows help to construct and legitimize a world in which technology is an abstract category of effects without any specific social and political context, rather than a critical part of a whole way of life. SF foregrounds technology as a special effect – magical, socially ungrounded – while naturalizing the technologies of domination themselves. This is also the way news and advertising work. Media coverage of the near catastrophe at Three Mile Island is one example. The news focused on the nuclear power plant as a complicated technical artefact (visual icon: the cooling towers) rather than as part of the political economy (that is to say, as a corporate asset – capital equipment – at the nexus of ratepayer, management, shareholder, banker, regulator, and energy strategist activity). This is also how advertising fetishizes commodities: it isolates them from the people and processes which produce them. Cars are displayed in grain fields as if they grazed there, frozen pre-cooked rolls are called 'home-made' because they are warmed up in a microwave in the consumer's kitchen, and so on. Like advertising, which is a crucial discourse for legitimizing the technical administration of daily life, SF makes technology into the source of magical objects which enter people's lives and transform them under the direction of higher, more powerful beings (whether aliens or ruling classes).

   Mission: Impossible is perhaps the most extreme contemporary version of this. Each of these TV programmes involves the creation of a closed, totally administered world in which the will of the IM Force (and, by proxy, of the US government) can be imposed on targets reduced to the status of experimental animals. This microcosm is often created by deluding subjects into believing they are in a submarine, boat, plane, train, bomb shelter, or other sealed-off setting. These are variations on the show's most basic environment (sometimes directly presented): the prison. The world taken for granted by the IM Force's targets is shown to be the carefully constructed artefact of a hegemonic elite. The target's consciousness is totally controlled – all perceptions are managed, all choices manipulated – in an unintended caricature of the depoliticized, reprivatized, wholly determined citizen of one-dimensional society, the utopia of cheerful robots or 'happy fascism'.

Calling *Mission: Impossible* SF is controversial, of course – in part because it challenges the genre chauvinism which left-wing critics have developed about SF as a privileged domain for raising the 'problem of reality' in a critical, utopian spirit. The problematic nature of reality is the focus of *all* the key discourses – ideology, realist fiction, and daily journalism – which construct the world-as-taken-for-granted in modern society. And these discourses, like SF, are constituted by the *tension* between affirmation and negation, legitimation of the way things are and a critique of them, rather than by some positivity or negativity inherent in them.

In any case, the experience of 'cognitive estrangement' is central to *Mission: Impossible*. The revelation of the world as an artefact constructed by a conspiratorial elite at the end of each episode approaches the plots of Philip K. Dick novels (*Time Out of Joint*, for example, where the characters live in an artificial underground environment imposed on them by a military government, and where Ragle Gumm's solutions to what he thinks are newspaper competitions are really the plotting of missile targets). But what is particularly interesting about *Mission: Impossible* is not just that the show reveals how the special effects (fake explosions, simulated wounds, artificial gunfire) naturalized on other action-adventure shows were accomplished, but also that it displays how problematic the idea of a special effect is in the first place. Each episode has a ritual opening meeting during which the IM Force members discuss the particular means of deception to be used on that week's targets. These special effects often involve simulating the infliction and the results of lethal violence, especially gunshot wounds. 'Barney' and 'Jim' display sacs and capsules of fake blood which, when bitten or broken, produce a realistic wound or flow from the mouth of a 'dying' IM Force member. In the same episode, however, the bad guys often shoot and kill each other, acts accompanied by the same signs of lethal violence manipulated by the IM Force: patches of blood on clothes, blood flowing from the mouths of dying victims, and so forth. The signifying power of these effects thus depends on whether they are taken by the audience to be 'special' or not. The show's producers, however, often undermine precisely this distinction in inadvertent ways. In one episode, involving the attempt to trick a scientist threatening to blow up Los Angeles into revealing the location of his atomic bomb, Jim pretends to shoot Willie. After firing at him (with the apparatus of fake blood, blanks, etc), Jim uses the same gun to shoot at a sniper. At this point, the camera shows his 'shots' hitting the tree trunk the sniper is hiding behind. The fake gun has suddenly turned into a real one – that is, a gun which is signified as 'real' by having little charges planted under the bark of a tree go off to simulate bullet impacts in one take (with suitable post-dubbed sound) when a gun is pointed at the trunk in a separate take. But the IM Force members have already used precisely these signs to fool their targets into thinking they have been shooting at each other, and have revealed to the audience how the signs are produced. In other words: all effects are special. This suggests that the prisons in *Mission: Impossible* are ultimately psychological rather than physical: the prison of the taken-for-granted. The show's subjects believe they are in a real prison – rather than a warehouse stocked with the appropriate props and actors – because they unquestioningly believe, as we all do most of the time, in appearances.

SF helps to create the world of appearances in advanced capitalist societies, but only indirectly. Like other forms of mass communications, SF does not precisely tell people what to think – about technology, say – but rather forestalls thinking about technology in ways that are outside authorized categories of reflection. The enthusiasm of SF film makers and SF audiences for special effects is one way the genre helps to naturalize these categories, making them inevitable, taken for granted, and hence invisible. But the invisible is never transparent, only unseen. To make visible the activity of differentiating effects into the special and the ordinary is one step in recovering social reality as well as film reality as an artefact, a form of practice, and thus enabling the imagination of alternative practices – and alternative realities.

Notes

1. Susan Sontag, 'The Imagination of Disaster' in *Against Interpretation*, London: Eyre and Spottiswoode 1966.

2. Budgets clearly have something to do with this distinction (*Star Wars*, for example, cost at least ten times as much as *Godzilla*), but not everything.

3. Stanley Fish, 'Normal Circumstances, Literal Language, Direct Speech Acts, the Obvious, What Goes Without Saying, and Other Special Cases', *Critical Inquiry*, vol. 4, no. 3, 1978.

4. Alvin W. Gouldner, *The Dialectic of Ideology and Technology*, New York: Seabury Press 1976, p. 107.

5. Harvey Molotch and Marilyn Lester, 'Accidents, Scandals, and Routines: Resources for Insurgent Methodology' in Gaye Tuchman, ed., *The TV Establishment*, Englewood Cliffs, NJ: Prentice-Hall 1974; Gaye Tuchman, *Making News: A Study in the Construction of Reality*, New York: MacMillan 1978.

6

Feminism, Humanism and Science in *Alien*

James H. Kavanagh

> One can and must speak openly of Marx's *theoretical anti-humanism*, and see in this *theoretical anti-humanism* the absolute (negative) precondition of the (positive) knowledge of the human world itself, and of its practical transformation. It is impossible to know anything about men except on the absolute precondition that the philosophical (theoretical) myth of man is reduced to ashes.
>
> Louis Althusser, *For Marx*

An aesthetically effective mass-cultural production, *Alien* (1979) cleverly fuses a number of disparate cultural semes into a cinematic narrative that has considerable visual and emotional impact. At the same time, the film cannot entirely conceal those other seams, the marks of its own internally overdetermined and contradictory construction, which allows criticism to expose its attempt to resurrect a specific ideological figure. For the death of the alien, as *Alien* has it, is the triumphant rebirth of humanism, disguised as powerful, progressive, and justifying feminism.[1]

The concept of humanism which functions as a crucial ideological trope in *Alien* is similar to that suggested by the Althusserian reflection above. Within a rigorous Marxist theory of history, society, and culture, it is a theoretical error to found a transformative programme for social liberation on the pseudo-concept 'man' – an ideological notion that conceals differences, contradictions, and struggles in the real under the sign of a generalized, shared essence. For Marxism, there is no such thing as man; there are specific men and women, distributed as differentially functioning agents into specific *classes*, with *class* standing as the significant category of an effective theory of social transformation. Whatever their good intentions, humanist theories are, in this Althusserian construction, inevitably ineffective and self-defeating grounds for transformative social practice. Even Stalinism is understood, in part, as an effect of irruptions of pre-Marxist humanist ideological categories into Marxist political theory and practice. In this problematic, the word *science* designates those forms of theoretical activity capable of producing knowledge that can actually be effective in various social practices, including revolutionary political practice. The Althusserian distinction between science and humanism thus signifies something more rigorous and challenging than the nasty/nice opposition it tends to register for those held within apparatuses whose task is precisely to reproduce a humanist ideology.

Alien initially figures humanism and science in terms that disrupt and even reverse the usual science fiction reproduction of humanist ideologies, in which reason-calculation-logic is inflected as bad, or at least inhuman, and in need of the good, corrective human figure who signifies emotion-passion-concern. *Star Trek*'s Spock and Kirk are the most familiar recent mass-cultural version of this humanist ideological couple reconstructed in signifying practice. In its earlier version, in the original *Invasion of the Body Snatchers* (1956), this split is reproduced with the even more stark assertion that the only distinguishing feature of those who are 'snatched' – that which is all of their horror – is lack of emotion. The obvious Cold War images of *Body Snatchers* and the more mediated, post-Cold War détente images of *Star Trek* suggest that fears about communism lurk behind certain typical humanist fears about science and rationality.

Thus, the ideological semes that *Alien* takes as its raw material tend to inflect negatively, for example, the signifying unit 'workers', whose black male voice insists that they want nothing to do with a rescue mission, which will only consume more of their time, unless they are paid for it: 'Our time is their time; that's the way *they* see it,' one of the workers says. There is no figure more offensive to an ideological humanism than this: workers attempting to withhold labour from ostensibly humanitarian services for mere material demands, and so implicitly marking humanism as a class luxury. Unless it be that other form of calculation, speaking here in the voice of a woman who firmly refuses to open the airlock through which a stricken friend and two other colleagues might pass to safety (including a man to whom she seems attracted); this refusal speaks from the theoretically antihumanist grounds of correct scientific procedure, assumption of legitimate authority, willingness to sacrifice friends, loved ones, the individual, on the basis of a rational definition of possible consequences, and so on. Her stand implicitly marks humanism as irrelevant. And the viewer held within a humanist ideology (as we all are) asks: 'Where are her feelings?'

Indeed, at first viewing one tends to sympathize with Ash (the science officer): his anxiety while monitoring the activities of the rescue team seems symptomatic of genuine concern; he takes a chance, makes the seemingly human, spontaneous gesture in opening the airlock hatch; and he seems genuinely hounded by Ripley when she complains about his acting inconsistently with his responsibilities as a science officer. All of this is visually reinforced by images of him wringing his hands, or on the verge of breaking into a sweat. Caught up in sympathy for Kane's (Cain's?) plight, the viewer cannot yet identify Ash's anxiety – and perspiration – as signs of anything more sinister than compassion.

As the nature and extent of the danger become clearer, however, the viewer gradually registers that the real heroes are not Ash, for all his seemingly humanitarian concern, nor even Dallas, the strong and attractive male figure who would normally function as the narrative's ego. The heroes are, rather, Ripley, the 'strong woman', and Parker, the 'black worker'. Theirs will be an uneasy alliance: 'Why don't they come down here?' Parker complains. 'This is where the *work* is'. And Ripley does come down – to supervise and be teased. But Ripley's hard line on opening the airlock hatch was right after all, and her assertive bickering with Ash stemmed from a proper suspicion of his stubborn scientific incompetence with the alien rather than, as we first suspect, an authoritarian pulling of rank. Parker's resistance to answering the distress call now seems more sensible than heartless; he too identifies Ash's failure to act in a scientifically correct – and safe – manner with the alien parasite: 'Why doesn't he freeze him?' Parker asks. To which Dallas replies, 'Shut up, and get back to work'. It is Dallas and Ash who act on behalf of power and greed. They accept protocols that have nothing to do with science or rationality but only with final obedience to the demands of the 'Company'. 'The money's safe!' is Dallas's exclamation of relief as they leave the 'Mother' ship to explore the alien planet. The film ultimately projects Ripley alone as its surviving hero, her authority now definitely seen by the viewer as grounded in intelligence and strength of character rather than in any intrinsic power hunger. When the alien kills Dallas, whose image inflects a deep cultural seme – nice, strong, attractive male; must be hero, can't be killed – the viewer registers definite subliminal surprise in realizing that the woman actually will be (and has been all along) the strong centre of the film, the ego through which the story will be resolved and our identification made.

As the power of the woman-signifier is foregrounded, the film's complex investment in the alien-signifier can be seen more clearly. The first part of the film, leading to the shocking birth of the alien, actually projects three images of birth, each with an increasingly confused and frightening set of sexual associations. The first is the lingering exploration of the inner body of the spaceship – and the ship is the computer is Mother – by the first-person camera that implicates the viewer as I/eye; this ends with a long tracking shot down the smooth, clean electronic corridor into an inner chamber, where six curiously unsexed bodies slowly come to life. The second birth scene – more a conception – involves two men and a woman collectively imaged as three clumsy spermlike figures entering the vaginal opening between the upstretched 'legs' of an alien spaceship. Entering a corridor that exudes the ooze of biology, they establish an effective visual trope: the confusion of organic and mechanical textures which gives the alien his camouflage. The three clumsy seekers find, in one chamber, death gigantic, and in another, the expectant egg of a new life grotesque. This conception – in which male and female, life and death are confused – is then reserved as the egg forces its own tenacious fertilizing instrument on the man, who as a passive receptacle must ingest its seed. Finally, the particularly horrifying confusion of the sexual-gynaecological with the gastrointestinal is patched onto the life-death, male-female confusions as Kane dies in agony enduring the forced 'birth' of the razor-toothed phallic monster that gnaws its way through his stomach into the light – a kind of science fiction *phallus dentatus.*

This patchwork of confusion serves on one level no other purpose than to invest the image of the phallus born from the stomach of the man with as many unconscious fears as possible, so as to produce more dramatically the horror effect. But precisely by so attempting to intensify fear, the film produces a monster in the image of a vicious phallic power articulated in a complex and contradictory relation to the female. Through grotesquely emphasized erectile images, the alien insistently registers psychosexually as a threatening phallus: it unfolds itself from a seemingly inert mass into a towering, top-heavy menace; extends its insidiously telescoping jaws; slithers its tail up the leg of its fear-paralysed female victim in a shot that visually and emotionally connotes rape as much as death. And the film sets up a final confrontation in which the strong woman alone must confront and obliterate this menace, assuming for herself the counterphallic power of the 'gun'.

Along the way, Ripley must also confront another enemy – one which leads the crew to, harbours and nurtures within itself, and assigns absolute priority to the alien; this other enemy, the alien's life support, is the ship itself, the computer Mother. Mother is the filmic presence that gives both life and death – freezing and resurrecting the crew in one womblike chamber, dispensing futile advice to the good boy and girl leaders in another – until Ripley confounds this oracle with a question that elicits its priorities. When its soothing, insistent female voice ignores her attempt to deactivate the self-destruct programme, Ripley finally addresses this presence as 'Mother, you bitch!' A minute or so later, screen time, Ripley prematurely addresses the alien she thinks she has destroyed: 'I got you, you son of a bitch!' The film thus presents a rather complex feminist version of the strong woman who must mobilize all her autonomous intellectual and emotional strength to resist and ultimately obliterate the voracious phallic monster forced on her by Mother as the representative of the will of the appropriately absent Father (the Company).

Interestingly, then, *Alien* operates as a feminist statement on a symbolic level that avoids both the trivializing, empiricist condemnation of men (typically, the men or man in her life) and the puritanical condemnation of sexuality and sexual attraction. Indeed, the film can be seen as almost postfeminist in its image of the relations between the men and women of the *Nostromo's* crew. There are strong and weak women and men on the ship, but the woman's right to assume authority is not even an issue; authority and power are ceded to persons irrespective of sex, solely in regard to their position and function. The way the film takes for granted Ripley's assumption of command, her right to order and even shove the men around, registers strongly as the absence of an unexpected problematic. The parallel assumption – again felt as an unusual noninsistence – that she is a sexually active woman, suggested in her understated but definite attraction to Dallas, avoids both the romantic tendency to turn every story about a woman into a love story and the repressive tendency to insist that every strong woman must be asexual (or at least aheterosexual, which is the same thing for Hollywood). *Alien* presents an image of an autonomous woman who has perfectly reasonable relations with men at all levels and who finds her most effective ally in a black male worker (with whom she is not sexually involved), even while she increasingly assumes the necessity of making her own stand against a threatening phallic power pressed on her through the agency of apparatuses called Mother and Company as much as by any particular man or group of men.

Alien seems to take up rather enthusiastically the ideological semes of feminism and to reproduce them in an interesting form. I would disagree with an ideological denunciation of the film as simply another exercise in conventional sexism on the basis of the scene in which Ripley removes her uniform to appear in T-shirt and panties. Such criticism would be hard-pressed to avoid repressive and self-defeating assumptions about what constitutes sexism, and irrelevant assumptions about what constitutes the film and its ideological discourse. The image presented to the viewer here is hardly sensational by any standards, and it seems senseless for a progressive criticism to construct from it a general condemnation of the film that denies all the other effects of a fairly consistent feminist statement. As I will suggest below, a suspicious ideological critique might more appropriately interrogate the discrepancy between the film's embrace of the woman-signifier and its more ambiguous, uncomfortable relation to the figure of the black worker.

An effective ideological analysis, and the more telling formal and substantive points it can make about *Alien*, do not reside in denunciation. A Marxist critique should be able to clarify the film's specific and contradictory production of an ideological reality, rather than focus on a single image that allows identification with some abstract, politicized evil. One first catches the ideological work of this film, and the generation of its formal and thematic contradictions in the process, in the attempt to alloy the rather consistent positive images of the strong woman with a contradictory set of messages on the humanism/science problematic.

In the scene in which Ash is revealed to be a robot, he suddenly appears at Ripley's side in Mother's womb; he first accepts her anger and trivial violence against him and then begins to lose control. In Ash's crazed pursuit of Ripley, the viewer senses a pathological force at work. Is he in some way possessed (another cultural seme the film plays with) by the alien? No, but he certainly possesses the same destructive phallic power: he forces Ripley onto a counter under a wall plastered with nude centrefolds, rolls up one of the magazines, and begins to shove it relentlessly down her throat. A scene that opens as a twist in a lagging plot becomes a forceful image relating pornography to violence against women. Parker, the black worker, rescues Ripley from this perverse rape, and we discover that Ash is *not* a man, but a robot sent by the Company to bring back the alien for their 'weapons research'. The film's throwaway anticorporatism and antimilitarism are thus strengthened: the Company as bad Father is now identified with the Company as imperialist (Nostromo, mining, and so on). But the terms in which Ash's head now reveals the secret of the alien's power and horror are more interesting: the alien is 'without remorse, conscience, morality ... a survivor'.

Here the film takes precisely those qualities associated with Ripley when she refused to open the airlock for her friends, and with Parker when he resisted being drafted for the rescue mission – qualities which were inflected positively – and reverses their value; it is now negative, bad, antihuman, to be a survivor, to use knowledge and power in a way that renders morality and guilt irrelevant. But this is exactly why we admire Ripley. The reversal of these inflections through the image of the science officer as robot reinvokes the entire ideological humanism/ science problematic. The scene thus attempts an impossible fusion of contradictory and heterogeneous ideological materials, a fusion whose impossibility is concealed by cinematic sleight of hand: Parker chased and strangled by a body with its head hanging off its neck – a startling image indeed. But the seam cannot be totally effaced: the slight flicker of that splice in the film where the robot's dummy head is exchanged for the actor's talking head is a reflection in technical practice of the central seam which marks the film as a specific aesthetic and ideological production.

Awareness of the film's contradictory ideological representation of humanism allows us to see the substantive importance of Ripley's last-minute return for a cat. This peculiar rescue mission is more than an annoying plot device to build suspense (although it is certainly that too). It achieves the suspense effect by presenting a supercharged image of that 'I brake for animals' ideology which signifies its humanism in a displaced concern for little furry creatures. Ripley's concern for the cat functions as a final sign of her recovery for an ideological humanism. The woman who would have let her friend(s) die rather than take a scientifically unacceptable risk in opening the airlock now risks disaster in order to be reunited with her pet. And the film insists, through the Macduffy effect, that no harm results from this gesture: it has no effect on Parker or Lambert's fate; the cat was not taken over by the alien; and so forth. Of course, Ripley's decision about the airlock was difficult and courageous precisely because the same arguments *might* have been made later. The film inflects the character, against the habitual humanist ideological reactions, as positive for making a decision on scientific, theoretically antihumanist grounds in the airlock situation and then reverses itself, against its own previous work, to approve her decision about the cat on contradictory grounds. This ideological double reverse marks a schizophrenia, not in the character's psychology (which does not exist), but in the film's relation to a dominant humanism.

A Greimasian semantic rectangle will foreground the structural importance of the cat in the complex of signifiers generated from the notion 'human':

The founding term in the film is *human* (S), represented by the image of Ripley as the strong woman. The antihuman (–S) is, of course, the alien, and the not-human ($\bar{S}$) is Ash, the robot. The cat, then, functions in the slot of the not-antihuman (–$\bar{S}$), an indispensable role in this drama.[2]

Alien's 'game of semiotic constraints' is thus played entirely around the problematic of humanism, with the strong woman now chosen over the attractive male captain (and the black worker) to represent the human. Humanism is smuggled back in with the cat, after the film has pivoted around the robot's speech – which turns the film from an implicitly antihumanist statement on the worker's class-interest and the intelligent woman's scientific knowledge into a vehicle for producing a newly adequated relation to that reality in which morality, remorse, and so on, are signs of the good. Now that the viewer is assured that Ripley really does have feelings, she is ready to go one-on-one against the alien in a scene which reconstructs the classic American cultural image of the gunfight. In the space western of the future, the sheriff is replaced by a woman, while what is important for ideological humanism is preserved – a tough gal, rather than a tough guy, but still with that soft spot in the heart. Gary Cooper goes home to his little boy, and Sigourney Weaver goes to bed with her kitty-cat.

Something of the good, of course, remains in this idyllic reconstruction of a radical feminist humanism: the black worker. For parallel with Ripley's sudden reversal from decision based on knowledge to choice based on feelings and impulse, the film also has Parker contradict his previous relation to humanist ethics. The worker who would not be drafted for a rescue mission unless his contract was redrawn suddenly throws down his weapon for a suicidal hand-to-hand combat with the alien, so as not to endanger the woman who cannot move from his line of fire. As with the strong woman, the film folds its positive inflection of the figure of the black worker back into ideological humanism. Unlike the strong woman, however, the black worker is hung up for meat by the alien. Like the *Nostromo*'s shuttle craft, the ideological system of bourgeois humanism can sustain only a limited number of living signs; nowhere are the class determinations of these limits more visible than in this film's willingness to present the strong woman as the good survivor – smarter than that mean old phallic monster – and the black worker as the good sacrificial victim – nice guy, but not as tough as he thought he was.

If it appears that all these narrative and ideological threads do not finally coalesce very well, that is because they do not. The film organizes a complex set of heterogeneous ideological and cultural semes into an overdetermined visual text that produces disparate, even contradictory, ideological effects, making it a terrain of potential ideological struggle. The film attempts to construct an imaginary unity for all these effects, and to efface that potential under the sign of the strong woman as a new type of humanist hero – this, after literally chewing up all other differences existing within the space of the human. One cannot assign *Alien*, then, to some pseudo-Marxist category of good or bad on the basis of an oblique anticorporate reference, or the portrayal of a woman in her underwear. Marxism seeks knowledge of the film as a specific aesthetic production, the specific ideologies to which it relates, and the transformative work it does with those ideologies to construct the illusion of a seamless reality. This illusion is dispelled precisely in those shifts, contradictions, and slippages that reveal the pressure of ideologies in and on the work of the text. To say that *Alien* is reactionary and/or sexist can give no new knowledge of either the film or those ideologies. To say that *Alien* broadcasts a very sophisticated set of overwhelmingly feminist signals articulated in contradictory relation to other signals about class, and about humanism and science, opens the way to knowledge of how this film, *and* those ideological raw materials it extracts from a specific field of social discourse, operate.[3]

To suggest, finally, that a cultural discourse on humanism is the *à dominante* with which this film finally sanctions for the viewer its specifically structured ideological reality is to indicate the potential allure, power, *invisibility* of humanist ideological semes, even for the radical critic. For distance from reaction or sexism comes easily enough. But there is a somewhat more difficult theoretical labour – one which perhaps carries less of the satisfying feeling of shedding and assigning guilt – in confronting the necessity to negotiate the theoretical (and potentially political) distance between the problematic of humanism and empathy and that of science and knowledge. That *Alien* can be seen as provoking such considerations makes it a very interesting film indeed.

Notes

1. For a theoretical reflection on the text's reworking of cultural-ideological semes, see Thomas E. Lewis, 'Towards A Theory of the Referent', *PMLA*, vol. 94, no. 2, 1979.

2. This application of the Greimasian semantic rectangle was suggested to me by Richard Astle.

3. Nothing in this essay is meant to deny the necessity in certain contexts of ideological practice to promote a certain politically skewed reading or evaluation of the film. Indeed, within such a practice, I would argue that the film, for its strong feminist signals as well as its vague anticorporatism, should be construed as generally positive and progressive. This must be distinguished, however, from the necessity within a theoretical practice to understand how the film *works* as an aesthetic and ideological production. Nor is anything here meant to suggest a denunciation of humanism, which in many contexts can be as indispensable as it is insufficient.

7

Feminism and Anxiety in *Alien*

Judith Newton

Ridley Scott's *Alien* (1979) is a paradigm of mass culture as 'a transformational work on social and political anxieties and fantasies', a work which is at once wish-fulfilling or utopian and protectively repressive in its thrust. The most obviously utopian element in *Alien* is its casting of a female character in the role of individualist hero, a role conventionally played by, and in this case specifically written for, a male. It is Ripley, third officer of the commercial towing vehicle *Nostromo*, who maintains her composure in the face of the monster, who ultimately defeats it on her own, and who achieves the film's imaginary resolution of anxieties.

On the most overt level, the anxieties which this female hero resolves are those having to do with work in a late capitalist society, anxieties which today can be consciously articulated by most of my own students (largely white working-class men and women, many of whom are majoring in accounting). The film evokes, in rather explicit fashion, their uneasy recognition that now everyone is forced to be a company man or company woman, somebody whose work is neither controlled nor understood by them, and somebody who is finally expendable in the name of profit. The title of the *Alien* ship, *Nostromo*, 'nostro homo', our man, makes allusion, of course, to Conrad's working-class hero, another company man, who dies understanding that he has been betrayed by 'material interests'.

What has changed most between Conrad's early imperialist concern and this late-capitalist operation – both are in the mining business – is the degree of alienation to which workers are inured. The Company in *Alien* represents capitalism in its most systemized, computerized, and dehumanizing form, a fact ironically enforced by the name of the Company computer, 'Mother'. Throughout the film, mechanization and technology, associated with the Company, are contrasted with the engaging humanity of the workers. Shots of blinking, computerized helmets are juxtaposed, in the film's opening sequence, with glimpses of empty coffee cups and hanging uniforms, both of which evoke the momentary absence of the sleeping crew. At several points, the impressive technology of the Company ship – impressive but liable to malfunction – is played off against the ingenuity and practical-mindedness of the crew, who are given to making use of pens or cattle prods or their hands during real emergencies. This tension between the human and the mechanical or technological, both associated with the Company, culminates in a vision of the mechanical as fatal – first in Ash, the Company android, a totally dehumanized worker, who threatens the collectivity represented by the human crew, and then in the alien itself. The alien, like Ash, is a piece of Company property, and in its later transformations it resembles a mechanical person. 'It's like a man,' Parker, the black, working-class character observes. Perfectly adaptable, perfectly defended, and (as Ash admiringly points out) 'unclouded by conscience, remorse, or delusions of morality', the alien is a 'perfect organism' for Company purposes. It is in fact a kind of ultimate Company Man, and the Company means to use it in its own defence, as part of 'the weapons division'.

When Ripley blasts this perfect organism into space, the film expresses two fantasies. The first is that individual action has resolved economic and social horrors, for all the anxieties which the film evokes about the dehumanizing force of late-capitalist labour have been deflected onto the alien. The second fantasy is that white middle-class women, once integrated into the world of work, will somehow save us from its worst excesses and specifically from its dehumanization. This fantasy has its roots in nineteenth-century ideologies about middle-class women, ideologies which maintained that women, as outsiders to the world of early capitalist competition, retained a moral purity which might redeem it – at first in the private sphere of the home, then in the quasi-public sphere of voluntary aid organizations, and ultimately in the public sphere itself.

Indeed, Ripley does betray residual traces of an outsider's sensitivity. She is the only crew member to distrust Ash, and her distrust and concern are juxtaposed against the cynicism of Dallas, a white, middle-class male, a traditional insider on his way to becoming a Company person. Dallas says, 'Standard procedure is to do what the Company wants you to do ... I just run the ship ... I don't trust anyone'. In allowing Ripley to defeat the Company's secret weapon *Alien* locates itself inside an ideology to which sectors of the twentieth-century women's movement has also subscribed. It is the belief that women, white middle-class women, will make it better. It is a mark of 1970s cynicism and despair, perhaps, that Ripley saves only her own humanity.

But the wish-fulfilling, utopian, seemingly feminist, content of *Alien* is more extensive than this; for the film not only breaks with the convention of having a male hero, it breaks with conventions of female heroism or female independence as well. It does so, moreover, in a way that draws attention to what it is doing, in a way that tends to leave even Marxist-feminist viewers feeling that the film is 'good on women'. Ripley's character, for example, appropriates qualities traditionally identified with male, but not masculinist, heroes. Ripley is skilled, she makes hard, unsentimental decisions; she is a firm but humane leader; she has the hero's traditional, and thrilling, resources in the face of the monster.

Her quest as hero, moreover, is not diluted by the introduction of a love plot although 'getting the man too' has been a standard qualification of female independence in women's fiction and women's movies since the 1930s. The female hero does not have a sexual involvement with anyone (nor does anyone else among the crew, despite what appears to have been a long flight – the crew is ten months from earth when the film opens). Finally, with the exception of Ash, none of Ripley's peers expresses resentment of her in her role as leader. Indeed, what *Alien* offers on one level, and to a white, middle-class audience, is a utopian fantasy of women's liberation, a fantasy of economic and social equality, friendship, and collectivity between middle-class women and men.

But the utopian and wish-fulfilling content of the film is accompanied by the covert expression of anxieties which are more primitive and more extreme than those which the film more overtly associates with work. This second set of anxieties, aroused by the film's specific fantasy of a redeeming female hero and by its more general feminist and utopian content, must be seen as a response to feminism as a collective force, as a force disruptive of traditional gender roles and the sexual division of labour and as a force which can oppose late capitalism itself. Although *Alien* appears, for example, to omit the private realm of the family, the family and domestic labour are evoked by scenes in which the crew gathers together for their meals. Since food simply appears on the table and since child care is displaced onto pouring milk for the collective cat, the film can be said to arouse and allay anxiety in relation to the family and the sexual division of labour by relieving men and women both of domestic responsibility. (At the same time, however, the film very indirectly retains the identification of domestic work with women since the cooking in this collective appears to be taken care of by the company computer – 'Mother'.)

Male – and especially white, middle-class male – hostility and anxiety over the erosion of traditional gender roles is also present in this film, and at the same time contained and managed. Resentment of Ripley's leadership, for example, is deflected onto the two working-class men and onto the android. These manoeuvres allow hostility to be ventilated and vicariously participated in, while protecting white, middle-class male viewers from having to identify with that ventilation. The two working-class men, who betray only a mild and ineffectual resentment of Ripley – 'She better stay the fuck out of my way,' says Parker – function, for the most part, as soothing reminders that white, middle-class men are still superior in position to *someone*. But Ash, who is ostensibly a white, middle-class male himself, scores a series of hostile victories over Ripley in which white male viewers can vicariously participate. Ash disobeys Ripley's orders by admitting the alien onto the space ship. He defers to Dallas even when Ripley is in command. He refuses to let Ripley look into his microscope. He even proves to be 'Mother's' favourite when the computer refuses to expose Special Order 937 to anyone but him. Ash's hostility reaches a violent climax when he beats Ripley up and simulates a rape by trying to shove a rolled-up girlie magazine down her throat. At this point, Ash is a covert emblem both of men dehumanized by their work and of men dehumanized by their rage at women; but it is at this point too that Ash is revealed to be an android, a figure safely dis-associated from the middle-class male viewer. Ultimately, it is Ripley who must triumph over the threats which Ash covertly represents, and she will do so by taking on that other mechanical man, the alien itself.

The alien is appropriately the locus of the most primitive – and alien – material which the film evokes, the sexual rage and terror, especially white male terror, which the threatened breakdown of gender roles provokes. With the exception of Parker, the alien is the focal point of all sexual energy in this movie. The alien, which is fond of womb-like and vagina-like spaces, is distinctly phallic, and it attacks Ripley, like a fantasy rapist, while she is undressing. But the alien is also equipped with a rather impressive set of vaginal teeth. It is born of eggs, and it continually gives birth to itself, once in a gory evocation of childbirth at the dining-room table. In this respect the alien is a potent expression of male terror at female sexuality and at castrating females in general. Finally, the alien becomes the site of all anxieties which the feminist gestures of the film evoke; and it is the female hero who must manage them, an allocation of responsibility which can be read as an expression of trust in women's capacity for taking care of business – or as an exasperated insistence that women clean up the mess they've made.

The mechanisms by which the female hero actually achieves this imaginary resolution are keys to the film's transformational work. In her first encounter with an enemy figure (Ash), Ripley is saved by Parker, the working-class black, and by Lambert, the other white female crew member. The film presents us with an intriguing coalition: two white middle-class women and a minority man. The coalition is especially promising because Parker, played by Yaphet Kotto, is the most vigorous and deliberately appealing member of the crew. He is also the member most in opposition to the Company's interests. Parker complains about the Company from the beginning. He gripes about the inequity in bonuses, about the class stratification on board, about the coffee. He complains that picking up aliens is not in his contract, and finally he is enraged that the Company has found its crew expendable: 'The damn Company, what about our *lives*?' Black and working class, Parker is also a traditional outsider, and yet he is not allowed to ally himself with Ripley.

Indeed the collectivity represented by Ripley, Parker, and Lambert is given us only to be exploded. Parker and Lambert are killed in the next sequence of the film while Ripley, despite the injunction that 'we have to stick together', is off looking for the cat. Ripley's previous relation to these two has prepared us, moreover, to feel very little emotional invest-ment in their momentary collectivity. She has had no particular sympathy for the two working-class men – 'You'll get what's coming to you', she tells them when they complain about their unequal share of bonuses. She has shown no emotional bonding with the other female. Lambert, who is passive and easily given to hysterics, functions for the most part to define what Ripley is not – emotional, feminine, unheroic. Ripley, as female hero, is not permitted to achieve imaginary resolution until she has been separated from an oppositional and potentially force-ful collective.

It is in these final moments that the film subtly reinvests Ripley with traditionally feminine qualities. First, while Parker and Lambert are racing to get off the ship, Ripley is sent on a prolonged search for Jonesey the cat. This is an impulsive, humanitarian, and therefore traditionally feminine action – 'Here kitty, kitty, here, sweetheart'. Also, immediately before Ripley's encounter with the alien on the space shuttle, we see her stripped to her bikini underpants, not standard gear for space duty perhaps, but exposing a long, and lovingly recorded, expanse of marvel-lous body. Finally, both before and after blowing the alien into space, Ripley is shown tucking her cat into bed. Ripley is not only divested of coalition and reinvested with feminity, she is also reaffirmed as a Company Woman. Despite the Company's betrayal of herself and of the entire crew, Ripley disposes of the alien only to sit down and complete her captain's log: 'Crew – and cargo – destroyed'.

What we have in *Alien* then, is wish-fulfilment and repression of a familiar order. In some respects the film is utopian, for it expresses, through its female hero, the fantasy that white, middle-class women, at their liberated best, can be harmoniously integrated into the late-capitalist world of work, a world they will then symbolically humanize with a residual sensitivity (although in this film the only humanity Ripley salvages is her own). But even this attenuated fantasy content evokes anxieties, and especially white, middle-class male anxieties, about feminism as a collective and potentially radical force, a force which opposes traditional gender roles, the sexual division of labour, and in some sectors, the oppression of minorities and late capitalism itself. Ultimately, this anxiety content of the film is managed by a figure who must be identified as a product of the women's movement – the liberated woman. But she is divested of the oppositional force which the women's movement can also represent.

Ripley, though in many ways a fine and thrilling hero, is robbed of radical thrust. Impulsive, nurturing, and sexually desirable, she is not so threatening to men after all. Unallied with minorities, with the working class, or with other women, she is also – and in contrast to Conrad's *Nostromo* – a Company Woman to the last. *Alien* is another demonstration of how late capitalism, through its 'dominant *cultural* forms and practices ... strives to sever social experience from the formation of counter-ideologies' and to 'pre-empt the effects of association'.[2] It is an example, to paraphrase John Brenkman, of how mass media establish a schism between what we hear and what we speak, so that we receive messages we would not speak and are made to read in them the figure of our needs, our desires, and our identity.[3]

Notes

1. Fredric Jameson, 'Reification and Utopia in Mass Culture', *Social Text*, no. 1. 1979, p. 141.

2. John Brenkman, 'Mass Media: From Collective Experience to the Culture of Privatization', *Social Text*, no. 1, 1979, p. 98.

3. Ibid., p. 105.

PART III

Repressions

I deological film criticism is predominantly text-based, taking films as the starting point of an analysis grounded in a distinction between surface and underlying meanings in representations. The cultural instrumentality assumed in this type of analysis is that films produce and reproduce ideologies, whilst simultaneously hiding this fact. The objective of ideological criticism is to expose the hidden meanings in, and thus the ideological operations of, film texts. It is a short, but decisive, step from this view of films and their cultural instrumentality to one which holds that texts are a site of repressions, a place where the unspoken and the unspeakable are occulted by the outwardly observable. In this view, representations 'speak' the repressions of culture, which by their very nature cannot be spoken directly; and texts become repositories of unconscious meanings.

This notion of an 'unconscious of the text' derives from psychoanalytic theory, and has become associated with a particular strand of psychoanalytic film criticism. It is largely in its adoption of a notion of the unconscious that this type of criticism differs from analysis directed at uncovering ideologies: the distinction lies in the two criticisms' respective views concerning the aetiology and formation of subtextual meanings. In the one, meaning is regarded as relating ultimately (if not in any obvious or direct way) to the social formation; while in the other it is traced back to unconscious processes whose relationship with the social, if any, is of no immediate concern. That there is a possibility of linking these two approaches was hinted at by Althusser in his work on the relationship between ideology and unconscious processes,[1] but this avenue remains largely unexplored in the critical literature.

But ideology and the unconscious are not to be conflated; and a notion of an 'unconscious of the text', as distinct from other kinds of subtexts, is a key component of cultural theory. It implies that cultural productions, such as films, may be regarded as sites of unconscious meanings – unconscious because repressed, and therefore inexpressible in direct form. Such meanings are there in the text, but appear in disguise – betraying themselves only in certain cues or clues, which have to be interpreted. Films, in this view, are in some ways similar to other unconscious productions, such as 'Freudian slips' and dreams: the one may be interpreted using the same techniques as are brought to bear on the other – namely, the methods of psychoanalysis, the science of the unconscious. The contents of repressed meanings in films reflect the classic concerns of psychoanalysis.

Psychoanalytic readings of films draw on concepts from psycho-analytic theory which describe unconscious processes – condensation, displacement, and so on – together with psychoanalytic methods for interpreting symptomatic expressions of these processes. Interpretation of films addresses itself to objects regarded in Freudian and other versions of psychoanalysis as characteristic of the repressed thoughts which constitute the unconscious: the primal scene and the mysteries of conception and birth, sexual drives and the desire for forbidden objects, the Oedipal scenario and sexual difference.

Science fiction cinema has proved a fertile ground for this type of criticism, probably because of some of its generic characteristics: for example, the strangeness, the fantastic nature, of the fictional worlds of science fiction films may endow them with some of the qualities of unconscious productions. To this extent, science fiction cinema posi-tively invites psychoanalytic readings. In an essay called 'Monsters from the Id' – a rare example of criticism directed at the genre as a whole, and unusual also in that it predates psychoanalytic film theory – Margaret Tarratt argued that science fiction films' very stock-in-trade is suppressed sexuality, that they are 'deeply involved with the concepts of Freudian psychoanalysis and seem in many cases to derive their struc-ture from it'.[2]

Aliens and extraterrestrial forces, argued Tarratt, are actually exter-nalizations of civilization's conflict with the primitive unconscious, the Id; and many of these science fiction monsters are disguised representa-tions of repressed sexual desires. Surveying the narrative contents of a large number of films, she concluded that much science fiction cinema is 'structured round coherent themes relating the tensions of sexual drives and the obligations on behavior imposed by civilized society'.[3] Tarratt's analysis suggests that as a genre, science fiction cinema is a peculiarly apt site for the return of culture's repressed, and that its cultural instru-mentality hinges on a working through, under seemingly innocent cover, of cultural taboos and obsessions which cannot be addressed openly.

The essays here by Daniel Dervin and by Vivian Sobchack take up and extend the approach taken by Tarratt, addressing science fiction cinema as a genre to whose understanding the concepts and methods of psychoanalysis can usefully be brought. Dervin's concern is with the ways in which unconscious fantasies associated with the primal scene – the moment when a child views its parents' sexual intercourse, or entertains fantasies about it – figure in the 'aesthetic conventions' of science fiction films. In psychoanalytic theory, the primal scene is part of the process through which the infant comes to regard itself as a separate being, and begins to be curious about its origins. Dervin argues that the motif of space travel in science fiction films (interpreted as separation of the self from Earth/mother) is a disguised expression of a primal scene fantasy; and that the genre's preoccupation with creation, gestation and procreation of alien beings and human substitutes speaks to primal scene wish-fulfilment fantasies of being on the scene of one's own conception. Vivian Sobchack's essay on sex – or its absence – in science fiction films is more explicit about its psychoanalytic methodology, treating the genre as a body of texts which work thematically in a fashion similar to the unconscious productions which form the object of psychoanalytic inquiry. Using the psychoanalytic techniques of free association and dream analysis, Sobchack reveals how repressions around sexuality return, in displaced and condensed forms, to the narratives of science fiction films.

The capacity of science fiction cinema to attract this sort of analysis is well illustrated by Judith Newton's ideological reading of *Alien* (1979) in Part II. Like Margaret Tarratt, Newton regards the alien monster of science fiction as a figure for something else – a 'disturbance in the sphere of sexuality', to use Freud's phrase. Unlike Tarratt, though, she pins her analysis specifically to male fears about female sexuality. Newton's reading is, of course, informed by feminist cultural theory, which did not yet exist when Tarratt wrote her essay; and the differences between their two approaches highlight some of the ways in which psychoanalytic film theory has been enriched – and challenged – by feminist concerns.

In her discussion of *The Terminator* (1984), Constance Penley draws on a number of psychoanalytic concepts, including – again – the primal scene. Unlike Daniel Dervin, however, she considers primal scene fantasies in their relation to sexual difference, which in Penley's view is a key feature of the unconscious of the science fiction film text. Although male–female differences and relations might, as Sobchack suggests, scarcely figure in the surface contents of science fiction films, they are actually deeply embedded in them: but 'the question of sexual difference ... is displaced onto the more remarkable difference between the human and the other'. Barbara Creed takes up the point about sexual difference and the human/other split in her essay here on *Alien*, a film which she says combines the conventions of science fiction and horror genres. Beneath its enactments of primal scene fantasies in scenes of birthing and exploration, says Creed, lurks the figure of a monstrous archaic femininity, in the shape of the alien – an infinitely fecund, parthenogenic mother, sadistic, phallic, and terrifying. The monstrous-feminine figures as a manifestation of fear of difference, fear of the feminine, the castrated 'other', described in the theory of the Oedipus complex. These unconscious processes of the text are characterized by Creed as patriarchal, as working ideologically to repress and control the feminine.

This reading of *Alien* indicates how feminist cultural theory can politicize psychoanalytic film criticism: feminist theory has demonstrated that unconscious processess – as they are worked through in cultural productions such as films and film genres – are not neutral, but deeply embedded in patriarchal discourses. Feminist psychoanalytic readings of films may be regarded as oppositional in the degree that, in excavating patriarchal meanings, they constitute a resistive practice of reading popular films 'against the grain' of hegemonic meanings. In fact, both ideological criticism and psychoanalytic criticism provide the means and the justification for 'readings against the grain', and thereby for laying bare the operations and contradictions of capitalism and patriarchy. However, these practices, in engaging with the very meanings they deconstruct, may be in some danger of getting caught up in them. To feminists wishing to move beyond critique of the dominant cultural order and towards newer forms of representation, this can seem a serious limitation.

It is perhaps worth noting that the psychoanalytic criticism at issue here represents only one of several uses to which psychoanalytic concepts have been put in film theory. The emphasis on film texts as repositories of unconscious meanings can be distinguished on the one hand from a view of films as expressing the collective psyche of an era (see Part I), and on the other from a psychoanalytic approach which concerns itself with the unconscious processes at work – the fantasies and the pleasures evoked – in the relationship between film spectator and film text. This type of cultural instrumentality is explored in Part IV.

Notes

1. Louis Althusser, 'Ideology and Ideological State Apparatuses' in *Lenin and Philosophy*, London: Verso 1971.

2. Margaret Tarratt, 'Monsters from the Id' in Barry K. Grant, ed., *Film Genre: Theory and Criticism*, Metuchen, NJ: Scarecrow Press 1977, p. 162. This essay was originally published in 1970–71.

3. Ibid., p. 178.

8

Primal Conditions and Conventions: The Genre of Science Fiction

Daniel Dervin

At some period in his or her development, every child either views the act of parental intercourse or entertains fantasies about it. Whether more real or imagined, the experience has come to be known in psychoanalysis as the primal scene. What makes the primal scene problematic for the child is that he experiences it through the psychosexual phase he is presently engaged in and interprets it accordingly, hence the infantile distortions of the sex act as an attack or beating, or involving oral and anal zones rather than those better suited to adult sexuality. The results may range from fixations of drives, phobias, to mental inhibitions or precocious awareness. In associating sex with violence, the child runs the risk of turning the sex act into a danger zone, fraught with peril. The primal scene is also so stimulating and exciting to the child, while at the same time excluding him, that he attempts to master this state of affairs by internalizing the total act, that is, by identifying with both parents, bisexually. Here is the basis for Edelheit's formulation that the primal scene forms mental structures especially adaptable to the creative enterprise.[1] The primal scene is often represented by the child as the monstrous act he senses it to be. Hence Medusas, Sphinxes, Chimaeras and other mythical composites represent primal scene phenomena.

Correctly perceived and interpreted, the primal scene reveals not only an Oedipal plight – mother with a formidable rival – but also procreation, the solution to the riddle of one's own origins as well as a (sneak) preview of genital activity.

The inevitable incursion of adult sexuality into the world of childhood need not *de facto* translate into numbing trauma, perversions, or an obsessive quest for origins that leads one back to unravelling the meaning of the combined parental act. Just as easily this ubiquitous discovery may lead to denial and those structured daydreams provided by the popular arts. In this context, one may encounter certain aesthetic *conventions* as derived from, analogous to, or coloured by, psychological *conditions* proper to the primal scene.

At this point I would like to draw on an earlier psychological study of movies by Martha Wolfenstein and Nathan Leites,[2] which, while limiting itself to the immediate postwar period (1945–49) and to an interpretation of films as shared daydreams with predictably concealed Oedipal triangular patterns, is by no means so naive nor so narrow as might now appear. Its 'Performers and Onlookers' section offers a limited and oblique treatment of movies as a 'primal situation of excited and terrified looking, that of the child trying to see what happens at night'. Movies re-excite because unlike other forms of art or experience 'so much of the lives of the fictional characters' appears on the screen. Hence the correlative wish to 'see actors as they really are', a wish partially satisfied in fan magazines, manifests the strength of pressures to penetrate 'fictional facades' and glimpse forbidden areas of privacy. But when performers appear as themselves in films, as the authors astutely observe, an 'unsettling of reality orientation' occurs. In effect, the wish to 'break through the aesthetic illusion' is ambivalent, and movies better succeed in maintaining conventions suitable to their medium.

Ever since George Méliès's *A Trip to the Moon* (1902) and Otto Rippert's *Homunculus* (1916), science fiction film has spun around the dual themes of other worlds and other beings. This interest may branch out into separate directions; or it may intertwine the same work as in the not-to-be-forgotten, *I Married a Monster from Outer Space* (1958).

While ranging from proximate planets to distant galaxies, from the depths of the ocean to the inner universe of the human body, such explorations presume two settings: one familiar and reliable, another mysterious and unpredictable. Analogies with early development from awareness of the maternal organism as a simple face-breast configuration to a vaginal-womb complexity are likely enough without one's enforcing a rule of reduction. The inner, pre-verbal experience of the child was encapsulated for me once when I heard an analyst who specialized in work with schizophrenics refer to the mother as the 'cosmic object' for the child.[3] The need for autonomy fuels space travels; curiosity pilots them. And the intermediate vehicle through which these adventures are conducted, in its blending of strangeness (to the audience) and familiarity (to the crew), may stand for the emerging self.

When hostile groups either control this new body of space, be it in the heavens or in the depths, or when hostile extraterrestrials penetrate the familiar atmosphere of Earth, one may begin inferring a primal scene ambiance. What is interesting, though, is less how films like the 1956 *Forbidden Planet* (outer space) or the 1966 *Fantastic Voyage* (through the body's inner spaces) implement general axioms than how such films vary, invert, and exceed anyone's psychological assumptions and manage to engage audiences' current political and cultural concerns. The 1954 to 1969 cycle of Japanese Godzilla films, with their inevitable destruction of Tokyo, has been interpreted as stages in a painful period of recovery from the traumatizing shock of atomic holocaust.[4] But metaphors, like monsters, enjoy the capacity for opening private worlds as well as illuminating public ones.

Along with the access to other mysterious worlds afforded by science fiction is the freedom to break out of the chain of time – be it of historical continuity or biological causality – to let one dwell in 2001 but also to visit lands that time forgot. Among other things, this permits one to revisit origins and revise the processes of conception, gestation, and birth. Such interests readily lead to science fiction's other major concern with alternative life forms.

It is also at this point that science fiction impinges on traditional mythology in at least two ways which are pertinent to this inquiry. On the one hand, there are all those fascinating sexual unions between humans and beasts (or gods in animal forms): Leda and the swan; Zeus as a bull ravaging Europa; Demeter as a mare, Poseidon as a stallion, and so on. These and composite figures like minotaurs and centaurs portray on various levels the marriage of humanity to nature. On the other hand, there are the reversals of the birth process in the patriarchal mode of Athene springing from the fertile brow of Zeus, Dionysus from his thigh, Aphrodite from the foam blood of Uranus's severed genitals, Eve from Adam's rib, Galatea from Pygmalion's sculpture, and so on. Science fiction varies the former by depicting variations of the marriage of man to the machine in such ways that the union of self and technology replaces our Freudian as well as our Darwinian origins. And from Frankenstein up to 'R2-D2', experiments with pseudoscientific alternatives to the biology of human conception and birth stand out as variations of the latter. The laboratory is hardly a bedroom, yet an operating table and various tubes and chemicals are always on hand; so is the launching pad hardly a birth ward, yet a helpless figure is strapped into position by white-coated scientists to await transmission from one state of being to another.

But the real basis for primal scene correspondences is that the experiments of science fiction often interface with the infantile distortions of adult sexuality and are presented as *faits accomplis*. The child's inability, or resistance, to resolving the riddles of adult sexual reproduction, and so fitting himself into the sequences of time and the cycles of nature, are

converted by the creative imagination into alternative modes of procreation. Simultaneously, a seemingly minor romantic-love plot may link the
discovery of adult sexuality in some socially appropriate form with the
destruction of the monster born from whatever bizarre union. The
monster concretizes the child's infantile sex fears, theories, and fantasies,
which dissolve when a 'better way' is found.[5] The double plots of science
fiction form a distinctive convention which permits a dual time sequence
to unfold. The adults and their intrigues are present-oriented and bound
by the rational mode of consciousness referred to in psychoanalysis as
secondary process thinking; while the fantastic material reproduces
infantile material of the primary mode. Simple narrative intercutting
allows the two modes to run concurrently, as they often do in life.

The thing in *The Thing* (1951) is a sort of unisex vegetable from
Mars, which reproduces itself from seed pollen it carries in its fist. 'No
pain, pleasure, emotions or heart. How superior!' exclaims a character,
but old-fashioned man–woman love triumphs in the end. In *The
Invasion of the Body Snatchers* (1956, 1978), a mysterious cosmic rain-
fall fertilizes the earth with bizarre plants which form pods bearing
resemblances to the nearest human beings whose bodies they proceed to
occupy during sleep. The original idea, in Pauline Kael's non-Freudian
view, 'comes from the fear of night and sleep',[6] an approach that is
explored generically in Harvey Greenberg's intensely Freudian chapters
on 'The Sleep of Reason' in his work on film;[7] but whether one attempts
to connect directly such fear with what occurs among adults at night
when children are struggling to fall asleep, the prospect of waking to
have one's own self invaded and occupied is certainly a primitive fear.
The original story was intended as a simpleminded parable against
communism during the Cold War, but Don Siegel's film version, in
removing it from the political arena, enlarged the psychological dimension.[8] The 1978 remake, notably set in San Francisco, with its associations of 1967 flower children and more recent cults, snipers, and
assassins, captures the ambiguity of seeing familiar faces undergo alien
conversions.

One clue as to why this might be happening in 1978 is planted in an
early scene. When Elizabeth (Brooke Adams) returns to Geoffrey (Art
Hindle), 'her laid-back lover is sprawled out watching basketball on TV;
he kisses Elizabeth without taking off his earphones and gets excited
only when he hears a terrific sound – he pushes her aside so he can see
it'.[9] Subsequently, he retires to the boudoir where he plugs into another
TV set and has Elizabeth fetch his headgear. Thus nursed, he falls asleep
and Elizabeth puts an arm over his unresponsive chest. The next
morning one of the deadly flowers brought back by Elizabeth and left at
their bedside has snatched the body of poor Geoffrey. The subtle

inference to be drawn is that his fate is a kind of retaliation for having already allowed the electronic milieu to encroach on his body and for failing to respond to the living, sexual otherness of Elizabeth. 'Something's missing', she senses. 'Emotion-feeling'. But there had been something missing before too. For a while she teams up with Matthew (Donald Sutherland), her boss at the Health Department, and he is able to gain time by taking her seriously as a woman (though the sexual element is largely suppressed) and by destroying his pod-spawn double. Clearly the threat is to a loss of the self and the assumption of a false self as a kind of living death. A psychiatrist, who ought to know about these Laingian distinctions, mistakes Elizabeth's motives for running away from Geoffrey and is blinded by the attention focussed on his self at a coming-out party for his how-to-be-happy book – signs that his body is up for snatching. But he is already a pod, despite his preaching about giving up the old concepts and evolving beyond good and evil. Meanwhile some business at a mud-bath and massage parlour advances primal-scene tableaux along the mobile/immobile axis. The curtained booths function as a birth ward, and instead of humans emerging from the regenerative mud, pods are being cultivated.

Two other scenes develop primal-scene motifs. In rescuing Elizabeth from the clutches of pod Geoffrey, Matthew hides in her bedroom where she lies in a drugged stupor, and watches as Geoffrey prepares her for re-inpodation. Later, Geoffrey dozes in a patio chair as his garden slowly comes alive. Huge Medusa-like flowers come into bloom, and viscous-enveloped humanoids emerge from the obscene plants. The danger of sleep now becomes clear: it permits the fiendishly accelerated process of conception, gestation, and birth to occur overnight. That one of these is Matthew's double, ready to occupy his slumbering frame before he hacks it to pieces, leads to an interpretation of the newborn pod as a newly arrived sibling ready to usurp the child's cherished position in the family. The fact that the pods are everywhere, taking over the whole planet, maintains a paranoid level of anxiety. Since pods in effect swallow up their victims, one returns to the primitive oral level of these cannibalistic fears. Nursing infants invade and snatch their mothers' breasts in the excitement of their aggressive wishes and fantasies, but at night when they are alone, their oral aggressions return to attack them. The way this attack is represented is through the nocturnally unavailable parents who are scheming to replace their human children with unnatural monsters; but behind these persecutory machinations are the orally distorted primal scenes of adult sexual behaviour.

By the movie's end only one woman is still humanly intact, and she is being fingered to the others by Matthew's pod, as if somehow the woman, as procreating and nursing mother, were responsible for the

dehumanization. Yet woman remains the only safe alternative to reproduction by the pod process. And so almost by default, the answer to the
threat of these latter-day body snatchers is the constancy and commitment that we like to believe adult sexuality renders possible, but fear is
missing from modern society, as **it is** particularly from the concentrated
chaos of California lifestyles.

Women who are impregnated by outer-space beings in *Village of the
Damned* (1960), and the parents of the drug-deformed *enfant terrible* in
It's Alive! (1974) work variations on horror films like *Rosemary's Baby*
(1968), which have common historical roots in the medieval supersti-
tions about dangerous females who have had intercourse with the devil.
The problematic status of the demon children[10] born of such union was
often resolved by casting them into water to see if they sank or swam.
The individual roots lend themselves to an interpretation of a father as a
negative superego image for the boy, as a forbidden love-object for the
girl: the primal scene as an obscene invitation to have congress with
Satan.

The preferred reproductive mode of the alien in *Alien* (1979) is
modelled on the insect world wherein spiders use wasps' bodies to lay
their eggs in, with a spaceman occupying the unhappy lot of the wasp.
The appalling emergence of 'the little bastard' alien from the spaceman's
ruptured chest-cavity may well push male birth fantasies to their
ultimate absurdity, but only after considerable ground has been covered.
Along the way the crudities of reproducing a human copy from corpses
a-mouldering in graveyards, as begun in *Frankenstein,* have progressed
so far as to become independent from the organic entirely. This began
with robots and achieved a zenith in *2001*'s Hal, a 9000 computer who
has to be killed before he becomes any more dangerously human. A
shorter route for man to repeat himself in his own image has been
suggested in cloning, and science fiction has been quick to explore these
possibilities in *Clones* (1973) and *The Boys from Brazil* (1978), though
the idea had already been adumbrated in *Seconds* (1966).

Narcissism, whether we trace it back to the boy who fell in love with
his image in a pool and died of starvation or to the flower he became,
whose scent is associated with stupor and stiffness (the *narco* in narcis-
sus), implies the reversal of mutual minglings and comminglings
between the sexes that lead to new generations. And *Boys* is remarkably
consistent in exposing the necrophiliac drift of cloning. The clones have
been produced from tissues taken from the body of Adolf Hitler, and
they are to form a crop of young führers who, after carefully being
placed in families through the civilized West, may be expected to
regenerate the master race. But when the moment of truth arrives and
the outwardly Nazi-stamped boys are found, the wholesome middle-

class environments prove stronger than the genetic programming, and a lad in Pennsylvania turns against his Nazi master (Gregory Peck). It is a triumph of nurture over nature-manipulation, and science fiction routinely allows such alternate birth practices to thrive long enough to gratify the audience's fantasies and arouse its fears, before exposing or eradicating them in the end.

While science fiction invites intricate variations on the gestation/birth process, there is one representation of birth that has become fairly standard and deserves the status of convention. Typically it occurs near the end of the action and functions as an escape motif in the plot. A crisis has been reached by the imminent destruction of the space station, the mother spacecraft, or the mother-planet itself. Simultaneously, a struggle with hostile forces engages all the energies of the worthy survivors. Seconds before a timed detonation of self-destruct, a collision or flaming holocaust, a miniature space capsule, rocket, or shuttle, is reached, manned, and launched into clear space as a backward look discloses a series of annihilating explosions. The emergence, often along a narrow canal and through a trap door, of the smaller body from the larger replicates birth in a technological medium. The battle, collision, and destruction may readily stand for the individual's excited emotional participation in primal scene activities. Either the parents are disguised as alien elements or are perceived as prehuman, cosmic forces which threaten to overwhelm the child's psyche.

The escape implicitly rests on grasping the fact that primal scene events precede birth, and the subsequent safety of the survivors suggests further steps along the separation–individual arc leading to selfhood.

Notes

1. Henry Edelheit, 'Mythopoesis and the Primal Scene', *The Psychoanalytic Study of Society*, vol. 5, 1972.

2. Martha Wolfenstein and Nathan Leites, *Movies: A Psychological Study*, Glencoe, Illinois: Free Press 1950.

3. John W.R. Love, at Chestnut Lodge, Rockville, Maryland.

4. Laurence Wharton, '*Godzilla* to *Latitude Zero*: The Cycle of the Technological Monster', *Journal of Popular Film*, vol. 3, no. 1, 1974.

5. Margaret Tarratt's article, 'Monsters from the Id' in Barry K. Grant, ed., *Film Genre: Theory and Criticism*, Metuchen, NJ: Scarecrow Press 1977, first started me thinking along these lines.

6. *New Yorker*, 25 December 1978.

7. Harvey R. Greenberg, *The Movies on Your Mind*, New York: E.P. Dutton 1975.

8. Ernesto G. Laura, '*Invasion of the Body Snatchers*' in William Johnson, ed., *Focus on the Science-Fiction Film*, Englewood Cliffs, NJ: Prentice-Hall 1972, pp. 71–3.

9. Pauline Kael, *New Yorker*, 25 December 1978.

10. The problematic status of children in the popular arts has been probed by James S. Gordon, a psychiatrist writing on 'Demonic Children', *New York Times Book Review*, 11 September 1977.

9

The Virginity of Astronauts:
Sex and the Science Fiction Film

Vivian Sobchack

Human biological sexuality and women as figures of its representation have been repressed in the male-dominated, action-oriented narratives of most American science fiction films from the 1950s to the present. Semiotically linked, insofar as each in our culture is conventionally reversible and may stand as a signifier for the other, sex and women and the significant connection between them is denied all but a ghostly presence in the genre. It is as if such a potent semiotic relation poses a threat to the cool reason and male camaraderie necessary to the conquest of space, the defeat of mutant monsters and alien invasions, and the corporate development and exploitation of science and technology. Thus, biological sexuality and women are often absent from science fiction film narratives, and when they do turn up they tend to be disaffiliated from each other, stripped of their cultural significance as a semiotic relation, carefully separated from each other so that biological sexuality is not linked to human women and human women are not perceived as sexual.

More than any other American film genre, then, science fiction denies human eroticism and libido a traditional narrative representation and expression. Sex and the science fiction film is, therefore, a negative topic. It points to a major absence in the genre, rather than a minimal presence. It surrounds a purposeful – if unconscious – repression. And it also suggests that such a marked – that is, noticeable – absence at the narrative level has left its trace, carved out its hollow, elsewhere in the films. Critical discourse, however, is not as a rule tuned to the analysis of negatives, of absences, of traces left by repression. Generally, it looks at what is there, at what is represented as present. Psychoanalysis, on the other hand, looks at what is there but represented as absent. As a mode of critical investigation that differs in focus and direction from other kinds of critical analysis, psychoanalysis, Michel Foucault tells us,

> points directly ... not towards that which must be rendered gradually more explicit by the progressive illumination of the implicit, but towards what is there and yet is hidden, towards what exists with the mute solidity of a thing, of a text closed in upon itself, or of a blank space in a visible text.[1]

A psychoanalytic approach to the topic of sex and the science fiction film would therefore seem an appropriate way to redeem the repressed to the realm of critical discourse and to explore its significance to the genre as a represented absence. Borrowing upon the psychoanalytic techniques of free association and dream analysis, such an approach should allow us to see how human sexuality and women return to the science fiction narrative in displaced and condensed forms, in an emotionally charged imagery and syntax that bears relation to the cryptic but coherent language of dream. And it should also help us to understand how – in their repressed and potent combination as a sign evoking male fear and desire – sex and women figure significantly, if covertly, in shaping the basic structure of the genre and initiating its major themes.

Let us return to what is represented as present in American science fiction films. (I should point out here that this recurrent cultural qualification is less patriotic than indicative of some particular conflicts localized in the American psyche and centred upon the opposition of biology and technology. Science fiction films from other countries do not seem to base themselves in a semiotic system in which biological reproduction and the female are linked as a sign opposed to the sign constituted by linking technological production to the male.) Certainly, at the overt level of plot and narrative, there are some human sexual dramas in American films of the genre, and there are some erotically articulated women. Human heterosexual relations are relatively important to the development of plot and narrative in *Forbidden Planet, The Incredible Shrinking Man, Colossus: The Forbin Project,* and *The Stepford Wives.* Becky, in the 1956 version of *Invasion of the Body Snatchers,* immediately comes to mind as a female character who functions centrally and erotically. But these are exceptions. For the most part, human heterosexual relations in the science fiction film are tepid – more obligatory than steamy. Indeed, those few science fiction films which deal overtly with sex and the sexuality of human women – their erotic appeal and their procreative function – generally do so outside the articulated context of human heterosexuality and within that of racial and spatial miscegenation. Hence we have not only films like *I Married a Monster from Outer Space* and *Mars Needs Women,* but also films like *The*

World, the Flesh, and the Devil and *Demon Seed.* Surely, in these latter two films, the titles say it all. Women who are erotically attractive or biologically fertile are subject only to an alien embrace – in the one instance (however liberal the film's surface message) to a black male, and in the other to a bronzed machine.

Generally, then, in the various overt dramas of science fiction film, the nature and function of human heterosexuality are either muted or transformed. While there are numerous boy-meets-girl encounters across the galaxy and the genre, they tend to be chaste and safe in their dramatization and peripheral to narrative concerns – no matter when the films were made. One gets the feeling that they are included either to satisfy the vague demands of formula or to answer the unspoken charges of homosexuality which echo around the edges of the genre. Science fiction films are full of sexually empty relations and empty of sexually full ones. In concert with this narrative de-emphasis on human sexuality and women, biological sexual functions – intercourse and reproduction – are avoided in their human manifestations and, instead, displaced onto mutant and alien life forms and into technological activity. In this way, women characters are narratively deprived of any problematic connection with sexuality. They rarely exist in the films to 'be made' or 'to make', as sexual objects or as sexual subjects.

Throughout the genre, human female biological difference from the male is literally covered up. (Women represented as alien, however, are often scantily and sexily clad.) The 1950s films are peopled by women restrained by shirtwaist dresses, peter pan collars, and occasional lab coats. Again, the only exception that comes immediately to mind is Becky in *Invasion of the Body Snatchers* – her strapless dresses and push-up bra a bold declaration of sexuality which perhaps forces the script to put her to sleep and turn her into a pod. With rare exceptions, female biological difference is de-emphasized in the films. The question it asks, the response it demands, the need and desire it evokes in the male are hidden and defused by sensible and functional attire, by rational occupations, and by the unprovocative, unquestioning, 'fulfilled' sexuality of a peripheral and occasional wife and mother.

This defusion of difference, this visual and narrative 'coding' of women in the science fiction film as not only peripheral but also asexual, might seem to be a function of the chronological and cultural context in which the films were made. But the de-emphasis on human female sexuality in the science fiction film is not limited to a particular period: rather it seems particular to the genre – sufficient at least if not necessary. Although less obvious than in films of the 1950s, say, this generic cover-up of biological difference is still present in recent films which feature central and narratively active female characters. Women are

sexually defused and made safe and unthreatening by costume, occupation, social position, and attitude – or they are sexually confused with
their male counterparts and narratively substituted for them. Princess
Leia of *Star Wars* and Ripley of *Alien* exemplify these alternatives which
both serve the same repressive ends – the disaffiliation of women and
sexuality and its corollary, the disguise of biological difference. For all
her aristocratic presence as a princess, Leia is also represented as one of
the boys. Whatever her narrative relations with Han Solo, her tough and
wisecracking character is not about to let her tightly-coiled hair down
nor expose her female flesh. It is only against her will that Leia wears the
scanty costume of a harem slave in *Return of the Jedi.* And it is not Han
Solo, but Jabba the Hutt – an alien – for whom she stands as an
unwilling erotic sign. She is simultaneously protected and desexed by her
social position (princesses are to fight for, not to sleep with) and by her
acerbic and pragmatically critical attitude. While she might be compared
in some ways to the Hawksian heroine, who through true grit and
stoicism gains acceptance by a male community, Carrie Fisher certainly
has none of the erotic presence of a Lauren Bacall. Leia, then, is
sexually defused and it seems safe to presume that no matter how
involved she gets with Han Solo in episodes to come, she will still come
off as chaste as her white robes.

Ripley in *Alien*, however, is subject to another sort of representation.
Narratively active as she is, she is no more a sexual being than are
2001's Bowman or Poole. It is telling that the original script of *Alien*
conceived Ripley as a male, and that few changes were made to accommodate the differences that such a sex change in the character might
present. Ripley, indeed, is hardly female (and considered by her
shipmates as hardly human). Unlike Leia, Ripley is not so much defused
in her sexuality as she is confused with her male companions and denied
any sexual difference at all. Instead of white robes that mark her both as
a woman and chaste or off-limits sexually, she wears the same fatigues as
the community of astronauts of which she is – from the beginning – a
part. She is not marked as either a woman or sexual – except for one
sequence at the climax of the film, a climax which has double meaning
and function since it is both narrative and sexual. It is truly disturbing
and horrific when Ripley takes her clothes off toward the end of *Alien*,
not only because, given the rules of genre, we suspect that her compla-
cent belief that she has destroyed the alien creature is unfounded. It is
also horrifying because she exchanges one kind of power for another,
her sudden vulnerability at the narrative level belied by her sudden
sexual potency as a visual representation on the screen. In becoming a
woman at the level of the narrative, Ripley is clearly marked as a victim;
however, in becoming a woman as a fleshly representation of biological

difference, Ripley takes on the concrete configuration of male need, demand, desire and fear, and she commands power at a deeper level of the film than that of its story. Stripping her narrative competence with her uniform, Ripley no longer represents a rational and asexual functioning subject, but an irrational, potent, sexual object – a woman, the truly threatening alien generally repressed by the male-conceived and dominated genre. It is no wonder that at the narrative level, the represented alien emerges phallic and erect and seeks to destroy and consume the fearsome difference that Ripley has so suddenly exposed. (And can one, then, forget that the alien was not of woman born – but erupted in violence and fury from a male belly?)

Sexuality, however, is not denied only to the few women characters in science fiction films. The male heroes who dominate almost all science fiction films are also remarkably asexual. Indeed, most of them are about as libidinally interesting as a Ken doll; like Barbie's companion, they are all jaw and no genitals. This sexlessness spans the occupational possibilities of the genre – from lab scientist to doctor, from amateur astronomer to geologist. It seems particularly radiant, however, in the superb physiques, wooden movements, hollow cheerfulness, and banal competence of science fiction astronauts. Certainly, although all science fiction films are – in one way or another – about space travel and the transgression of those established boundaries and markers which give shape and identity to mind, body, and place, not all science fiction films have astronauts in them. Yet, astronauts are clearly those figures who centralize and visually represent the values and virtues common to all the male protagonists of the genre in a single archetypal presence. They are cool, rational, competent, unimaginative, male, and sexless. These qualities make them the heroes of the genre, as they are heroes of our popular culture. Whereas the semiotic link between biological sexuality and women has been repressed or broken by the genre, the semiotic link between biological asexuality and men has been forged by it and allowed a full range of representation. Thus, much as one can productively free associate around the absence in the science fiction film that the female body represents, the virginal astronaut presents an opportunity to free associate around a dominant and significant presence.

Virginal astronauts are not to be taken literally: rather they are visual signs that systemically and systematically function in a conscious and unconscious narrative syntax. That is, they are simultaneously icon, index, and symbol. In their visual representation and narrative activity, they embody, dramatize, and stand for the science fiction film's secondary and conscious – or textual – conflict. And they also embody, dramatize, and stand for the genre's primary and unconscious – or subtextual – thematic problem and the narrative momentum it generates. That major generic problem centres around the male desire to break free from biological dependence on the female as Mother and Other, and to mark the male self as separate and autonomous. The realization of this desire – certainly at the level of science fiction narrative – necessitates the rejection and repression of female difference and its threat to male autonomy as being, indeed, the difference which makes a difference. In the genre, only women represent difference and so are outcasts at the edges of the narrative, or are covered up in overalls and lab coats so they might share a bit of narrative space. This connection of the female with difference, sexual difference and biological power, suggests perhaps why we tend to think of astronauts in the plural. They usually come in teams, representing similitude on the screen rather than difference. Maleness in its clean-cut asexuality is visually coded as assembly-line sameness.

These virginal astronauts, then, tend to be more corporate than corporeal. Indeed, it is their interchangeable blandness, their programmed cheerfulness, their lack of imagination, their very banality (think of that reductive language they all use), that makes them heroes, that gives them that aura of mechanical and robotic competence which insists that nothing can go wrong, that everything is A-OK. They all look as if they can accomplish the unthinkable without ever having to think about it. They are a team, all the same – and certainly never separated by real sexual rivalry. Offscreen or on, these men who figure in our public myths neither appeal to prurient interest nor really seem to have any. They are never 'sexy'. Their wooden postures and – dare I say it – tight-assed competence disallow any connection with the sexual and sensuous. *2001*'s astronaut Poole, basking nearly naked under a sunlamp, is hardly a piece of beefcake. Thus, whether named Buzz or Armstrong, Buck, Flash, or Bowman, our public astronauts reek of locker-room camaraderie, but hardly of male sweat or semen. As if in training for the big game, they have rejected their biology and sexuality – pushed it from their minds and bodies to concentrate on the technology required to penetrate and impregnate not a woman, but the universe.

The virginal astronauts of the science fiction film are a sign of penetration and impregnation without biology, without sex, and without the opposite, different, sex. They signify a conquering, potent, masculine and autonomous technology which values production over reproduction, which creates rather than procreates in a seeming immaculate conception and a metaphorically autocratic caesarian birth. As signs, asexual astronauts give concrete form and presence in both culture and film to this public – if unspoken – disaffiliation of rational technological enterprise from human biological activity. Not only does the technological man want to make his own babies, but he wants to do so without the hormones and flesh, without lust and arousal, and his most heroic representatives, the astronauts, embody this distrust of women, of the biological, and of the irrational dependencies of the flesh.

It is understandable, then, that women pose a particular narrative threat to science fiction heroes and their engagement with technology. They are figures who – as mothers, wives, girlfriends – arouse male need, demand, and desire. They represent the Mother and the Other whose very presence points to the puny and imitative quality of male endeavour, of technological creation and its inanimate products. Their power to originate life is envied and emulated. Thus, their absence from a central position in science fiction narrative creates an indelible and deeply significant space. Women cannot be avoided in the science fiction film, no matter how many spaceships leave them behind. They also serve who only stand and wait – or who actively emerge from narrative exile to occupy the paradigmatic space of the imagery. Thus, if human females and Mother Earth are abandoned, if male heroes escape them, it is to yet another female presence: the dark womb of space both beckons and menaces – yielding and receptive to phallic exploration and reunion, or as consuming and destructive as a black hole in its eradication of male potence and presence. Women do not disappear from the science fiction film – nor does sex. They may be repressed, but they return to the narrative in what Foucault called 'the mute solidity of a thing', in the condensed and displaced imagery and action of the genre that are themselves sensuous and sexual though no longer human in their overt and articulated form of signification.

Repression is the psychoanalytic term for the 'active process of keeping out and ejecting, banishing from consciousness, ideas or impulses that are unacceptable to it'.[2] An attempt is made to push the entire painful and emotionally charged idea – the whole being called an 'instinct-presentation' – into the realm of the unconscious. Psychoanalysis tells us:

> It is possible to reduce to a minimum the influence of such an instinct-presentation by first breaking it up into its two basic components: the idea and the affective charge. This means that there are three things that are subject to repression: (1) the instinct-presentation; (2) the idea; (3) the affect. In many instances, when the entire instinct cannot be successfully repressed, either the ideational or the affective part may be. If the idea is repressed, the affect with which it was associated may be transferred to another idea (in consciousness) that has no apparent connection with the original idea. Or, if the affect is repressed, the idea, remaining, so to speak, alone in consciousness may be linked to a pleasant affect. Finally, if the whole instinct-presentation is repressed, it may at some later time return to consciousness in the form of a symbol.[3]

This psychoanalytic description describes precisely what has been entertained here about the presence and absence of women in the science fiction film. The instinct-presentation is comparable to what I have earlier described as the complete sign of sexual woman, the semiotic bearer – in her bodily difference – of a biological power which demands the painful male recognition of dependence and impotence and their corollaries, desire and envy. The influence of this instinct-presentation is minimized when the films break down the semiotic connection between its two parts, when they separate biology and sexuality from women, the affective charge from the idea. When human women are present in the narrative, when they remain as an idea but their affect, their biological difference and sexuality, is repressed, they are merely pleasant or indifferent presences and representations. When biological difference and sexuality are present in the narrative, when they remain as an affect but their idea, their traditional semiotic representation as female, is repressed, they are usually transferred to another idea that seems unrelated to the original one. Thus, sexuality can be transferred to a giant mutant insect about to lay eggs, or to the biologically different sexuality of an alien creature like the Thing which can breed from its hand and whose offspring we see pulsating tumescently during a sequence of *The Thing From Another World* (1951). (Consider the film's counter to this: the hero's human male hands are literally tied by his very aware girl friend, because in their last encounter he couldn't keep those hands off her.) Nearly all of *Alien*'s imagery is organic and/or sexual, whereas the humans are not – except for Ripley's climactic emergence as female toward the end of the narrative.

Finally, as I have suggested, if both women and human sexuality are repressed from the narrative as a whole, as a sign, as the entirety that is the instinct-presentation, then that whole may return in another form to the narrative – in some symbolic representation. The narrative enterprise of space exploration and its accompanying visuals may be viewed as a symbolic representation of birth and/or intercourse: the expulsion from the body as well as the penetration of space, the infant's separation from the Mother or the adult male's reunion with the Mother in the form of the female Other. Similarly, the alien invasion of the planet or the alien mind/body 'takeover' may be viewed as the symbolic enactment of the fear of femaleness – both as all-consuming, castrating, possessive, and potent (having the power of breast *and* penis), and as an 'inverted' rape fantasy in which the invasion of the planet, mind, and body represent the negative, passive, vulnerable, and female side of penetration, represent 'being screwed' rather than 'screwing'. And, of course, female sexuality may return symbolically in the representations of the alien or mutation. These representations return the repressed to the narrative, then, but they are returned in visual disguise – transformed by the semiotic processes of the unconscious known as condensation and displacement.

Condensation is the term given by psychoanalysis to that process in which a single idea, word, or image 'is made to contain all the emotion associated with a group of ideas', or a conversation, or a lived scene or experience.[4] Thus, one representation comes to stand for many. A single signifier is substituted for a number of signifiers and comes, therefore, to have attached to its manifest form a number of meanings – multiple signifieds. In addition, it condenses and compresses all the emotion connected with each of the individual signifiers and signifieds for which it alone has come to stand. The similarities that are perceived between single ideas, words, or images, between emotional associations and life experiences, provide the attraction which brings a particular group of signifiers and signifieds together under the symbolic umbrella of a single supercharged representation. This process is certainly characteristic of all dreams, but it can be seen also in the metaphorical nature and function of conscious language – a structural and functional similarity which has been emphasized by French neo-Freudian Jacques Lacan, and which allows me to justify the pertinence of condensation to the science fiction film without going so far as to claim that film is identical to either dream or human psyche.[5] Rather, we are looking at cinematic signification of a particular type. We are looking in most science fiction films at a powerfully charged or cathected imagery that is not consciously articulated as metaphorical, at an imagery which is meant in the narrative to denote precisely that for which it iconically stands.

Think, for example, of the Rhedosaurus in *The Beast from 20,000 Fathoms*. At the denotative level of the narrative, the creature is a signifier – an image or visual representation – of a single signified: a prehistoric giant reptile. However, that visual representation carries a great emotional charge – and not only because it wrecks Coney Island. It has the visual force it does because it represents other things and ideas and associations in addition to its denotative function. It also signifies primeval origins, the primal sink and slime from which life first emerged. It also signifies atomic force and destruction and extinction (it was aroused by an atomic blast), and the fear of an avenging nature which has been disturbed by technology. It signifies, too, something unnameably alien, inhuman, unknowable in its scaliness and reptilian being, something Other (perhaps the female Other, the bad Mother – since the creature's destructive path leads to its ancient breeding ground). While these semiological claims should be argued in an analysis of the entire film, proposing them here helps clarify the idea of condensation as it relates to science fiction imagery. In addition, insofar as this particular film never overtly articulates these signifieds at the level of the narrative, never deals with the origins of life or the perils of atomic power or the hideousness that mere difference represents (be it of species or sex), we can see how condensation emerges as an imagery of the repressed.

Displacement similarly emerges as an expression of the repressed, and it too is characteristic of dreams. Lacan has likened it in structure and function to the metonymic nature and function of conscious language, to the way in which signifier follows signifier in a contiguous chain of substitutive movement. Displacement is the 'transference of the emotions ... from the original ideas to which they are attached – to other ideas'.[6] Emotion or psychic energy can be transferred from its source in an original event and that event's original representation to something else, something less originally meaningful. In such a manner, psychoanalysis tells us, the emotions 'may be able to gain the realm of consciousness, attaching themselves to ideas to which the patient is ordinarily indifferent. By such an arrangement the patient is spared the pain of knowing the original source of the affects'.[7] Often, in the science fiction film, the emotions generated by the narrative and the visual imagery in regard to being, for example, in a spaceship are those of confinement, of discomfort, of dependence (upon the ship and computer to sustain life support – think of the lifeline and the 'umbilical' which links technological man to the mother machine). Powerlessness is also evoked, visualized in the helpless and dependent sleep of those aboard. It is more than likely that the original source of these emotions – not attached to technology – comes from a deeper level than the narrative and can be related to the original and repressed representation of human biology and its process: the passage from womb to tomb, the infantile intimations of original being and not-being that merge in the biological space travel which results in birth and also, finally, in death.

Displacement also involves not only the transference of emotion from an original to a secondary representation, but also 'the shifting of id impulses from one pathway to another'.[8] Someone who is civilized is not supposed to hit an antagonist and so will curse him roundly. In the science fiction film, someone who is rational is not supposed to destroy things irrationally or ravage them – and so will raise a creature or machine who can do it for him. Of particular interest to biology, sex and science fiction, displacement often involves transferences at the level of the body, in relation to both the organic and erotogenic. We are told:

> The instincts shift, for example, from the oral to the anal, to the genital zones, or to any other erotogenic zone. In conversion hysteria a psychic complex may be displaced upon a potentially organic structure. Or, all the issues connected with genitality may be displaced to the oral zone. Displacement 'from below upward' is a common phenomenon.[9]

In *Invaders From Mars,* one sequence of images shows a woman about to be 'taken over' (that is, possessed, taken) by the aliens. She is shown lying on a platform, the nape of her neck about to be penetrated by some long, tubular sort of mechanical mind probe which will place the red crystal it holds at its tip into her body. Supervising this enterprise is the 'head' alien creature – who is, literally, a head encased in a glass ball and moved about by mutants who obey its telepathic commands. In this film (as in many other science fiction films), the head – narratively the place of reason as opposed to libido – has become the representation of the penis. The nape of the neck in this instance (which is an eroto-genic zone in some cultures) has become the representation of the womb and anus (it is, after all, the back of the neck). The action, what we see on the level of the narrative as an alien invasion, an appropriation of the mind, is a displacement of sexual erotic activity, particularly in its negative implications as rape and sodomy. While it is never consciously articulated in the films, such displacements 'from below upward' are articulated in the absolutely sensitive – if vulgar – locutions of such phrases as 'giving head' or 'mind-fuck' or even in such an innocent synonym as 'conception' for 'idea'.

The point to be made here is that both displacement and condensa-tion work at once in the entirety of the narrative and concentrate their efforts on the complete or partial repression of the instinct-presentation and its component parts: female sexuality and fertility, female biology and its representation in a body that is different, that is difference itself. What results is a basic structure which informs the genre – a kind of push-pull configuration in which what is repressed will return in disguise to become overtly articulated. This basic structure, however, is also able to accommodate historical and cultural change – for what will be repressed (the sexual female, or sexuality itself) will alter with the times and will also emerge in a disguise which responds to historical concerns. While these changes may be marked, however, the structure itself remains constant. Displacement and condensation will occur or the genre will not exist – in the same way that metonymy and metaphor exist or there can be no language.

Earlier I suggested that all science fiction films were about space travel whether or not they had rockets or spaceships in them, whether or not they were manned by virginal astronauts. By space travel, I was referring to the passage across known and marked boundaries that give identity to the world and to ourselves – as Earth and space, as inside and outside, as self and other, as male and female. Borders and markers in the science fiction film are seen as extendable – and their contents as spilling over into each other, possibly merging. This is what is so thrilling about the genre, and what is so threatening, what structures its narratives

as a play of fear and desire. It is also what affixes the genre to
infantile and pre-Oedipal dramas in which the female – as Mother and
Other – becomes the focal point and origin of questions the infant must
answer regarding its own sexuality, its selfness, its very identity as
human and biologically gendered. In repressing women and sexuality, in
a culture which semiotically links biology and sexuality to women and
technology to men, most American science fiction films play out
scenarios which focus on infantile experience while pretending to adult
concerns.

Freud, Melanie Klein, and others have noted the following features
which characterize infantile experience. One can see immediately how
they are paralleled by the action and imagery of the American science
fiction film in its various dramatic manifestations. The infant feels a
sense of helplessness, impotence, and dependence; a sense of insignifi-
cance and smallness in relation to the monstrous size and physical
importance of the mother. The infant has a confused image of gender
identity, its own and its mother's, and tends to collapse the penis and
breast into a bisexual imagery in which body parts and power are interchangeable. The infant has difficulty in distinguishing boundaries
between itself and its mother, between inside and outside, mind and
body, body and tool or toy. It has extreme ambivalence toward maternal
power in its relation to the infant's own limited power, resulting in a
tension between its sense of its own desire and destructive potential and
its dependent demands upon one who can destroy. Thus, the infant has
a tendency to introject or project maternal power, to see itself as powerful and potent and autonomous like the mother or to fear the other as
monstrous, destructive, and all-powerful. As well, the infant is both
curious and afraid in its lack of knowledge – it wants to know, but is
afraid of what it does not know or what it may find out. And this lack of
knowledge is most focused around sexual and body imagery and
concern for its own origin.[10] 'Where did I come from?' is a question
penultimately connected with another: 'Who and what am I?'

These questions lie repressed in the narratives of the science fiction
film. At the level of conscious representation, the one is articulated as
'Where are we *going*?' or 'Where did *It* (or *They*) come from?' The first
is a positive and the second a negative disguise for the infant's 'Where
did I come from?' The second question takes the disguised form of
'Who and what is *It* (or *They*)?' instead of 'Who or what am I?' If these
questions were exposed in their original form, in the 'true speech' that
Lacan sees as the unconscious, the genre could not exist at the narrative
level as the kind of exploration it is. Thus, those questions of origin and
identity and the conventional sign of the sexual female which provokes
those questions must be repressed.

Notes

1. Michel Foucault, *The Order of Things*, New York: Vintage Books 1973, p. 374.

2. Leland E. Hinsie, MD and Robert J. Campbell, MD, *Psychiatric Dictionary*, 4th edn, New York: Oxford University Press 1970, p. 660.

3. Ibid.

4. Ibid., p. 149.

5. For a clear exploitation of Lacan and his semiotic psychoanalysis, see Anika Lemaire, *Jacques Lacan*, trans. David Macey, London: Routledge & Kegan Paul 1979.

6. *Psychiatric Dictionary*, p. 219.

7. Ibid.

8. Ibid., p. 220.

9. Ibid.

10. I should like to thank Zoë Soufoulis, who brought these characteristics to my attention in a presentation, 'Science Fiction, Psychoanalysis and the (M)other', for my Film Genre course at the University of California, Santa Cruz, Fall 1981.

10

Time Travel, Primal Scene and the Critical Dystopia

Constance Penley

If the sure sign of postmodern success is the ability to inspire spinoffs, *The Terminator* was a prodigy. The film was quickly replicated by *Exterminator, Re-animator, Eliminators, The Annihilators*, and the hard-core *The Sperminator*, all sound-alikes if not look-alikes. It then went on to garner one of popular culture's highest accolades when a West Coast band named itself *Terminators of Endearment*. And just to show that postmodernity knows no boundaries, national or otherwise, an oppressively large (2ft × 3 ft) and trendy new Canadian journal has appeared, calling itself *The Manipulator*.

For some science fiction critics, Fredric Jameson among them, *The Terminator*'s popular appeal would represent no more than American science fiction's continuing affinity for the dystopian rather than the utopian, with fantasies of cyclical regression or totalitarian empires of the future. Our love affair with apocalypse and Armageddon, according to Jameson, results from the atrophy of utopian imagination, in other words, our cultural incapacity to imagine the future.[1] Or, as Stanislaw Lem puts it, in describing the banality and constriction of most American science fiction, 'The task of an SF author today is as easy as that of the pornographer, and in the same way'.[2] But surely there are dystopias and dystopias, and not all such films (from *Rollerball* to *The Terminator*) deserve to be dismissed as trashy infatuations with an equally trashy future. While it is true that most recent dystopian films are content to revel in the sheer awfulness of The Day After (the Mad Max trilogy and *A Boy and His Dog* come readily to mind), there are others which try to point to present tendencies that seem likely to result in corporate totalitarianism, apocalypse, or both. Although *The Terminator* gives us one of the most horrifying post-apocalyptic visions of any recent film, it falls

116

into the latter group because it locates the origins of future catastrophe in decisions about technology, warfare and social behaviour that are being made today. For example, the new, powerful defence computer that in *The Terminator* is hooked into everything – missiles, the defence industry, weapons design – and trusted to make all the decisions, is clearly a fictionalized version of the burgeoning Star Wars industry. This computer of the near future, forty years hence, gets smart – a new order of intelligence. It 'began to see all people as a threat', Reese tells Sarah as he tries to fill her in on the future, 'not just the ones on the other side. It decided our fate in a microsecond. Extermination'.

A film like *The Terminator* could be called a 'critical dystopia' inasmuch as it tends to suggest causes rather than merely reveal symptoms. But before saying more about how this film works as a critical dystopia, two qualifications need to be made. First, like most recent science fiction from *V* to *Star Wars*, *The Terminator* limits itself to solutions that are either individualist or bound to a romanticized notion of guerilla-like small-group resistance. The true atrophy of the utopian imagination is this: we *can* imagine the future but we *cannot* conceive ✓ the kind of collective political strategies necessary to change or ensure that future. Second, the film's politics, so to speak, cannot be simply equated with those of the 'author', James Cameron, the director of *The Terminator*, whose next job, after all, was writing *Rambo* (his disclaimers about Stallone's interference aside, he agreed to the project in the first place). Instead *The Terminator* can best be seen in relation to a set of cultural and physical conflicts, anxieties and fantasies that are all at work in this film in a particularly insistent way,

What are the elements, then, of *The Terminator*'s critical dystopian vision? Although the film is thought of as an exceptionally forward-thrusting action picture, it shares with other recent science fiction films, like *Blade Runner*, an emphasis on atmosphere or 'milieu', but not, however, at the price of any flattening of narrative space. (In this respect it is closest to *Alien*.) *The Terminator* is studded with everyday-life detail, all organized by an idea of 'tech noir'. Machines provide the texture and substance of this film: cars, trucks, motorcycles, radios, TVs, time clocks, phones, answering machines, beepers, hair dryers, Sony Walkmen, automated factory equipment. The defence network ✓ computer of the future which decided our fate in a microsecond had its humble origins here, in the rather more innocuous technology of the film's present. Today's machines are not, however, shown to be agents of destruction because they are themselves evil, but because they can break down, or because they can be used (often innocently) in ways they were not intended to be used. Stalked by a killer, Sarah Conner cannot get through to the police because the nearest phone is out of order. When she finally reaches the LA Police Department emergency line, on a phone in the Tech Noir nightclub, it is predictably to hear 'All our lines are busy ... please hold ...'. Neither can she get through to her room-mate, Ginger, to warn her because Ginger and her boyfriend have put on the answering machine while they make love. But Ginger wouldn't have been able to hear the phone, in any case, because she'd worn her Sony Walkman to bed. Tech turns noir again when the Terminator, not Ginger, takes the answering machine message that gives away Sarah's location. Later Sarah will again reveal her whereabouts when the Terminator perfectly mimics her mother's voice over the phone. And in one of the film's most pointed gestures toward the unintentionally harmful effects of technology, the police psychiatrist fails to see the Terminator entering the station when his beeper goes off and distracts him just as their paths cross. Lacking any warning, scores of policemen are killed and the station destroyed. The film seems to suggest that if technology can go wrong or be abused, it will be.

But the film does not advance an 'us against them' argument, man versus machine, a Romantic opposition between the organic and the mechanical, for there is much that is hybrid about its constructed elements. The Terminator, after all, is part machine, part human – a cyborg. (Its chrome skeleton with its hydraulic muscles and tendons of flexible cable looks like the Nautilus machines Schwarzenegger uses to build his body.) And Kyle's skills as a guerrilla fighter are dependent upon his tech abilities – hot-wiring cars, renovating weapons, making bombs. If Kyle himself has become a fighting machine in order to attack the oppressor machines, Sarah too becomes increasingly machine-like as she acquires the skills she needs to survive both the Terminator and the apocalypse to come. The concluding irony is that Kyle and Sarah use machines to distract and then destroy the Terminator when he corners them in a robot-automated factory. At the end of one of the most harrowing, and gruellingly paced, chase scenes on film, Sarah terminates the Terminator between two plates of a hydraulic press. This interpenetration of human and machine is seen most vividly, however, when Sarah is wounded in the thigh by a piece of exploding Terminator shrapnel. Leaving aside the rich history of sexual connotations of wounding in the thigh,[3] part of a machine is here literally incorporated into Sarah's body. While the film addresses an ultimate battle between humans and machines, it nonetheless accepts the impossibility of clearly distinguishing between them. It focuses on the partial and ambiguous merging of the two, a more complex response, and one typical of the critical dystopia, than the Romantic triumph of the organic over the mechanical, or the nihilistic recognition that we have all become automata (even if those automata are better than we are, more human than human, as in *Blade Runner*).[4]

The Terminator, however, is as much about time as it is about machines. Because cinema itself has the properties of a time machine, it lends itself easily to time travel stories, one of the staples of science fiction literature. Compared to the complexity of many literary science fiction time travel plots, *The Terminator*'s story is simple: in 2010 a killer cyborg is sent back to the present day with the mission of exterminating Sarah Conner, a part-time waitress and student, the future mother of John Conner, the man who will lead the last remnants of humanity to victory over the machines which are trying to rid the world of humans. John Conner chooses Kyle Reese, a young and hardened fighter, to travel back in time to save Sarah from the Terminator. If the Terminator succeeds in his mission, John Conner, of course, will never be born, and the humans will never be able to fight back successfully against the machines. Kyle has fallen in love with Sarah through her photograph, given to him by John Conner. He says he always wondered what she was thinking about when the photo was taken for she has a faraway look on her face and a sad smile. 'I came across time for you', he professes. 'I love you. I always have.' They make love, he is killed soon after, Sarah destroys the Terminator and leaves for the mountains to give birth to her son and wait out the holocaust to come. The film ends South of the Border with a Mexican boy taking a Polaroid of Sarah as she is thinking of Kyle. It is the photograph that John Conner will give to Kyle, forty years later, knowing that he is sending his own father to his death.

This sort of story is called a time-loop paradox because cause and effect are not only reversed but put into a circle: the later events are caused by the earlier events, and the earlier by the later.[5] If John Conner had not sent Kyle Reese back in time to be his father, he would never have been born. But he was born, so Kyle Reese must *already* have travelled back to the past to impregnate Sarah Conner. As another instance of paradox, John Conner's fighting skills were taught him by his mother. Sarah Conner, however, learned those skills from Kyle Reese, who had himself learned them while fighting at John Conner's side. Small wonder then that Sarah looks slightly bewildered when Kyle says he has 'always loved' her. How could this be true when, from the perspective of her point in time, he hasn't been born yet?

What is the appeal of time loop paradox stories? They are so fascinating that many people who used to read science fiction but have long since given it up will usually remember one story in particular, Ray Bradbury's 'A Sound of Thunder', even if they can no longer recall the author or the title (others have also noted this phenomenon). In this famous story, big game hunters from the future travel back to the age of the dinosaurs. They don't have to fear that their shooting and bagging will affect the future, however, because dinosaurs will soon be extinct anyway. They are strictly warned, though, not to step off the walkway that has been prepared for them over the primeval jungle. One hunter disobeys and in doing so crushes a tiny butterfly under his boot. When the hunting party returns to the future, everything is ever so slightly different, the result of killing one small insect millions of years earlier.

The essential elements of time travel and its consequences are witnessed in a very succinct way in 'A Sound of Thunder'. That is why the story is remembered. But when plots of this kind become more complex, one theme tends to predominate: what would it be like to go back in time and give birth to oneself? Or, what would it be like to be one's own mother and father? Robert Heinlein has given us the seminal treatment of this paradoxical situation in the story 'All You Zombies'. A time traveller who has undergone a sex-change operation not only encounters both earlier and later versions of himself but turns out to be his own mother and father. Similarly, in David Gerrold's *The Man Who Folded Himself*, each time the protagonist travels in time, he reduplicates himself. Eventually this results in a large group of identical men who find each other to be ideal lovers. One of them goes very far back in time and meets a lesbian version of himself. They fall in love, have children, and then break up, to return to their copy-lovers. (As the narrator says in 'All You Zombies', 'It's a shock to have it proved to you that you can't resist seducing yourself'.) The appeal of a film like *Back to the Future* is quite apparent – it is only a more vulgar version of the desire manifested in these stories. There is of course a name for this desire; it is called a primal scene fantasy, the name Freud gave to the fantasy of overhearing or observing parental intercourse, of being on the scene, so to speak, of one's own conception. The desire represented in the time travel story, of both witnessing one's own conception and being one's own mother and father, is similar to the primal scene fantasy, in which one can be both observer or one of the participants. The reconstruction of a patient's primal scene assumes, in fact, a great deal of time travel. (Freud said the most extreme primal scene fantasy was that of observing parental intercourse while one is still an unborn baby in the womb.)[6] The Wolf-Man, supine on the analytic couch, is sent further and further back in time to 'remember' the moment when, as a child, he saw his parents having sex. Although Freud's interpretation depends upon the Wolf-Man witnessing such a scene, he decides, finally, that it was not necessary for the event to have actually occurred for it to have had profound effects on the patient's psychical life. A patient can consciously fabricate such a scene only because it has been operative in his or her unconscious, and this construction has nothing to do with its actual occurrence or nonoccurrence. The idea of returning to the past to generate an event that has already made an impact on one's identity lies at the core of the time-loop paradox story.

What is *The Terminator*'s primal scene? The last words that Kyle Reese throws at the Terminator, along with a pipe bomb, are 'Come on, motherfucker!' But in the narrative logic of this film it is Kyle who is the mother fucker. And within the structure of fantasy that shapes the film, John Conner is the child who orchestrates his own primal scene, one inflected by a family romance, moreover, because he is able to choose his own father, singling out Kyle from the other soldiers. That such a fantasy is an attempted end-run around Oedipus is also obvious: John Conner can identify with his father, can even *be* his father in the scene of parental intercourse, and also conveniently dispose of him in order to go off with (in) his mother.

Recent film theory has taken up Freud's description of fantasy to give a more complete account of how identification works in film.[7] An important emphasis has been placed on the subject's ability to assume, successively, all the available positions in the fantasmatic scenario. Extending this idea to film has shown that spectatorial identification is more complex than has hitherto been understood because it shifts constantly in the course of the film's narrative, while crossing the lines of biological sex; in other words, unconscious identification with the characters or the scenario is not necessarily dependent upon gender. Another element of Freud's description of fantasy that also deserves attention, particularly in discussing fantasy in relation to popular film, is the self-serving or wish-fulfilling aspect of fantasy. In 'The Paths to the Formation of Symptoms', Freud constructs two analogies between the creation of fantasy and instances drawn from 'real life'. He begins by saying that a child uses fantasies to disguise the history of his childhood, 'just as every nation disguises its forgotten prehistory by constructing legends'. (p. 368) A fantasy is thus not 'just a fantasy' but a story *for* the subject. The fantasy of seduction, for example, serves to deny the subject's acts of autoeroticism by projecting them onto another person. (Such fantasy constructions, Freud says, should be seen separately from those real acts of adult seduction of children that occur more frequently than is acknowledged.) Similarly, in the 'family romance' the subject creates another parent, an ideal one, to make up for the perceived short-comings of the real mother or father. Thus a film like *The Terminator* that is so clearly working in relation to a primal fantasy, is also working in the service of pleasure (already a requirement for a mass audience film), a pleasure that depends upon suppressing conflicts or contradictions. (Because such suppression does not always work, and because desire does not always aim for pleasure – the death drive – much recent film analysis is devoted to examining those aspects of film that go distinctly 'beyond the pleasure principle'.[8]

Take, for example, the seemingly contradictory figure of Kyle Reese. The film 'cheats' with his image in the same way that Ford's *The Searchers* 'cheats' with Martin Pauley's image, which is, variously, wholly Indian, 'half-breed', 'quarter-blood' Cherokee, one-eighth Cherokee, or wholly white, depending upon the unconscious and ideological demands of the narrative at any given moment.[9] In *The Terminator* Kyle is the virile, hardened fighter barking orders to the terrified Sarah, but alternately he is presented as boyish, vulnerable, and considerably younger in appearance than her. His childishness is underscored by Sarah's increasingly maternal affection for him (bandaging his wounds, touching his scars), and in the love scene, he is the young man being initiated by the more experienced, older woman. Kyle is thus both the father of John Conner and, in his youth and inexperience, Sarah's son, John Conner. The work of fantasy allows the fact of incest to be both stated and dissimulated. It is only in fantasy, finally, that we can have our cake and eat it too. Or as the French equivalent puts it, even more aptly, that we can be and have been – *peut être et avoir été.*

Freud also compared the mental realm of fantasy to a 'reservation' or 'nature reserve', a place set aside where 'the requirements of agriculture, communication and industry threaten to bring about changes in the original face of the earth which will quickly make it unrecognizable' (almost a description of a post-apocalyptic landscape). 'Everything, including what is useless and even what is noxious, can grow and proliferate there as it pleases. The mental realm of fantasy is just such a reservation withdrawn from the reality principle' (p. 372). Can a film like *The Terminator* be similarly dismissed as merely escapist, appealing as it does to a realm of fantasy 'withdrawn from the reality principle', where even our incestuous desires can be realized? For one possible answer we can turn to the end of Freud's essay on symptom formation, where he tells us that there is 'a path that leads back from fantasy to reality – the path, that is, of art'. An artist, he says, has the ability to shape a faithful image of his fantasy, and then to depersonalize and generalize it so much that it is made accessible to other people. Even if we do not have as much faith in 'art' or the 'artist' as Freud has, we can still draw some useful conclusions from what he says.

One could argue that *The Terminator* treads the path from fantasy back to reality precisely because it is able to generalize its vision, to offer something more than this fully, though paradoxically, resolved primal fantasy. This generalizing of the fantasy is carried out through *The Terminator*'s use of the topical and everyday: as we have seen, the film's texture is woven from the technological litter of modern life. But this use of the topical is not, for example, like *E.T.*'s more superficial referencing of daily life through brand name kid-speak, that is, topicality for topicality's sake. Rather, it is a dialogue with Americana that bespeaks the inevitable consequences of our current technological addictions. To give another example, the shopping mall in George Romero's *Dawn of the Dead* is more than a kitsch ambience, it is a way of concretely demonstrating the zombification of consumer culture. By exposing every corner of the mall – stores, escalators, public walkways, basement, roof – the location becomes saturated with meaning, in a way that goes far beyond *E.T.*'s token gesturing toward the commodification of modern life. If *The Terminator*'s primal scene fantasy draws the spectator into the film's paradoxical circle of cause and effect and its equally paradoxical realization of incestuous desire, its militant everydayness throws the spectator back out again, back to the technological future.

In the realm of the unconscious and fantasy, the question of the subject's origin, 'Where do I come from?' is followed by the question of sexual difference. 'Who am I (What sex am I)?' It is by now well known that the narrative logic of classical film is powered by the desire to establish, by the end of the film, the nature of masculinity, the nature of femininity, and the way in which those two can be complementary rather than antagonistic.[10] But in film and television, as elsewhere, it is becoming increasingly difficult to *tell the difference.* As men and women are less and less differentiated by a division of labour, what, in fact, makes them different? And how can classical film still construct the difference so crucial to its formula for narrative closure? Ironically, it is science fiction film – our hoariest and seemingly most sexless genre – that alone remains capable of supplying the configurations of sexual difference required by the classical cinema. If there is increasingly less practical difference between men and women, there is more than enough difference between a human and an alien (*The Man Who Fell to Earth, Starman*), a human and a cyborg/replicant (*Android, Blade Runner*), or a human from the present and one from the future (*The Terminator*). In these films the question of sexual difference – a question whose answer is no longer 'self-evident' – is displaced onto the more remarkable difference between the human and the other. That this questioning of the difference between human and other is sexual in nature, can also be seen in the way these films reactivate infantile sexual investigation. One of the big questions for the viewer of *Blade Runner*, for example, is 'How do replicants *do it*?' Or, of *The Man Who Fell to Earth*, 'What is the sex of this alien who possesses nothing that resembles human genitals (its sex organs are in its hands)?'

But if recent science fiction film provides the heightened sense of difference necessary to the classical narrative, it also offers the reassurance of difference itself. In describing one important aspect of the shift in the psychical economy from the nineteenth century to the twentieth century, Raymond Bellour maintains that in the nineteenth century men looked at women and feared they were different, but in the twentieth century men look at women and fear they are the same.[11] The majority of science fiction films work to dissipate that fear of the same, to ensure that there is a difference. A very instructive example is the NBC mini-series 'V' broadcast in the US during the 1983–84 season. A rare instance of science fiction on television ('Star Trek' notwithstanding, the television industry insists that science fiction does not work on television), 'V' tried to be as topical and up-to-date as possible, particularly in the roles it gave to women. The Commander of the alien force that takes over Earth's major cities, the Supreme commander of the aliens, the leader of the Earthling guerrillas, and the leader of the alien fifth column aiding the Earthlings, are all played by women. They are seen performing the same activities as the men (planning, fighting, counter-attacking, infiltrating, etc), thus removing the most important visible signs of difference. The only difference remaining in 'V' is that between the aliens (scaly, green reptiles in human disguise) and the humans. That difference, however, comes to represent sexual difference, as if the alien/human difference were a projection of what can no longer be depicted otherwise.[12] The leader of the guerrillas is captured and brainwashed by the alien commander. Although she is eventually rescued by her comrades, it is feared that the brainwashing has turned her into an alien. She even begins using her left hand rather than her right one, a reptile-alien characteristic. Thus when she and her boyfriend, the second in command of the guerrillas, are shown making love, we realize, as they do, that this could be interspecies sex – the blond, all-American Julie may be a lizard underneath it all, whether in fact or in mind. It gives the otherwise banal proceedings a powerful source of dramatic tension, while it reassures TV-viewing audiences everywhere that there is a difference. (Such a radical disposition of difference always risks, of course, tipping over into the horror of *too much* difference.)

Similarly, it is instructive to see how *Aliens*, directed by James Cameron following his success with *The Terminator*, cracks under the strain of trying to keep to the very original lack of sexual differentiation in its precursor, Ridley Scott's *Alien* (not counting, of course, the penultimate scene of Ripley in her bikini underwear). Dan O'Bannon's treatment for the first film was unique in writing each role to be played by either a man or a woman.[13] Ridley Scott's direction followed through on this idea, producing a film that is (for the most part) stunningly egalitarian. In attempting to repeat the equal-opportunity camaraderie of the first film, Cameron's sequel includes a mixed squad of marines, in which the women are shown to be as tough as the men, maybe tougher. And Ripley is, again, the bravest and smartest member of the team. But this time there is a difference, one that is both improbable and symptomatic. Ripley 'develops' a maternal instinct, risking her life to save the little girl who is the only survivor of a group of space colonists decimated by the aliens. Tenaciously protective, she takes on the mother alien, whose sublime capacity for destruction is shown nonetheless to result from the same kind of maternal love that Ripley exhibits. Ripley is thus marked by a difference that is automatically taken to be a sign of femininity. *Aliens* reintroduces the issue of sexual difference, but not in order to offer a newer, more modern configuration of that difference. Rather, by focusing on Ripley alone, the question of the couple is supplanted by the problem of the woman as mother. What we get finally is a conservative moral lesson about maternity, futuristic or otherwise: mothers will be mothers, and they will always be women. We can conclude that even when there is not much sex in science fiction, there is nonetheless a great deal about sexuality, here reduced to phallic motherhood: Ripley in the robot-expediter is simply the Terminator turned inside out.

Just as it is ironic that science fiction film can give us the sharper notion of sexual difference lost from contemporary classical film, so too it is ironic that when this genre does depict sexual activity, it offers some of the most effective instances of eroticism in recent film. The dearth of eroticism in current film making is pointed up by Woody Allen's success in providing the paradigm of the only kind of sexual difference we have left: the incompatibility of the man's neuroses with the woman's neuroses. Understandably, this is not very erotic. But science fiction film, in giving us an extreme version of sexual difference, coincides with the requirements of the erotic formula, one which describes a fantasy of absolute difference and absolute complementarity (the quality of being complementary, of course, depending upon the establishment of difference). Unlike in classical cinema, the science fiction couple is often not the product of a long process of narrative differentiation; rather, the man and the woman are different from the very beginning. The narrative can then focus on them together and the exterior obstacles they must overcome to remain a couple. The erotic formula has, in fact, two parts: first, the two members of the couple must be marked as clearly different. (In non-science fiction film, for example, she is a nun, he is a priest; she is white, he is black; she is a middle-class widow, he is a young working-class man; she is French, he is German/Japanese, etc.) Second, one of the two must die or at least be threatened by death. If the man and the woman, in their absolute difference, are absolutely complementary, then there is nothing left to be desired. Something has to be taken away to regenerate desire and the narrative. Thus, although the lovemaking scene in *The Terminator* is not a very distinguished one in terms of the relatively perfunctory way that it was filmed, it nonetheless packs a strong erotic charge in its narrative context because it is a kiss across time, a kiss between a man from the future and a woman from the present, an act of love pervaded by death. For Kyle has to die in order to justify the coda, in which Sarah ensures the continuity of the story, now a legend, of their love for each other.

The Terminator harnesses the power of 'imaginary reminiscence' (the primal scene fantasy of time travel) in a way that allows it to present one of the most forceful of recent science fiction tales about the origins of techno-apocalypse. The film is able to do so, as I have argued, by generalizing its core of fantasy through the systematic use of the topical and everyday, reminding us that the future is now. As a critical dystopia, *The Terminator* thus goes beyond the flashy nihilism of apocalypse-for-the-sake-of-apocalypse to expose a more *mundane* logic of technological modernity, even if it is one that is, finally, no less catastrophic.

Notes

1. Fredric Jameson, 'Progress Versus Utopia; Or, Can We Imagine the Future?', *Science Fiction Studies*, vol. 9, no. 2, 1982.

2. Stanislaw Lem, 'Cosmology and Science Fiction', trans. Franz Rottenstein, *Science Fiction Studies*, vol. 4, no. 2, 1977.

3. See Jessie L. Weston, *From Ritual to Romance: An Account of the Holy Grail from Ancient Ritual to Christian Symbol*, Cambridge: Cambridge University Press 1920, pp. 42–8.

4. For a full and very interesting discussion of the political dimensions of the cyborg, see Donna Haraway, 'A Manifesto for Cyborgs: Science, Technology, and Socialist Feminism in the 1980s', *Socialist Review*, no. 80, 1985.

5. Useful essays on time travel and its paradoxes include Stanislaw Lem, 'The Time Travel Story and Related Matters of SF Structuring', *Science Fiction Studies*, vol. 1, no. 2, 1974; Monte Cook, 'Tips for Time Travel', in *Philosophers Look at Science Fiction*, Chicago: Nelson-Hall 1982; David Lewis, 'The Paradoxes of Time Travel' in Fred D. Miller, Jr and Nicholas D. Smith, eds, *Thought Probes*, Englewood Cliffs, NJ: Prentice-Hall 1981.

6. Sigmund Freud, 'The Paths to the Formation of Symptoms', *The Standard Edition of the Complete Psychological Works of Sigmund Freud*, London: Hogarth Press 1958, vol. 16, p. 370.

7. See, among others, Elisabeth Lyon, 'The Cinema of Lol V. Stein', *Camera Obscura*, no. 6, 1980; Elizabeth Cowie, 'Fantasia', *m/f*, no. 9, 1984; Stephen Neale, 'Sexual Difference in Cinema', *Oxford Literary Review*, vol. 8, nos. 1–2, 1986.

8. For the best formulation of this idea, see Joan Copjec, '*India Song/Son nom de Venise dans Calcutta désert*: The Compulsion to Repeat', *October*, no. 17, 1981.

9. Brian Henderson, '*The Searchers*: An American Dilemma', *Film Quarterly*, vol. 34, no. 2, 1980–81.

10. There are, of course, important exceptions to this standard narrative logic, as Jacqueline Rose has shown, for example, in her analysis of *The Birds*, in which Mitch's 'successful' attainment of a masculine and paternal identity comes at the price of regression and catatonia for Melanie: 'Paranoia and the Film System', *Screen*, vol. 17, no. 4, 1976–77.

11. Raymond Bellour, 'Un jour, la castration', *L'Arc*, no. 71, 1978.

12. This wholly unremarkable series seems surprisingly capable of taking on a great deal of cultural resonance in its radical presentation of 'difference'. Andrew Kopkind, in *The Nation*, 22 November 1986, reports that 'V' is one of the most popular shows in South Africa. He speculates that the show's success lies in the unconsciously ironic, allegorical reading that it allows. Robin Hairman, in *The Voice*, 13 January 1987, also reports on the cult that has grown up around 'V' in South Africa because of the allegorical readings that escaped the government censors. Before the series was over, anti-government forces were spraying slogans from the series on walls in Johannesburg and Soweto, and T-shirts with a large V painted on front and back became a feature on the streets: '"V" joined the mythology of the resistance'.

13. Danny Peary reports this in his interview with Sigourney Weaver, 'Playing Ripley in *Alien*' in Danny Peary, ed., *OMNI's Screen Flights/Screen Fantasies: The Future According to Science Fiction Cinema*, Garden City, NY: Doubleday 1984, p. 162.

11

Alien and the Monstrous-Feminine

Barbara Creed

The science fiction horror film *Alien* (1979) is a complex representation of the monstrous-feminine in terms of the maternal figure as perceived within a patriarchal ideology. She is there in the text's scenarios of the primal scene of birth and death; she is there in her many guises as the treacherous mother, the oral sadistic mother, the mother as the primordial abyss; and she is there in the film's images of blood, of the all-devouring vagina, the toothed vagina, the vagina as Pandora's box; and finally she is there in the chameleon figure of the alien, the monster as fetish-object of and for the mother. But it is the archaic mother, the reproductive/generative mother, who haunts the *mise-en-scène* of the film's first section, with its emphasis on different representations of the primal scene.

According to Freud, every child either watches its parents in the act of sexual intercourse or has fantasies about that act – fantasies which relate to the problem of origins. Freud left open the question of the cause of the fantasy but suggested that it may initially be aroused by 'an observation of the sexual intercourse of animals'.[1] In his study of the Wolf-Man, Freud argued that the child did not initially observe his parents in the act of sexual intercourse but that he witnessed the copulation of animals whose behaviour he then displaced onto his parents. In situations where the child actually witnesses sexual intercourse between its parents, Freud argued that all children arrive at the same conclusion: 'They adopt what may be called a *sadistic view of coition*'.[2] If the child perceives the primal scene as a monstrous act – whether in reality or fantasy – it may fantasize animals or mythical creatures as taking part in the scenario. Possibly the many mythological stories in which humans copulate with animals and other creatures

(Europa and Zeus, Leda and the Swan) are reworkings of the primal scene narrative. The Sphinx, with her lion's body and woman's face, is an interesting figure in this context. Freud suggested that the Riddle of the Sphinx was probably a distorted version of the great riddle that faces all children – Where do babies come from? An extreme form of the primal fantasy is that of 'observing parental intercourse while one is still an unborn baby in the womb'.[3]

One of the major concerns of the science fiction horror film (*Alien, The Thing, Invasion of the Body Snatchers, Altered States*) is the reworking of the primal scene in relation to the representation of other forms of copulation and procreation. *Alien* presents various represent-ations of the primal scene. Behind each of these lurks the figure of the archaic mother, that is, the image of the mother in her generative func-tion – the mother as the origin of all life. This archaic figure is somewhat different from the mother of the semiotic chora, as posed by Kristeva,[4] in that the latter is the pre-Oedipal mother who exists in relation to the family and the symbolic order. The concept of the parthenogenetic, archaic mother adds another dimension to the maternal figure and presents us with a new way of understanding how patriarchal ideology works to deny the 'difference' of woman in her cinematic representation.

The first birth scene occurs in *Alien* at the beginning, where the camera/spectator explores the inner space of the mother-ship whose life support system is a computer aptly named 'Mother'. This exploratory sequence of the inner body of the 'Mother' culminates with a long track-ing shot down one of the corridors which leads to a womb-like chamber where the crew of seven are woken up from their protracted sleep by Mother's voice monitoring a call for help from a nearby planet. The seven astronauts emerge slowly from their sleep pods in what amounts to a re-birthing scene which is marked by a fresh, antiseptic atmosphere. In outer space, birth is a well controlled, clean, painless affair. There is no blood, trauma or terror. This scene could be interpreted as a primal fantasy in which the human subject is born fully developed – even copulation is redundant.

The second representation of the primal scene takes place when three of the crew enter the body of the unknown space-ship through a 'vaginal' opening: the ship is shaped like a horseshoe, its curved sides like two long legs spread apart at the entrance. They travel along a corridor which seems to be made of a combination of inorganic and organic material – as if the inner space of this ship were alive. Compared to the atmosphere of the *Nostromo*, however, this ship is dark, dank and mysterious. A ghostly light glimmers and the sounds of their movements echo throughout the caverns. In the first chamber, the three explorers find a huge alien life form which appears to have been dead for a long time. Its bones are bent outward as if it exploded from the inside. One of the trio, Kane, is lowered down a shaft into the gigantic womb-like chamber in which rows of eggs are hatching. Kane approaches one of the eggs; as he touches it with his gloved hand it opens out, revealing a mass of pulsating flesh. Suddenly, the monstrous thing inside leaps up and attaches itself to Kane's helmet, its tail penetrating Kane's mouth in order to fertilize itself inside his stomach. Despite the warnings of Ripley, Kane is taken back on board the *Nostromo* where the alien rapidly completes its gestation process inside Kane.

This representation of the primal scene recalls Freud's reference to an extreme primal scene fantasy where the subject imagines travelling back inside the womb to watch her/his parents having sexual intercourse, perhaps to watch her/himself being conceived. Here, three astronauts explore the gigantic, cavernous, malevolent womb of the mother. Two members of the group watch the enactment of the primal scene in which Kane is violated in an act of phallic penetration – by the father or phallic mother? Kane himself is guilty of the strongest transgression; he actually peers into the egg/womb in order to investigate its mysteries. In so doing, he becomes a 'part' of the primal scene, taking up the place of the mother, the one who is penetrated, the one who bears the offspring of the union. The primal scene is represented as violent, monstrous (the union is between human and alien), and is mediated by the question of incestuous desire. All restagings of the primal scene raise the question of incest, as the beloved parent (usually the mother) is with a rival. The first birth scene, where the astronauts emerge from their sleep pods, could be viewed as a representation of incestuous desire *par excellence*: the father is completely absent; here, the mother is sole parent and sole life-support.

From this forbidden union, the monstrous creature is born. But man, not woman, is the 'mother' and Kane dies in agony as the alien gnaws its way through his stomach. The birth of the alien from Kane's stomach plays on what Freud described as a common misunderstanding that many children have about birth, that is, that the mother is somehow impregnated through the mouth – she may eat a special food – and the baby grows in her stomach from which it is also born. Here, we have a third version of the primal scene.

A further version of the primal scene – almost a convention[5] of the science fiction film – occurs when smaller craft or bodies are ejected from the mother-ship into outer space; although sometimes the ejected body remains attached to the mother-ship by a long lifeline or umbilical chord. This scene is presented in two separate ways: one when Kane's body, wrapped in a white shroud, is ejected from the mother-ship; and the second, when the small space capsule, in which Ripley is trying to escape from the alien, is expelled from the underbelly of the mother-ship. In the former, the 'mother's' body has become hostile; it contains the alien whose one purpose is to kill and devour all of Mother's children. In the latter birth scene the living infant is ejected from the malevolent body of the 'mother' to avoid destruction; in this scenario, the 'mother's' body explodes at the moment of giving birth.

Although the 'mother' as a figure does not appear in these sequences – nor indeed in the entire film – her presence forms a vast backdrop for the enactment of all the events. She is there in the images of birth, the representations of the primal scene, the womb-like imagery, the long winding tunnels leading to inner chambers, the rows of hatching eggs, the body of the mother-ship, the voice of the life-support system, and the birth of the alien. She is the generative mother, the pre-phallic mother, the being who exists prior to knowledge of the phallus.

In explaining the difficulty he had in uncovering the role of the mother in the early development of infants, Freud complained of the almost 'prehistoric' remoteness of this 'Minoan-Mycenaean' stage:

> Everything in the sphere of this first attachment to the mother seemed to me so difficult to grasp in analysis – so grey with age and shadowy and almost impossible to revivify – that it was as if it had succumbed to an especially inexorable repression.[6]

Just as the Oedipus complex tends to hide the pre-Oedipal phase in Freudian theory, the figure of the father, in the Lacanian rewriting of Freud, obscures the mother-child relationship of the imaginary. In contrast to the maternal figure of the Lacanian imaginary, Kristeva posits another dimension to the mother – she is associated with the pre-verbal or the semiotic and as such tends to disrupt the symbolic order.[7]

I think it is possible to open up the mother-question still further and posit an even more archaic maternal figure, to go back to mythological narratives of the generative, parthenogenetic mother – that ancient archaic figure who gives birth to all living things. She exists in the mythology of all human cultures as the mother-goddess who alone created the heavens and earth. In China she was known as Nu Kwa, in Mexico as Coatlicue, in Greece as Gaia (literally meaning 'earth') and in Sumer as Nammu. In 'Moses and Monotheism', Freud attempted to account for the historical existence of the great mother-goddesses.

> It is likely that the mother-goddesses originated at the time of the curtailment of the matriarchy, as a compensation for the slight upon the mothers. The male deities appear first as sons beside the great mothers and only later clearly

assume the features of father-figures. These male gods of polytheism reflect the conditions during the patriarchal age.[8]

Freud proposed that human society developed through stages from patriarchy to matriarchy and finally back to patriarchy. During the first, primitive people lived in small hordes, each one dominated by a jealous, powerful father who possessed all the females of the group. One day the sons, who had been banished to the outskirts of the group, overthrew the father – whose body they devoured – in order to secure his power and to take his women for themselves. Overcome by guilt, they later attempted to revoke the deed by setting up a totem as a substitute for the father and by renouncing the women whom they had liberated. The sons were forced to give up the women, whom they all wanted to possess, in order to preserve the group which otherwise would have been destroyed as the sons fought amongst themselves. In 'Totem and Taboo', Freud suggests that here 'the germ of the institution of matri-archy'[9] may have originated. Eventually, however, this new form of social organization, constructed upon the taboo against murder and incest, was replaced by the re-establishment of a patriarchal order. He pointed out that the sons had: 'thus created out of their filial sense of guilt the two fundamental taboos of totemism, which for that very reason inevitably corresponded to the two repressed wishes of the Oedi-pus complex'.[10]

Freud's account of the origins of patriarchal civilization is generally regarded as mythical. Lévi-Strauss points out that it is 'a fair account not of the beginnings of civilization, but of its present state' in that it expresses 'in symbolic form an inveterate fantasy' – the desire to murder the father and possess the mother.[11] In her discussion of 'Totem and Taboo', Kristeva argues that a 'strange slippage' has taken place, in that although Freud points out that morality is founded on the taboos of murder and incest his argument concentrates on the first to the virtual exclusion of the latter. Yet, Kristeva argues, the 'woman – or mother – image haunts a large part of that book and keeps shaping its back-ground'. She poses the question:

> Could the sacred be, whatever its variants, a two-sided formation? One aspect founded by murder and the social bond made up of a murderer's guilt-ridden atonement, with all the projective mechanisms and obsessive rituals that accompany it; and another aspect, like a lining, more secret and invisible, non-representable, oriented toward those uncertain spaces of unstable identity, toward the fragility – both threatening and fusional – of the archaic dyad, toward the non-separation of subject/object, on which language has no hold but one woven of fright and repulsion?[12]

From the above, it is clear that the figure of the mother in both the history of human sociality and in the history of the individual subject poses immense problems. Freud attempts to account for the existence of the mother-goddess figure by posing a matriarchal period in historical times while admitting that everything to do with the 'first attachment to the mother' is deeply repressed – 'grey with age and shadowy and almost impossible to revivify'. Nowhere does he attempt to specify the nature of this 'matriarchal period' and the implications of this for his own psychoanalytical theory, specifically his theory of the Oedipus complex which, as Lacan points out, 'can only appear in a patriarchal form in the institution of the family'.[13] Kristeva criticizes Freud for failing to deal adequately with incest and the mother-question while using the same mystifying language to refer to the mother; the other aspect of the sacred is 'like a lining', 'secret and invisible', 'non-representable'. In his re-reading of Freud, Lacan mystifies the figure of woman even further: '... the woman is not-all, there is always something with her which eludes discourse'.[14] Further, all three writers conflate the archaic mother with the mother of the dyadic and triadic relationship. They refer to her as a 'shadowy' figure (Freud); as 'non-representable' (Kristeva); as the 'abyss of the female organ from which all life comes forth' (Lacan[15]), then make no clear attempt to distinguish this aspect of the maternal imago from the protective/suffocating mother of the pre-Oedipal or the mother as object of sexual jealousy and desire as she is represented in the Oedipal configuration.

The maternal figure constructed within/by the writings of Freud, Lacan and Kristeva is inevitably the mother of the dyadic or triadic relationship – although the latter figure is more prominent. Even when she is represented as the mother of the imaginary, of the dyadic relationship, she is still constructed as the *pre-Oedipal* mother, that is, as a figure about to 'take up a place' in the symbolic – as a figure always in relation to the father, the representative of the phallus. Without her 'lack', he cannot signify its opposite – lack of a lack or presence. But if we posit a more archaic dimension to the mother – the mother as originating womb – we can at least begin to talk about the maternal figure as *outside* the patriarchal family constellation. In this context, the mother-goddess narratives can be read as primal-scene narratives in which the mother is the sole parent. She is also the subject, not the object, of narrativity.

For instance in the 'Spider Woman' myth of the North American Indians, there was only the Spider Woman, who spun the universe into existence and then created two daughters from whom all life flowed. She is also the Thought Woman or Wise Woman who knows the secrets of the universe. Within the Oedipus narrative, however, she becomes the

Sphinx, who also knows the answers to the secret of life; but here her situation has been changed. She is no longer the subject of the narrative; she has become the object of the narrative of the male hero. After he has solved her riddle, she will destroy herself. The Sphinx is an ambiguous figure; she knows the secret of life and is thereby linked to the mother-goddess but her name, which is derived from 'sphincter', suggests she is the mother of toilet training, the pre-Oedipal mother who must be repudiated by the son so that he can take up his proper place in the symbolic. It is interesting that Oedipus has always been seen to have committed two horrific crimes: patricide and incest. But his encounter with the Sphinx, which leads to her death, suggests he is also responsible for another horrific crime – that of matricide. For the Sphinx, like the Medusa, is a mother-goddess figure; they are both variants of the same mythological mother who gave birth to all life. Lévi-Strauss has argued that a major issue in the Oedipus myth is the problem of whether or not man is born from woman. This myth is also central to *Alien*:

> Although the problem obviously cannot be solved, the Oedipus myth provides a kind of logical tool which relates the original problem – born from one or born from two? – to the derivative problem: born from different or born from same?[16]

The Medusa, whose head, according to Freud, signifies the female genitals in their terrifying aspect, also represents the procreative function of woman. The blood which flows from her severed head gives birth to Pegasus and Chrysaor. Although Neptune is supposed to be the father, the nature of the birth once again suggests the parthenogenetic mother. In *Alice Doesn't*, Teresa de Lauretis argues that:

> to say that narrative is the production of Oedipus is to say that each reader – male or female – is constrained and defined within the two positions of a sexual difference thus conceived: male-hero-human, on the side of the subject; and female-obstacle-boundary-space, on the other.[17]

If we apply her definition to narratives which deal specifically with the archaic mother – such as the Oedipus and Perseus myths – we can see that the 'obstacle' relates specifically to the question of origins and is an attempt to repudiate the idea of woman as the source of life, woman as sole parent, woman as archaic mother.

In his article, 'Fetishism in the Horror Film', Roger Dadoun also refers to this archaic maternal figure. He describes her as:

> a maternal thing situated on this side of good and evil, on this side of all organized form, on this side of all events – a totalizing, oceanic mother, a

'mysterious and profound unity', arousing in the subject the anguish of fusion and of dissolution; the mother prior to the uncovering of the essential *béance* [gap], of the *pas-de-phallus*, the mother who is pure fantasm, in the sense that she is posed as an omnipresent and all-powerful totality, an absolute being, only in the intuition – she does not have a phallus – which deposes her ...[18]

If Dadoun places emphasis on her 'totalizing, oceanic' presence, I would stress her archaism in relation to her generative powers – the mother who gives birth all by herself, the original parent, the godhead of all fertility and the origin of procreation. What is most interesting about the mythological figure of woman as the source of all life (a role taken over by the male god of monotheistic religions) is that, within patriarchal signifying practices, particularly the horror film, she is reconstructed and represented as a *negative* figure, one associated with the dread of the generative mother seen only in the abyss, the monstrous vagina, the origin of all life threatening to reabsorb what it once birthed. Kristeva also represents her in this negative light, and in this context it is interesting to note that Freud linked the womb to the *unheimlich*, the uncanny. Freud also supported, and elaborated upon, Schelling's definition of the uncanny as 'something which ought to have remained hidden but has come to light'.[19] In horror films such as *Alien*, we are given a representation of the female genitals and the womb as uncanny – horrific objects of dread and fascination. Unlike the mythological mother-narratives, here the archaic mother, like the Sphinx and the Medusa, is seen only in a negative light. But the central characteristic of the archaic mother is her total dedication to the generative, procreative principle. She is outside morality and the law. Ash's eulogy to the alien is a description of this mother: 'I admire its purity; a survivor unclouded by conscience, remorse or delusions of morality.'

Clearly, it is difficult to separate out completely the figure of the archaic mother, as defined above, from other aspects of the maternal figure – the maternal authority of Kristeva's semiotic, the mother of Lacan's imaginary, the phallic woman, the castrated woman. While the different figures signify quite separate things about the monstrous-feminine, each one is also only part of the whole – a different aspect of the maternal figure. At times the horrific nature of the monstrous-feminine is totally dependent on the merging together of all aspects of the maternal figure into one – the horrifying image of woman as archaic mother, phallic woman and castrated body represented as a single figure.

The archaic mother – constructed as a negative force – is represented in her phantasmagoric aspects in many horror texts, particularly the science fiction horror film. We see her as the gaping, cannibalistic bird's mouth in *The Giant Claw*; the terrifying spider of *The Incredible Shrinking Man*; the toothed vagina/womb of *Jaws*; and the fleshy, pulsating, womb of *The Thing* and the *Poltergeist.* What is common to all of these images of horror is the voracious maw, the mysterious black hole which signifies female genitalia as a monstrous sign which threatens to give birth to equally horrific offspring, as well as threatening to incorporate everything in its path. This is the generative archaic mother, constructed within patriarchal ideology as the primeval 'black hole'. This, of course, is also the hole which is opened up by the absence of the penis; the horrifying sight of the mother's genitals – proof that castration can occur.

However, in the texts cited above, the emphasis is not on castration; rather it is the gestating, all-devouring womb of the archaic mother which generates the horror. Nor are these images of the womb constructed in relation to the penis of the father. Unlike the female genitalia, the womb cannot be constructed as a 'lack' in relation to the penis. The womb is not the site of castration anxiety. Rather, the womb signifies 'fullness' or 'emptiness' but always it is its own point of reference. This is why we need to posit a more archaic dimension to the mother. For the concept of the archaic mother allows for a notion of the feminine which does not depend for its definition on a concept of the masculine. The term 'archaic mother' signifies woman as sexual difference. In contrast the maternal figure of the pre-Oedipal is always represented in relation to the penis – the phallic mother who later becomes the castrated mother. Significantly, there is an attempt in *Alien* to appropriate the procreative function of the mother, to represent a man giving birth, to deny the mother as signifier of sexual difference – but here birth can exist only as the other face of death.

The archaic mother is present in all horror films as the blackness of extinction – death. The desires and fears invoked by the image of the archaic mother, as a force that threatens to reincorporate what it once gave birth to, are always there in the horror text – all pervasive, all encompassing – because of the constant presence of death. The desire to return to the original oneness of things, to return to the mother/womb, is primarily a desire for non-differentiation. If, as Georges Bataille[20] argues, life signifies discontinuity and separateness, and death signifies continuity and non-differentiation, then the desire for and attraction of death suggests also a desire to return to the state of original oneness with the mother. As this desire to merge occurs after differentiation, that is after the subject has developed as a separate, autonomous self, then it is experienced as a form of psychic death. In this sense, the confrontation with death as represented in the horror film, gives rise to a terror of self-disintegration, of losing one's self or ego – often represented cinematically by a screen which becomes black, signifying the obliteration of self, the self of the protagonist in the film and the spectator in the cinema. This has important consequences for the positioning of the spectator in the cinema.

One of the most interesting structures operating in the screen-spectator relationship relates to the sight/site of the monstrous within the horror text. In contrast to the conventional viewing structures working within other variants of the classic text, the horror film does not constantly work to suture the spectator into the viewing processes. Instead, an unusual phenomenon arises whereby the suturing processes are momentarily undone while the horrific image on the screen challenges the viewer to run the risk of continuing to look. Here, I refer to those moments in the horror film when the spectator, unable to stand the images of horror unfolding before his/her eyes, is forced to look away, to not-look, to look anywhere but at the screen. Strategies of identification are temporarily broken, as the spectator is constructed in the place of horror, the place where the sight/site can no longer be endured, the place where pleasure in looking is transformed into pain and the spectator is punished for his/her voyeuristic desires.

Confronted by the sight of the monstrous, the viewing subject is put into crisis – boundaries, designed to keep the abject at bay, threaten to disintegrate, collapse. The horror film puts the viewing subject's sense of unified self into crisis in those moments when the image on the screen becomes too threatening or horrific to watch, with the threat that the viewing subject will be drawn to the place 'where meaning collapses', the place of death. By not-looking, the spectator is able momentarily to withdraw identification from the image on the screen in order to reconstruct the boundary between self and screen and reconstitute the 'self' which is threatened with disintegration. This process of reconstitution of the self is reaffirmed by the conventional ending of the horror narrative in which the monster is usually 'named' and destroyed.[21]

Alien collapses the image of the threatening archaic mother, signifying woman as 'difference', into the more recognized figure of the pre-Oedipal mother; this occurs in relation to two images of the monstrous-feminine: the oral-sadistic mother and the phallic mother. Kane's transgressive disturbance of the egg/womb initiates a transformation of its latent aggressivity into an active, phallic enemy. The horror then played out can be read in relation to Kristeva's concept of the semiotic chora. Kristeva argues that the maternal body becomes the site of conflicting desires (the semiotic chora). These desires are constantly staged and restaged in the workings of the horror narrative where the subject is left alone, usually in a strange hostile place, and forced to confront an unnameable terror, the monster. The monster represents both the subject's fears of being alone, of being separate from the mother, and the threat of annihilation – often through reincorporation. As oral-sadistic mother, the monster threatens to reabsorb the child she once nurtured. Thus, the monster is ambiguous; it both repels and attracts.

In *Alien*, each of the crew members comes face to face with the alien in a scene whose *mise-en-scène* is coded to suggest a monstrous, mal-evolent maternal figure. They watch with fascinated horror as the baby alien gnaws its way through Kane's stomach; Dallas, the captain, encounters the alien after he has crawled along the ship's enclosed, womb-like air ducts; and the other three members are cannibalized in a frenzy of blood in scenes which emphasize the alien's huge razor-sharp teeth, signifying the monstrous oral-sadistic mother. Apart from the scene of Kane's death, all the death sequences occur in dimly lit, enclosed, threatening spaces reminiscent of the giant hatchery where Kane first encounters the pulsating egg. In these death sequences the terror of being abandoned is matched only by the fear of reincorporation. This scenario, which enacts the conflicting desires at play in the semiotic chora, is staged within the body of the mother-ship, the vessel which the space-travellers initially trust, until 'Mother' herself is revealed as a treacherous figure programmed to sacrifice the lives of the crew in the interests of the Company.

The other face of the monstrous-feminine in *Alien* is the phallic mother. Freud argued that the male child could either accept the threat of castration, thus ending the Oedipus complex, or disavow it. The latter response requires the (male) child to mitigate his horror at the sight of the mother's genitals – proof that castration can occur – with a fetish object which substitutes for her missing penis. For him, she is still the phallic mother, the penis-woman. In 'Medusa's Head' Freud argued that the head with its hair of writhing snakes represented the terrifying genitals of the mother, but that this head also functioned as a fetish object. He also noted that a display of the female genitals makes a woman 'unapproachable and repels all sexual desires', referring to the section in Rabelais which relates 'how the Devil took flight when the woman showed him her vulva'.[22] Perseus's solution is to look only at a reflection, a mirror-image of her genitals. As with patriarchal ideology, his shield reflects an 'altered' representation, a vision robbed of its threatening aspects. The full difference of the mother is denied; she is constructed as other, displayed before the gaze of the conquering male hero, then destroyed. The price paid is the destruction of sexual hetero-geneity and repression of the maternal signifier. The fetishization of the mother's genitals could occur in those texts where the maternal figure is represented in her phantasmagoric aspects as the gaping, voracious vagina/womb. Do aspects of these images work to mitigate the horror by offering a substitute for the penis? However, it is possible that we could theorize fetishism differently by asking: Who is the fetish-object a fetish for? The male or female subject? In general, the fetishist is usually assumed to be male, although Freud did allow that female fetishism was a possibility.[23] The notion of female fetishism is much neglected although it is present in various patriarchal discourses.[24]

In *The Interpretation of Dreams*,[25] Freud discusses the way in which the doubling of a penis-symbol indicates an attempt to stave off castration anxieties. Juliet Mitchell refers to doubling as a sign of a female castration complex: 'We can see the significance of this for women, as dreams of repeated number of children – "little ones" – are given the same import.'[26] In this context, female fetishism represents an attempt by the female subject to continue to 'have' the phallus, to take up a 'positive' place in relation to the symbolic.

Female fetishism is clearly represented within many horror texts – as instances of patriarchal signifying practices – but only in relation to male fears and anxieties about women and the question: What do women want? (*The Birds, Cat People, Alien, The Thing.*) Women as yet do not speak their own 'fetishistic' desires within the popular cinema – if, indeed, women have such desires. The notion of female fetishism is represented in *Alien* in the figure of the monster. The creature is the mother's phallus, attributed to the maternal figure by a phallocentric ideology terrified at the thought that women might desire to have the phallus. The monster as fetish object is not there to meet the desires of the male fetishist, but rather to signify the monstrousness of woman's desire to have the phallus.

In *Alien*, the monstrous creature is constructed as the phallus of the negative mother. The image of the archaic mother – threatening because it signifies woman as difference rather than constructed as opposition – is, once again, collapsed into the figure of the pre-Oedipal mother. By relocating the figure of woman within an Oedipal scenario, her image can be recuperated and controlled. The womb, even if represented negatively, is a greater threat than the mother's phallus. As phallic mother, woman is again represented as monstrous. What is horrific is her desire to cling to her offspring in order to continue to 'have the phallus'. Her monstrous desire is concretized in the figure of the alien; the creature whose deadly mission is represented as the same as that of the archaic mother – to reincorporate and destroy all life.

If we consider *Alien* in the light of a theory of female fetishism, then the chameleon nature of the alien begins to make sense. Its changing appearance represents a form of doubling or multiplication of the phallus, pointing to the mother's desire to stave off her castration. The alien is the mother's phallus, a fact which is made perfectly clear in the birth scene where the infant alien rises from Kane's stomach and holds itself erect, glaring angrily around the room, before screeching off into the depths of the ship. But the alien is more than a phallus; it is also coded as a toothed vagina, the monstrous-feminine as the cannibalistic mother. A large part of the ideological project of *Alien* is the represent-ation of the maternal fetish object as an 'alien' or foreign shape. This is why the body of the heroine becomes so important at the end of the film.

Much has been written about the final scene, in which Ripley/Sigourney Weaver undresses before the camera, on the grounds that its voyeurism undermines her role as successful heroine. A great deal has also been written about the cat. Why does she rescue the cat and thereby risk her life, and the lives of Parker and Lambert, when she has previously been so careful about quarantine regulations? Again, satisfac-tory answers to these questions are provided by a phallocentric concept of female fetishism. Compared to the horrific sight of the alien as fetish object of the monstrous-feminine, Ripley's body is pleasurable and reassuring to look at. She signifies the 'acceptable' form and shape of woman. In a sense the monstrousness of woman, represented by Mother as betrayer (the computer/life-support system) and Mother as the uncontrollable, generative, cannibalistic mother (the alien), is controlled through the display of woman as reassuring and pleasurable sign. The image of the cat functions in the same way; it signifies an acceptable, and in this context a reassuring, fetish object for the 'normal' woman. Thus, Ripley holds the cat to her, stroking it as if it were her 'baby', her 'little one'. Finally, Ripley enters her sleep pod, assuming a virginal repose. The nightmare is over and we are returned to the opening sequence of the film where birth was a pristine affair. The final sequence works, not only to dispose of the alien, but also to repress the nightmare image of the monstrous-feminine within the text's patriarchal discourses.

Kristeva's theory of abjection, if viewed as description rather than prescription, provides a productive hypothesis for an analysis of the monstrous-feminine in the horror and the SF horror film.[27] If we posit a more archaic dimension to the mother, we can see how this figure, as well as Kristeva's maternal authority of the semiotic, are both constructed as figures of abjection within the signifying practices of the horror film. We can see its ideological project as an attempt to shore up the symbolic order by constructing the feminine as an imaginary 'other' which must be repressed and controlled in order to secure and protect the social order. Thus, the horror film stages and re-stages a constant repudiation of the maternal figure.

Notes

1. Sigmund Freud, 'From the History of an Infantile Neurosis' in *Case Histories II*, Pelican Freud Library, vol. 9, Harmondsworth: Penguin 1981.

2. Sigmund Freud, 'On the Sexual Theories of Children' in *On Sexuality*, Pelican Freud Library, vol. 7, Harmondsworth: Penguin 1981, p. 198.

3. Sigmund Freud, 'The Paths to the Formation of Symptoms' in *Introductory Lectures on Psychoanalysis*, Pelican Freud Library, vol. 1, Harmondsworth: Penguin 1981, p. 417.

4. Julia Kristeva, *Powers of Horror: An Essay on Abjection*, New York: Columbia University Press 1982, p. 14.

5. Daniel Dervin argues that this structure does deserve the status of a convention. For a discussion of the primal scene fantasy in science fiction cinema, see 'Primal Conditions and Conventions: the Genre of Science Fiction' in this volume.

6. Sigmund Freud, 'Female Sexuality' in *On Sexuality*, Pelican Freud Library, vol. 7, p. 373.

7. For a discussion of the relation between 'the semiotic' and the Lacanian 'Imaginary', see Jane Gallop, *Feminism and Psychoanalysis: the Daughter's Seduction*, London: MacMillan 1983, pp. 124–5.

8. Sigmund Freud, 'Moses and Monotheism', *The Standard Edition of the Complete Psychological Works of Sigmund Freud*, London: Hogarth Press 1958, vol. 23, p. 83.

9. Sigmund Freud, 'Totem and Taboo' in *The Origins of Religion*, Pelican Freud Library, vol. 13, Harmondsworth: Penguin 1985, p. 206.

10. Ibid., p. 205.

11. Lévi-Strauss, quoted in Georges Bataille, *Death and Sensuality: A Study of Eroticism and the Taboo*, New York: Walker & Company 1962, p. 200.

12. Kristeva, pp. 57–8.

13. Jacques Lacan, in Anthony Wilden, ed., *The Language of the Self*, Baltimore: Johns Hopkins University Press 1970, p. 126.

14. Jacques Lacan, *Le Seminaire XX*, p. 34, translated by Stephen Heath, 'Difference', *Screen*, vol. 19, no. 3, 1978, p. 59.

15. Jacques Lacan, *Le Seminaire II*, translated in Heath, p. 54.

16. Claude Lévi-Strauss, *Structural Anthropology*, trans. C. Jacobson and B.G. Schoepf, New York: Doubleday 1976, p. 212.

17. Teresa de Lauretis, *Alice Doesn't: Feminism, Semiotics, Cinema*, Bloomington: Indiana University Press 1984, p. 121.

18. Roger Dadoun, 'Fetishism in the Horror Film', *Enclitic*, vol. 1, no. 2, 1977, pp. 55–6.

19. Sigmund Freud, 'The "Uncanny"', *The Standard Edition*, vol. 17, p. 245.

20. Bataille, *Death and Sensuality*.

21. For a discussion of the relationship between the female spectator, structures of looking and the horror film, see Linda Williams, 'When the Woman Looks' in Mary Anne Doane, Patricia Mellencamp and Linda Williams, eds, *Re-Vision: Essays in Feminist Film Criticism*, Los Angeles, CA: American Film Institute 1984.

22. Sigmund Freud, 'Medusa's Head', *The Standard Edition*, vol. 18, p. 105.

23. Sigmund Freud, 'An Outline of Psychoanalysis', *The Standard Edition*, vol. 23, p. 202.

24. Mary Kelly, 'Woman–Desire–Image', *Desire*, London: ICA 1984.

25. Sigmund Freud, *Interpretation of Dreams*, Pelican Freud Library, vol. 4, Harmondsworth: Penguin 1982.

26. Juliet Mitchell, *Psychoanalysis and Feminism*, Harmondsworth: Penguin 1974, p. 84.

27. For an analysis of the horror film as a 'return of the repressed', see Robin Wood's articles, 'Return of the Repressed', *Film Comment*, July–August 1978; and 'Neglected Nightmares', *Film Comment*, March–April 1980.

PART IV

Spectators

One of the cultural instrumentalities attributed to science fiction cinema is its capacity to do things for its consumers – form them in certain ways, perhaps, or evoke particular responses: fascination, curiosity, awe, suspense, fear. Two premises underlie this view. The first is that meanings in film texts are not already there, but are produced in a relationship between text and spectator. The second is that films speak to, or address, spectators in particular ways; and therefore that a text is not open to all possible readings, but may privilege some meanings over others: though this, as has been noted, does not preclude the readings 'against the grain' of 'preferred' meanings produced by ideological and psychoanalytic criticism. Attention to questions of address, negotiation, and the relationship between film texts and spectators signals a move away from a criticism centred on film texts – however conceptualized – towards a more interactive model of the reception, the uses, of films. How might this model work? Cultural theory has looked at this question in a number of ways, and in film theory two approaches have been predominant: an attention on the one hand to cinematic enunciation, and on the other to the cinematic apparatus.

Cinematic enunciation refers to mechanisms of address to spectators. Narrative viewpoint, which is a key element of enunciation, governs the extent to which, and the ways in which, enunciation provides spectators with knowledge about what is going on in the story. We may, for instance, be 'told' more than some or all of the story's characters about what is 'really' happening (a 'view behind'); we may know only as much as the hero (a 'view with'); or – rarely in classical cinema – we may know less than any of the characters.[1] Narrative viewpoint is a key condition of spectator response. For example, Tzvetan Todorov, writing about the literary genre of the Fantastic, argued that in this genre narrative knowledge is characteristically withheld from the reader, who is thereby put in a position of uncertainty as to what is 'really' going on in the story,[2] a state which may be associated with responses of disquiet and anxiety. Enunciation works rather differently in films, however, because of cinema's specific signifying qualities, notably its 'codes of visibility': stories are told by showing events, by making them visible. This, as will be demonstrated, inflects spectator response in a variety of ways.

Meanwhile, we might inquire whether any consistent modes of enunciation are associated with science fiction as against other film genres. This question, unfortunately, appears to have received little or no attention – another gap in critical work on science fiction. Looking at narrative viewpoint in individual science fiction films, however, reveals quite a wide range of enunciative modes; from the suspense-generating 'view behind' of *Alien* (1979), to the narrative 'view with' the hero in parts of *Blade Runner* (1982), and the unstable narrative viewpoint of *Videodrome* (1982). This might suggest that as a genre, science fiction cinema is not associated with any particular enunciative processes, but perhaps takes its cue in this respect from other film genres. It is often noted that science fiction overlaps with other genres: *Alien* is a horror film as well as a science fiction film; *Blade Runner* incorporates elements of film noir. This points to what has been regarded as a key characteristic of science fiction cinema, particularly in recent years: its intertextuality. *Alien* and *Blade Runner* are both cases in point; and *Blade Runner* in particular operates on at least two enunciative levels, one of them a kind of 'meta-enunciation' in which the spectator is addressed as knowing – not just about events in the narrative, but also about the history of cinema and the conventions of certain film genres.

Cinematic enunciation and the various spectator-text relationships it proposes form part of the cinematic apparatus. The notion of the apparatus is associated with a totalizing model of cinema as a system, a machine with many working parts: the economics of the film industry, its structures of production, distribution and exhibition, its technologies and signifying practices, its modes of reception, and the interconnections between all of these. The spectator occupies a pivotal place in this system, because its mode of consumption is what makes cinema a special kind of commodity. Consumers pay to enter a space – a cinema auditorium – and look at images projected onto a screen. As a commodity, cinema is intangible: it is sold on the spectator's expectation of pleasure or diversion. In this sense, with cinema the exchange object is really pleasure.

If meanings – and pleasures – are produced in the interaction of film and spectator, spectatorship must be the central activity of the cinematic apparatus. How, then, does spectatorship work? Film theorists inquiring into the ways the apparatus produces pleasures for the spectator have looked to psychoanalytic theory for answers, drawing on such concepts as narcissism, voyeurism, fetishism and scopophilia. For example, the analogical quality of the film image, its capacity to reproduce the appearance of the 'real world', is seen as evoking narcissistic fantasies, the pleasure of looking at oneself or one's likeness. But spectators see only shadows: what appears on the screen is 'primordially elsewhere'. This combination of visibility and absence evokes voyeuristic fantasies, the pleasure of looking at something that cannot return the look.

All these pleasures depend not only on visibility, but also on another key component of the cinematic apparatus: the context in which films are consumed, the darkened auditorium. These are the very qualities that make cinema different from other forms of representation: the pleasures evoked by cinema are precisely the pleasures of looking, under cover of darkness – 'lawless seeing'. In psychoanalytic theory, the desire for pleasurable looking – scopophilia – is classified as a sexual drive, whose impulse derives from repressions associated with the Oedipal moment and the castration complex. Looking in cinema is therefore associated with repression, sexual pleasure, and sexual difference.[3] This highly superficial sketch of a complex body of theory should at least highlight the extent to which spectatorship in cinema is both dependent upon, and productive of, certain pleasures. Theories of spectatorship, however, relating as they do to the totality of the cinematic apparatus, have a very broad sweep. Is it feasible, using their terms, to inquire into modes of spectatorship proposed by a single film genre?

In 'The Doubles of Fantasy and the Space of Desire', J.P. Telotte attempts to do exactly this by taking up the question of narcissism as a mode of spectatorship, as it informs the peculiar pleasures of science fiction cinema. Telotte's contention is that the thematic motif of doubling, characteristic of many science fiction films, speaks in certain ways to the pleasure of looking at one's own likeness proposed by the mimetic qualities of the cinematic image. Science fiction as a genre speaks to a spectatorial desire for likeness which is worked through in stories about human substitutes – androids, cyborgs, replicants – that are outwardly indistinguishable from real human beings. In the doubling theme, argues Telotte, is found the image of cinema's 'mimetic problem and of the visual desire which powers its narratives'. Cinema's articulation of this theme involves both visibility and a particular narrative viewpoint: the spectator is unable to tell by looking who is human and who is not, unless additional information is provided through the enunciation. A genre-specific narrative theme, in this argument, speaks to a

fantasy – the desire for self as other – which informs spectator-text
relations across the entire apparatus of cinema. But, if, as Telotte himself
concedes, all films appeal to such desires, does the specificity of science
fiction cinema lie only in a combination of desire in the cinematic
apparatus with thematics in the genre? Does this particular intertwining
of desire and narrative set science fiction apart from other film genres?
In science fiction, does the relationship between spectatorial pleasure
and genre come into play outside the sphere of narrativity?

Science fiction cinema distinguishes itself from other film genres –
and indeed from science fiction writing – by its appeal to special effects
technology in creating the appearance of worlds which either do not
exist, or cannot for one reason or another be recorded, as it were, live:
vessels travelling through deep space, otherworldly landscapes, beings of
alien appearance. Not all science fiction films use special effects, though
recently they seem increasingly to do so, and the technology of special
effects in films is the object of obsessive attention of the 'golly-gosh'
variety in science fiction fan literature. For the fans, special effects are
the *raison d'être* of the genre. Not so, however, for the critics, who have
devoted a great deal more attention to the narratives of science fiction
films than to their qualities as spectacle.

Among the numerous readings of *Alien*, for example, it is rare to
encounter discussion of the film's special effects sequences. And yet the
narrative of this film is periodically, and significantly, halted by episodes
whose only function must be to invite the spectator's awed gaze: these
include lengthy special effects sequences early in the film devoted to the
business of getting characters out of the mother space ship and onto the
alien planet, sequences which in narrative terms are quite clearly exces-
sive. What sort of appeal to scopophilia is being made in such displays of
cinema's codes of visibility?

Special effects sequences like these, while appealing to notions of
cinema as a kind of magic, are commonly quite 'readerly' in the literal-
ness of their descriptions of settings and spatial and temporal transitions.
To this extent, they belong to classical cinema's project of setting up
coherent fictional worlds, comprehensible through their visibility, in
which stories are enacted. Hollywood science fiction tends to anchor the
'magic' of cinema in the classical narrative rather than freeing it into the
poetic possibilities of film language. Nevertheless, special effects in
science fiction cinema always draw attention to themselves, inviting
admiration for the wizardry of the boffins and the marvels of a technology that translates their efforts onto the screen. They call forth
wonder at the fictional machines of space travel, and also at the
'machine' of the cinematic apparatus itself. In fact, there is never any
pretence that special effects spectacles are anything other than artefacts;

and yet at the same time (as Michael Stern points out in his essay on the ideological work of special effects in Part II), the illusionism of classical cinema works to persuade us otherwise. In this sense, the visual pleasures proposed by special effects are twofold, and incorporate contradictory beliefs held simultaneously: 'I know, but ... '

In *Genre*, Steve Neale argued that cinema can be exhibitionistic, putting its codes of visibility on display, inviting the spectator's gaze, engaging particular pleasures and fantasies. Special effects do this in a peculiarly pristine manner, and in deploying them science fiction cinema as a genre occupies a key role in the cinematic apparatus's 'mechanisms of institutionalised exhibitionism'.[4] Neale takes up this argument here in his essay on knowledge, belief and judgement in science fiction. He suggests that special effects in science fiction films, whilst incorporating an element of self-reflexivity in their display of cinema's powers, also counter the spectator's awareness of their artifice. These divisions of knowledge and belief are structured like the disavowal characteristic of fetishism: 'Just as the fetish both avows and disavows an absence, a lack (the lack, for the fetishist proper, of the phallus wished for in the object of sexual desire), so the fictional representation, the cinematic image, and the special effect both avow and disavow something that does not exist'.

In an era of television and home video, spectacular special effects – combined as they usually are with sophisticated sound systems and state-of-the-art technologies of film stocks, cameras, and so on – are an important selling point for science fiction films as *cinema*. Special effects propose that for maximum pleasure films should be viewed in cinema auditoria, not at home on a television set. Films' status as commodities hinges not only on their technologies of production, then, but also on their technologies of consumption. The question of where and how science fiction films are consumed becomes as important as the fact of their production. First-run movie houses are equipped with large screens and sophisticated sound and projection systems. The films not only depend on, but are instrumental in the production of, the hardware that makes their consumption possible. But developments in the technologies of film production and consumption do not take place in isolation from other developments.

Nowhere is this clearer than in the case of the film projection systems Imax and Omnimax. Both are large-screen formats using 70mm film stock: Imax is projected onto a flat screen; Omnimax onto the inside of a dome, which allows spectators to 'experience an undistorted, natural perspective, as if the subjects on the screen were actually there'.[5] 'Soon it may be difficult to tell the technology of the future from the technology of film; illusion may replace reality', says Albert J. LaValley, heralding the entry of a postmodern sensibility into film spectatorship.[6] In enhancing cinema's illusionistic qualities, whilst simultaneously drawing attention to the very technologies through which the illusions are produced, Imax and Omnimax express at its utmost the double and contradictory quality of the visual pleasures proposed by special effects.

In the instance of special effects, the cinematic apparatus and the technological future represented in the fictional worlds of science fiction films begin to coincide. The Imax/Omnimax film *The Dream Is Alive* (1984) is about space travel; though it is not a science fiction film, but a documentary which charts three voyages of the US space shuttle *Challenger*. Many of the film's images, however, look exactly like science fiction film images. Which is real, and which is the copy? What is the relationship here between 'real' space travel, its representation in a context of spectatorship that proposes enhanced realism, and fictionalized space travel?

In his essay here on the Géode, Paul Virilio discusses *The Dream Is Alive*, which was commissioned by the Smithsonian Institution's National Air and Space Museum and funded by the Lockheed Corporation. The Géode is an Omnimax auditorium which forms part of the Cité des Sciences, a science and technology museum complex at La Villette on the outskirts of Paris. Virilio explores the chain of connections which links a film about the US space programme, the Géode, and the Omnimax system's state-of-the-art technologies of film production and consumption, with other technologies, notably those of military training programmes.[7] These connections between the cinematic apparatus and the military machine highlight some of the ways in which the cinematic apparatus participates in an entire network – an intertext – of discourses and practices. In Part V, science fiction cinema is considered in its intertextuality.

Notes

1. Annette Kuhn, *Women's Pictures: Feminism and Cinema*, London: Routledge & Kegan Paul 1982, pp. 50–53.

2. Tzvetan Todorov, *The Fantastic: A Structural Approach to a Literary Genre*, Ithaca, NY: Cornell University Press 1975.

3. Christian Metz, 'The Imaginary Signifier', trans. Ben Brewster, in *Psychoanalysis and Cinema*, London: MacMillan 1982; Laura Mulvey, 'Visual Pleasure and Narrative Cinema', *Screen*, vol. 16, no. 3, 1975; Judith Mayne, 'Feminist Film Theory and Criticism', *Signs*, vol. 11, no. 1, 1985.

4. Stephen Neale, *Genre*, London: British Film Institute 1980, p. 34. See also Christian Metz, '*Trucage* and the Film', trans. Françoise Meltzer, *Critical Inquiry*, vol. 2, no. 4, 1977.

5. Alan Stegeman, 'The Large-screen Film: A Viable Entertainment Alternative to High Definition Television', *Journal of Film and Video*, vol. 36, no. 2, 1984.

6. Albert J. La Valley, 'Traditions of Trickery: The Role of Special Effects in the Science Fiction Film' in George E. Slusser and Eric S. Rabkin, eds, *Shadows of the Magic Lamp: Fantasy and Science Fiction Film*, Carbondale, IL: Illinois University Press 1985.

7. See also Paul Virilio, *War and Cinema: The Logistics of Perception*, trans. Patrick Camiller, London: Verso 1989.

12

The Doubles of Fantasy and the Space of Desire

J.P. Telotte

> Filmic space is divided between two fields ... specular space and blind
> space. Specular space ... is everything we see on the screen ... blind space
> is everything that moves (or wriggles) outside or under the surface of
> things, like the shark in *Jaws*. If such films 'work', it is because we are more
> or less held in the sway of these two spaces.[1]

The fundamental principle of film, according to André Bazin, is a kind
of visual desire, what he terms our 'obsession' or 'appetite for illusion'.[2]
This perspective sees film as catering to man's persistent desire to
double the self and his world, and thus as representing a development of
the age-old dream for a perfect mimesis or 'total cinema'. Read in
another fashion, however, Bazin's theory offers more than simply an
aesthetic of reality; it testifies as well to the medium's potential for
fantasy or 'illusion'. The mimetic desire of film, after all, draws not only
on the 'specular space' of reality. As the current popularity of horror,
science fiction, and heroic adventure films indicates, we are at least
equally moved by an appetite for images drawn from the 'blind space' of
the imagination. Fantasy films, for instance, draw into a cinematically
real context 'copies' which have no originals, by way of suggesting what
could be, 'what if' they inhabited our own specular space. Moreover, the
prevalence of sequels and cycles in the horror and science fiction genres
argues for another dimension to this desire, the extension of its reach to
the real world as well, as it elicits additional images of those desired
images. Still, if such films seem less obviously to serve that human desire
to 'catch' reality, they are not less concerned with desire itself: they
attest to our urge to gain access to the meeting ground between the
specular and the blind, the very realm of desire in our own lives as in
the world of film.

The fantasy formula's particular investment in this play of desire shows through the commentaries on its various manifestations. In analysing the visual structures of film fantasy, for instance, Mark Nash describes the singular linking of the seen and unseen underlying the form and contributing to its attraction. He traces out a characteristic dialectic between 'impersonal shots' and 'point of view structures' which serves to undermine our normal comfortable perspective on reality.[3] Building upon this notion of fantasy's subversively attractive vision, Rosemary Jackson finds a link in its literary form to the subtle workings of desire; this formula, she holds, 'tells of the impossible attempt to realize desire, to make visible the invisible and to discover absence'.[4] Psychologist James Hillman disagrees, however, finding in both dreams and the impulse for fantasizing not a frustration of desire, but a necessary psychic accommodation to it operating through an 'imaginal' process. He holds that fantasy draws us into the self where archetypal images speak to our dayworld situation. Within this dark or 'vesperal' region of the psyche, we encounter images of the human mystery which help us to a new perspective on, and indeed a completion of the self.[5] Hillman's theory seems to hold equal importance for film, with its mimetic grounding, and the field of fantasy, as it suggests that from this meeting of man's own specular and blind spaces, there emerges not just an alternate reality, but significant, desired, and even necessary images of our involvement in the world.

What this perspective points up is that a crucial attraction of the fantasy film is not simply the fear or awe it commonly inspires in viewers, but the images of desire it raises, since they engender that new perspective and the understanding it brings. As a case in point, the horror genre typically conjures up monstrous 'copies' that, we would prefer to think, have no originals, no correspondence in our world. Their anomalous presence, however, fascinates us even while it challenges our lexicon of everyday images. In this pattern we can discern a subtle desire to remodel the world by projecting into it, cinematically, the doubles of our imagination. It also helps explain why the most effective threats in the genre are seldom the clearly visible monsters or noonday devils, but dark patches and vague presences which invite projection and suggest an interweaving of specular and blind space – on the screen just as in our psyches. The fantasy film, then, generally depicts not a physical desire, nor even a consciously psychic one – that way lies either pornography or voyeurism – but a desire that is itself almost an absence because of its deep-rootedness in the unconscious. It is that archetypal imagery of which Hillman speaks, 'the fantasy aspect of all natural substances',[6] that speaks of the ineffable, calls to mind the unreality of much that we commonly think real, and reveals the blind space that promises to deconstruct our usual vision of the specular.

To illustrate this imaginal confluence of desire and mimesis, we might turn particularly to the horror and science fiction genres, where the copy or double is peculiarly prominent, usually as a threat to the human realm in which it phenomenally claims a place. Specifically, the normal locus of desire – the human body – assumes a new significance as both the most natural and potentially most menacing image in the genres' specular field. In depicting an attempt to recreate human life by forging a monstrous double, an early horror film like *Frankenstein* (1931) reveals the larger outline of a design whose cinematic development we may periodically trace in films like *The Body Snatcher* (1945), *Invasion of the Body Snatchers* (1956), and *Blade Runner* (1982). As exemplary texts, these films are commonly concerned with the human body as a double, and thus as an emblem of man's own blind space disconcertingly brought into contact with the specular. As adaptations of literary works which similarly dwell on this problem of doubling, they particularly point up cinema's ongoing fascination with its own limits and driving forces and the manner in which fantasy has tapped this substrate. Literary sources like Mary Shelley's *Frankenstein*, Robert Louis Stevenson's 'The Body-Snatcher', Jack Finney's *Invasion of the Body Snatchers*, and Philip K. Dick's *Do Androids Dream of Electric Sheep?* have furnished a fantasy motif that is especially suggestive for film, which finds in the doubling theme an image of its own mimetic problem and of the visual desire which powers its narratives. In the persistent concern with doubling that the science fiction and horror film genres manifest, therefore, we might locate a mirror of those basic desires to which film, apparently successfully, caters.

With a science fiction film like *Blade Runner* the ultimate consequence of a desire for doubling occupies the narrative's foreground, by way of emphasizing that the double – or 'replicant', as it is here termed – represents the very image of desire. The film evokes a world wherein desires are incessantly raised to the surface, as its very landscape is dominated by advertisements and commercial exploitation. Flying billboards, for example, constantly hover over the city, flashing various slogans, while loudspeakers blare out commercial messages, and entire sides of skyscrapers are little more than monumental neon advertisements. Even that typical locus of desire, the copy, seems pervasive here, as we see mechanical snakes, birds, dogs, and people – in fact, one avenue of the city is given over to the manufacture and sale of these indistinguishable copies of the real. This indistinguishability, a nearly perfect mimesis, gives birth to the film's central conflict, as the replicants, created to satisfy man's every desire – for entertainment, companionship, relief from labour, sexual outlet – threaten to render their creators superfluous and take their place. In his study of violence in human history, René Girard argues for a link between the double and a subversive menace, noting that 'the double and the monster are one and the same being', so that there is 'no double who does not yield a monstrous aspect upon close scrutiny'.[7] If desire can engender such a potential threat in its doublings, then, it can also call from within a counter violence. In this case, that force drawn from the blind space in man takes the form of hired killers, or blade runners, whose task is to track down and destroy the replicants who rebel against their servile status and seek a normal human life. With the bounty hunters society sets about a task which points up its own inherent contradiction; it seeks to rid a world marked by specular desire of the very embodiment of desire.

In an ironic contrast, normal human desire seems practically absent from this future society, as if it had been displaced by a sheer fascination with doubling and its emblems. Despite the pervasive advertisements and commercial lures, despite too the easy accessibility of doubles which cater to man's desires, including the need for others, alienation, isolation, and depression are manifestly common. The major figures in the film, for instance, the blade runner Rick Deckard, Dr Tyrell, master designer of replicants, and J.F. Sebastian, a chief genetic engineer, are all isolates who seem to derive their only comforts and indeed their sole purpose from those doubles which they either create or destroy; these people apparently have little alternative, since this is the way of their society rather than an aberration from the norm. While some people have abandoned this world, where everything seems doubled and every desire modelled on another real or illusory desire, they have simply left Earth in favour of one of its clones, an 'off-world' colony which, like the other copies fashioned in this future society, is supposedly better than its model. Those who remain, consequently, feel much like aliens in their own world. In a subtle, self-induced fashion, a creeping sameness seems to have worked its will, as the people, displaced by desire, gradually become deprived of it, save for an empty obsession with duplications. What director Ridley Scott suggests is a circumstance in which Girard's dictum on the double as a monster might almost be reversed, so that it is the original in a world of copies – man himself – who begins to assume an equally aberrant, life-denying aspect.

One consequence of this ambivalent vision of man – and a measure of just how far we have come since *Frankenstein*'s simple, melodramatic working out of this conflict – is that our sympathies find no sure anchor here; rather, they shift uneasily between the world-weary Deckard and his replicant antagonists, especially as it becomes increasingly clear that essentially they share a single fate. Forced to act as that force of violence which, Girard asserts, doubling inevitably evokes, Deckard reluctantly goes about his job, even as he meditates on the nature of his quarry and wonders about his own place in the confusing welter of being. More than their human counterparts, though, the replicants are possessed by these ontological questions, as they apparently frequently rebel against their shallow, servile status and seek to lead human lives. The particular group of escaped androids which Deckard pursues have learned not only of their engineered origins, but also of their programmed mortality – a safety feature to ensure their demise after a short, useful career. Faced with the sort of knowledge man has always had to abide with, that of an inevitable and onrushing death, the replicants become questors, seeking out their creators – Tyrell and Sebastian – in hope of gaining just what man has always sought, the secret of longer life. In their driving desire for life, in fact, they come to seem even more human than many of the real people here. What *Blade Runner* thereby suggests is how man's fascination with doubling might fashion not only copies of humanity, but models of real desire – for life, love, and meaning – which may indeed seem better than the original, as these desires are so ardently asserted that they threaten to supplant the jaded and flickering ones to which man tentatively clings.

In the character of Rachael, a nearly perfect replicant, as Tyrell proudly asserts, this problem finds its clearest and most troubling expression. Although he learns she is an android, Deckard finds himself attracted to Rachael, fascinated not by her nature as a copy so much as by the way in which she mirrors something significantly human within him; a loneliness and a longing for others wherewith that loneliness might be overcome. She, in turn, apparently falls in love with Deckard and even kills one replicant to save his life. Her reception of the knowledge that she is herself an android prepares for this elemental sign of humanity, for unlike the replicants Pris and Roy Batty who, after the fashion of the pod people in *Invasion of the Body Snatchers*, want nothing more than to survive, she simply accepts what is, after all, the quite human fate of inevitable death. The order to kill her like the others, consequently, elicits a different response from Deckard, a refusal as if it meant killing another human. By listening to his human desires, which speak of an ultimate concern for life and for others, he manages to assert his own humanity in the face of an increasing dehumanization. While it seems ironic that a double or android should represent the stimulus for this awakening of a proper human desire, this circumstance indicates how far we may have come in our fascination with doubling and what effect that particular desire might work on man. No longer viewed simply as the aberrant concern of monstrous types, to be kept hidden from the specular world at all costs, as in *Frankenstein*, doubling and its coeval desire for sameness, *Blade Runner* suggests, threaten to become common and pernicious influences, displacing any real desire and a concern for others.

This film thereby makes explicit a theme running through a great many horror and science fiction films – that the double or copy represents a menace in direct proportion to the abdication from real desire which occurs in man himself. If this ongoing fascination with doubling becomes a dominant force in man's life, distancing him from the real rather that bringing him closer to it, he runs the risk of becoming little more than a copy himself, potentially less human than the images fashioned in his likeness. More than simply the exploration of a fashionable topic, the morality of genetic engineering, then, *Blade Runner* envisions, in the best traditions of these genres, the disconcerting displacement of a desire for others, for life itself, by a narcissistic preoccupation with doubles that could well lead to our destruction – as it does for Tyrell and Sebastian – or at least to a dehumanization, as we abdicate from all desire and leave it as the province of our proxies. As in the other films discussed here, desire clearly assumes two opposed dimensions – a narcissistic fascination with doubling and a human need for others – and the former threatens to blot out the latter, as man unthinkingly sets about reducing his own measure.

At the same time, *Blade Runner* holds out a promise as well. It is one seen most clearly in Rachael, who awakens Deckard's slumbering desires and effectively serves as a mirror in which he might see his humanity. In Deckard's fight with Roy Batty, though, we see dramatized both the danger and the promise latent in these doubles. After a lengthy combat, Deckard slips from atop a building and dangles precariously above the dark city streets; however, instead of plunging his adversary to destruction, the replicant pulls him back to safety, just before his own life gives out. It is with that curious, saving grasp that Roy Batty reminds us of the positive potential originally seen for such human artifice. Brought back from the brink of extinction in this unexpected way, Deckard seems to gain a new perspective on his life and that of his replicant adversaries – one that enables him to set aside his bounty hunter role. What the copy offers in that last, dying surge of strength is more than a life-saving grip; it is a saving grace that brings a new sense of self, of life, and an unexpected but necessary redemption.[8]

The moral thrust of the horror and science fiction genres abides in this complex mirroring of man and taking of his measure. John Carpenter's 1982 remake of the 1951 film *The Thing*, for example, explicitly employs the motif of doubling to pose a challenge to our normal perceptions of the self that sums up the various formulations we have seen here. Confronted by an alien creature that, as one character notes, 'wants to hide inside an imitation' and can easily do so because of its capacity to 'shape its own cells to imitate' its prey, an isolated group of humans desperately looks for 'some kind of test' to determine precisely who is real and who only a copy. To those around him, MacReady, Carpenter's protagonist, asserts, 'I know I'm human', but it is a declaration that has a forced ring to it, hinting at the sort of uncertainty about the self that also marks *Blade Runner*'s Deckard and much of modern society. His later question, 'So how do we know who's human?' speaks more directly of this anxiety which horror and science fiction films, in response to audiences' misgivings today, have increasingly brought to the foreground – an uncertainty about a human nature that easily finds itself prey to dehumanization, even to a monstrous potential arising from that blind space within the self. In the recurrent fantasizing about doubles, copies, or replicants, these films evoke both a fascination and a fundamental fear, the latter a natural defensive reaction to the former. In its narcissistic dimension, the interest in doubles denotes a concern with the self that potentially threatens to shut out others and, as it draws man ever deeper into the unknown realms of his own Id, eventually brings his destruction. At the same time, that interest recalls our abiding fascination with film itself, and especially our constant but unspoken hope that in the medium's fleeting images we might momentarily glimpse something previously unseen, something perhaps of the self, something vital. In dramatizing such possibilities, the horror and science fiction genres hold up a mirror to man, reflecting the disturbing double of his proclivity for doubling. Through this reflexive effect, however, they hold out a hope of quelling certain dangerous impulses, almost cathartically, by permitting us to view an aspect of the self which we are normally too blind to perceive.

This essay has suggested that a major attraction of certain forms of film fantasy rests in their concern with attraction itself, that is, with the varieties of human desire which always try to press into the specular world from their blind, internal origins. Persistently, this concern translates into a depiction of the human body as a double or as the very emblem of man's fascination with doubling. From seeing our own image *in* our own image, of course, we might come to recognize a potential danger in that doubling. While all films obviously answer to this basic mimetic desire, then, certain forms of the fantasy film find in it their very *raison d'être*; they locate in the normal specular space of film, a realm of blindness and lost perspective that is at once frightening and fascinating, and that holds the potential both to alarm and to instruct us. By raising the spectre of a desire to replicate the self, possibly at the cost of the self, they promise to counter this tendency, to snatch our bodies back from a fall to which man seems all too prone.

Notes

1. Pascal Bonitzer, 'Partial Vision Film and the Labyrinth', trans. Fabrice Ziolkowski, *Wide Angle*, vol. 4, no. 4, 1980, p. 58.

2. André Bazin, *What is Cinema?*, trans. Hugh Gray, Berkeley: University of California Press 1967, vol. 1, p. 11.

3. Mark Nash, '*Vampyr* and the Fantastic', *Screen*, vol. 17, no. 3, 1976, p. 34.

4. Rosemary Jackson, *Fantasy: The Literature of Subversion*, London: Methuen 1981, p. 4.

5. James Hillman, *The Dream and the Underworld*, New York: Harper & Row 1979, pp. 1–3; and *Re-Visioning Psychology*, New York: Harper & Row 1975, p. x.

6. Ibid., p. 91.

7. René Girard, *Violence and the Sacred*, trans. Patrick Gregory, Baltimore: John Hopkins University Press 1977, p. 160. See also Girard's explanation for the connection between sameness and the impulse for violence: 'all losses of difference also involve violence, and this violence is contagious' (p. 281). I am indebted to Girard's work for much of my approach in this essay. For his more complex formulation of the doubling impulse, see *Deceit, Desire and the Novel*, trans. Yvonne Freccero, Baltimore: Johns Hopkins University Press 1965.

8. A Christian iconography pointedly marks the last scenes of the film: see particularly the dove which Roy Batty produces, recalling the symbol of the Holy Spirit. In fact, Batty invokes certain Christ-like resonances which point up his subtle function as a redeemer here.

13

'You've Got To Be Fucking Kidding!' Knowledge, Belief and Judgement in Science Fiction

Steve Neale

In John Carpenter's version of *The Thing* (1982), there is, as Philip Brophy has pointed out, one particularly telling line uttered during the course of one particularly telling and spectacular scene.[1] *The Thing* concerns an alien that first invades and then imitates both human and animal forms. It has infiltrated the base camp – and the crew – of a scientific observation post in Antarctica. At one point, in the guise of the body of an ailing crew member, it tears off the hands of the doctor who attempts to revive him; then, awakened, sprouts all manner of tentacles and limbs through the muscles and flesh of its host. It is shot down in flames. But one of its tentacles latches on to the crew member's head, which is now lying under the table:

> the tentacle lashes out of the head onto a door, and drags itself on its side. Just as it reaches the doorway, the crew see it and are transfixed by it. The head slowly turns upside down and, suddenly, eight insect-like legs rip through the head using it like a body. The sight is of an upside-down severed human head out of which have grown insect feet. As it 'walks' out the door, a crew member says *the* line of the film: 'You've got to be fucking kidding!'[2]

As Brophy goes on to show, the significance of this line lies in its twofold status. It is on the one hand a narrative event: a fictional remark made by a fictional character about a specific, fictional entity. As such it is a sign of the character's astonishment, an acknowledgement of what is for him the reality of the creature and its powers. On the other hand, it is what one might call both a 'textual' and an 'institutional' event: a remark addressed to the spectator by the film, and by the cinematic apparatus, about the nature of its special effects. As such it is the sign of a number of things. It is a sign that the film is, at this point at least, 'violently self-conscious' (to use Brophy's words):[3] it is aware that the Thing (and the world it inhabits) are cinematic fabrications, the product, in particular, of an up-to-date regime of special effects; it is aware that the powers of this regime have here been stretched to their limit; and it displays both those powers – and that awareness – to the full. It is a sign also of an awareness on the part of the spectator (an awareness often marked at this point by laughter): the spectator knows that the Thing is a fiction, a collocation of special effects; and the spectator now knows that the film knows too.

Despite this awareness, the special effects have had an effect. The spectator has been, like the fictional character, astonished and horrified. An effect of this kind is fundamental to science fiction in the cinema. So too, though, is the awareness. In fact, as I shall go on to argue, the effect and the awareness are interdependent. Indeed, one of the keys to understanding the attraction, the pleasure – the lure – of science fiction lies precisely in the intricate intercalation of different forms, kinds and layers of knowledge, belief and judgement that a line like the one from *The Thing*, together with the effect it accompanies, serves both to correlate and mark. In order to identify a little more precisely the nature and function of these forms, kinds and layers, it is necessary to say something about narrative fiction and genre, about cinema and the nature of its images and sounds, and about the status and role of its special effects.

All narratives involve the representation of events and their agents. The primary purpose of these agents and events is to provide links in a narrative chain (a plot) on the one hand, and to occasion a range of aesthetic effects (like suspense, surprise and pathos) on the other. Narrative events and their agents are understood and adjudged on the basis of a variety of types of knowledge, and in accordance with a variety of different criteria. This knowledge and these criteria can either be internal and overt or external and implicit. Thus on the one hand the narrative can have its characters comment on one another, on the world they inhabit, and on the events that they encounter, thereby providing the spectator with an array of explicit information and judgements. Alternatively, it can rely on the spectator's own knowledge and values, appealing implicitly to information and criteria of judgement it presumes it shares with its audience. Most narratives in most genres in the cinema involve both kinds of knowledge and judgement. Thus, for example, two of the members of the crew in *The Thing* are called doctors, but the film does not at any point explain what a doctor is or does. It assumes we will know. However, soon after the Thing's first transformation on the base, one of the doctors performs an autopsy on its partially incinerated body.

He is needed to provide both spectator and crew with the kind of information that the narrative cannot presume. He says:

> 'You see what we're talking about: here is an organism that imitates other life forms. And it imitates them perfectly. When this thing attacked our dogs it tried to digest them, absorb them, and in the process shape its own self to imitate them.'

This information is treated as authoritative, in part because it is delivered, precisely, by an expert, and in part because it remains uncontested: it is the only explanation we are offered. However, a little later in the film there is both speculation and dispute. Two members of the crew are sent out onto the ice to investigate what looks like the remains of some kind of spaceship:

> 'Jesus, how long you figure this has been in the ice?'
> 'I'd say the ice this is buried in is a hundred thousand years old. At least.'

They return to base. The helicopter pilot, MacReady, explains what he thinks might have happened; and crewmen Childs and Palmer comment on what he says:

> 'I don't know. Thousands of years ago it crashes and this thing gets thrown out, or crawls out, and it ends up freezing in the ice.'
> 'I just can't believe any of this voodoo bullshit.'
> 'Happens all the time, man. They're falling out of the sky like flies. Government knows all about it. Right, Mac?'
> 'You believe any of this voodoo bullshit, Blair?'
> 'Childs, Childs. Chariots of the gods, man.'

In line with Colin MacCabe's argument that in conventional narrative films (or what he calls 'classic realist texts') the truthful view is the view confirmed by the camera, by what we ourselves see, it is significant that we tend here to accept MacReady's account.[4] We do so not only because it is the only coherent account we are given – because all Childs offers is doubt – though this is important. Nor do we do so only because MacReady is played by the star of the film, Kurt Russell, though this is important too. We do so primarily because we have been shown MacReady actually looking at the spaceship's remains, and because we have been shown, in a pre-credit sequence, the spaceship crash. Thus this particular conversation, and the judgement it involves, is significant for what it can tell us about the articulation and acquisition of knowledge in any kind of narrative film. It is significant also, though, for what it can tell us about the nature and function of knowledge in science fiction in particular.

All fiction to some extent involves what has traditionally been called 'suspension of disbelief', by virtue of the fact that its agents and events are, by definition, unreal. In actual fact, while disbelief may well be involved, it is often knowledge and judgement that the spectator is required to suspend, as Ben Brewster has pointed out.[5] Thus in Minnelli's film, *The Cobweb* (1955), we have no choice but to accept the judgement of the film and of a number of the characters that the designs for a new set of curtains show artistic promise and skill, whether or not we may personally like them.[6] Similarly, we have no choice but to accept that the unconventional behaviour of many of the film's characters is due to neurosis, whether or not we have any precise knowledge of mental states and conditions, and whether or not we agree with the way they are portrayed and explained in the film. In *The Thing*, we have no choice but to accept the doctor's explanation that the Thing can absorb and imitate other life forms, and MacReady's thesis that it came from outer space, crashing to Earth in a spaceship. However, while *The Cobweb* is a contemporary drama, *The Thing* is science fiction. The cultural status of the events and narrative agents involved in the two films are therefore distinct. While they are in both films equally unreal, spaceships and shape-changing aliens – unlike curtains, neurotically inspired artistic talent, and mentally disturbed behaviour – are conventionally adjudged in our culture as also inherently improbable.[7]

It is in this context that the conversation between Childs, MacReady and Palmer is particularly significant. For what is at stake here is precisely the improbability, not only of the film's own events, but of the reasons it gives for their occurrence. Childs's scepticism is especially important. For it articulates a position of doubt, a refusal to suspend disbelief, that is shown to be mistaken. But Palmer's ready acceptance of MacReady's explanation is also important. If Childs is sceptical, Palmer is naive (and slightly deranged). His enthusiastic evocation of the 'chariots of the gods' is thus merely the equally unacceptable obverse of Childs's dismissive evocation of voodoo. MacReady's position, based as it is on direct observation and a coherent assessment of the facts – not on a refusal to face those facts, or on an acceptance of them only because they fit neatly into a pre-existing framework of irrational beliefs – emerges, therefore, by contrast, as all the more balanced, all the more credible, all the more convincing; all the more probable.

Like MacReady, *The Thing* is here engaged in a process of persuasion. Major aspects of its fictional world are, from a general cultural point of view, not only unlikely or impossible, but also, therefore, unknowable in advance and thus in need of explanation. The film is therefore involved both in establishing its own credibility, and in establishing its own regime of credence – the rules, the norms and the laws by which its events and agents can be understood and adjudged. What is probable or possible in this world? How does it operate? What is regarded within it as unusual, unlikely, inexplicable? How do we know when the explanations we are offered for the events that occur are right or wrong? And so on.

Such a process is of course very common in science fiction (as it is in other genres, like the horror film, which involve the depiction of improbable or 'marvellous' events). Common also is the twofold nature of this process, one in which exposition, explanation and the establishment of internal norms are coincident with the negotiation of a position of credibility – and the acknowledgement of positions of incredulity and doubt. Thus in *Close Encounters of the Third Kind* (1977), Roy Neary tries to explain to his wife what it is that he has witnessed. 'You're not going to believe what I saw', he says. And in the 1978 remake of *Invasion of the Body Snatchers*, Elizabeth Driscoll and others try to explain to a sceptical David Kibner that human beings are somehow being copied. 'Don't you think we know how insane this sounds?', she says. 'But what do you think we're doing? Do you think we're making it up?'

One of the reasons why we know that Elizabeth and the others are not 'making it up', one of the reasons why we, at least, believe what Roy has to say, is that, as in *The Thing*, we ourselves have seen what it is that is being referred to, what it is that is being explained. Inasmuch as this is the case, the processes and issues of judgement and belief are ultimately focussed – and founded – on what it is we see, and hence ultimately also on the cinematic image and its powers.

In his essay 'The Imaginary Signifier', the film theorist Christian Metz has addressed in general terms the nature and the powers of the cinematic image – and cinematic sound – and the extent to which they involve, and depend on, specific regimes and structures of knowledge and belief.[8] Metz points out that the cinema is in many ways 'more perceptual' than other arts like music, literature, sculpture, painting and photography. It involves both vision and audition, and it involves the representation, in detail, of sound, of speech, of objects in space, and of movement and temporal progression. However, this 'numerical superiority' disappears when cinema is compared to arts like opera and theatre. For opera and theatre, too, involve several axes of perception, and are possessed of similar representational capacities. Thus

Their difference from the cinema lies elsewhere: they do not consist of *images*, the perceptions they offer to the eye and the ear are inscribed in a true space (not a photographed one), the same as that occupied by the public during the performance; everything the audience hear and see is actively produced in their presence, by human beings or props which are themselves present.[9]

In the cinema, by contrast, 'everything is recorded',[10] everything, therefore, is absent:

> Thus the cinema, 'more perceptual' than certain arts according to the list of its sensory registers, is also 'less perceptual' than others once the status of these perceptions is envisaged rather than their number or diversity; for its perceptions are all in a sense 'false'. Or rather, the activity of perception it involves is real (the cinema is not a phantasy), but the perceived is not really the object, it is its shade, its phantom, its double, its *replica* in a new kind of mirror. It will be said that literature, after all, is itself only made of replicas (written words, presenting absent objects). But at least it does not present them to us with all the really perceived detail that the screen does. . . . The unique position of the cinema lies in this dual character of its signifier: unaccustomed perceptual wealth, but at the same time stamped with unreality to an unusual degree, and from the very outset.[11]

In the cinema, therefore, a dual and contradictory status is accorded its images and sounds. These images and sounds thus incrementally redouble the already contradictory status of any fiction they may be used to present: 'In the cinema it is not just the fictional signified, if there is one, that is thus made present in the mode of absence, it is from the outset the signifier.'[12]

Inasmuch as this is the case, the 'suspension of disbelief' required by any fiction – or more accurately, the suspension of judgement, on the one hand, coupled with a splitting or division of knowledge on the other (as can be encapsulated in a formula like 'I know this is fictional, unreal, but will nevertheless treat it as worthy of judgement, and therefore as worthy of credence') – is given, in the cinema, an additional twist ('I know that what is presented by means of these images and sounds is not really there, but nevertheless ... '). Yet further twists are added when it comes to a genre like science fiction, which by definition deals, as we have seen, with the unlikely, and hence the unbelievable; and when it comes to the mobilization, in cinematic science fiction, of a regime of special effects, of specially fabricated images and sounds, both to present and to authenticate its events, its agents and its settings.

Metz has discussed special effects in the cinema in '*Trucage* and the Film'.[13] He points out that '*trucages*' in the cinema are of various kinds, and can operate in a variety of different ways at a variety of distinct and different levels. Some, like the effects involved in fades and dissolves, are meant to be perceived. Others, like the use of stuntmen and stand-ins, are not. Some, like back projection, are involved at the point of filming. Others, like wipes, are not. Some, like the use of models and make-up, are primarily profilmic (effects produced in front of the camera, but without the aid of its own particular technological capabilities). Others, like slow-motion and mattes, depend either upon the specific capacities of the camera, or upon other cinematographic devices and processes. And so on. At the moment of viewing, as opposed to the moment of production, the spectator is engaged in a number of mental operations. In the case of 'visible *trucages*', 'the spectator undertakes a type of spontaneous sorting out of the visible material of which the text is composed and ascribes only a portion of it to the diegesis [the fictional world]'.[14] In the case of the majority of effects usually termed, and regarded, as 'special effects', by contrast (the use of mattes, make-up, back projection, models and the like), 'the spectator *ascribes to the diegesis the totality of the visual elements furnished him*'.[15] Metz goes on to argue:

> In films of the fantastic, the impression of unreality is convincing only if the public has the feeling of partaking, not of some plausible illustration of a process obeying a nonhuman logic, but of a series of disquieting or 'impossible' events which nevertheless unfold before him in the guise of eventlike appearances.[16]

Thus here, once again, the spectator's credibility is subject to division: 'The spectator is not the victim of the machination to the point of being unaware that it exists, but he is not sufficiently conscious of it for it to lose its impact.'[17]

With this particular combination of forms of awareness and 'impact', we are back again at the point in *The Thing* at which the character utters his self-reflexive line. Here it is worth stressing, once more, the element of display the line involves. As Metz himself points out, while there is always a degree of duplicity, of secrecy, of the hidden attached to the use of special effects, there is always also 'something which flaunts itself'.[18] This flaunting both caters to – and counters – the spectator's awareness, while ensuring at the same time that cinema will take the credit for the impact. Either way, cinema gains. It is worth also stressing that, of course, both the impact itself, and hence the particular – and delicate – balance between impact and awareness, is always relative both to the capacities of cinema's special effects regimes as they exist at any point in time, and to the amount of capital expended on effects in production. As has already been pointed out, *The Thing* is concerned, among other things, not only to display the latest special effects, but also to display an awareness that they *are* the latest. It is also concerned, like other, often cheaper, science fiction and horror films to build in an element of camp, a tongue-in-cheek knowingness. This element is designed to protect the spectator (and hence the film) both from disappointment, should the effects fail to convince, or should their convincingness serve merely to highlight the improbable nature of that which they are used to represent; and also from genuine trauma, should the effects and what they represent be taken too seriously.

Metz draws on the psychoanalytic concept of disavowal, and on its model of the fetish, to pinpoint the nature of the divisions of knowledge and belief that the cinema, its fictions, and its special effects all, in their various ways, involve. Just as the fetish both avows and disavows an absence, a lack (the lack, for the fetishist proper, of the phallus wished for in the object of sexual desire), so the fictional representation, the cinematic image, and the special effect both avow and disavow something that does not actually exist.[19] Although, as a clinical perversion, fetishism is a specific psychic formation (and practice), it is, like all perversions, only a particular response to a universal human experience (in this case the experience of castration – of insufficiency, loss and lack); only a particularized extension of a universal disavowal (the disavowal of the lack of the phallus – the mark of power and self-sufficiency – initially imagined as belonging to the mother). It thus provides a paradigm for

> all the splittings of belief which man will henceforth be capable of in the most varied domains, of all the infinitely complex unconscious and occasionally conscious interactions which he will allow himself between 'believing' and 'not believing' and which will on more than one occasion be of great assistance in resolving (or denying) delicate problems.[20]

Inasmuch as the institution of the cinema is one of the 'domains' to which Metz goes on to refer, a thesis such as this accounts both for the spectator's general capacity to believe (and at the same time to know), and for the extent to which that capacity can be exercised, multiplied, doubled and redoubled in a genre like science fiction. It accounts, too, for the extent to which knowledge and belief are foregrounded – highlighted as issues – in science fiction films, the extent to which, for instance, as we have seen, the characters themselves have often to suspend disbelief, have often to undergo a process of learning, have often to revise the habitual basis of the judgements that they make. What it cannot do, though, is predict how any one individual film will draw on this capacity and deal with these issues. As a final comment, it is perhaps worth suggesting in this context that the more interesting films will be those which work not, like *E.T.* (1982), simply to affirm belief (and the cinema's capacity to feed it), but those which, like *Invasion of the Body Snatchers* (in particular the 1956 version), work instead to link habitual perceptions, assumptions and judgements to issues and forms of social conformity – and in the process offer a challenge to both.

Notes

1. Philip Brophy, 'Horrality – the Textuality of Contemporary Horror Films', *Screen*, vol. 27, no. 1, 1986.
2. Ibid., p. 11.
3. Ibid.
4. Colin MacCabe, 'Realism and Cinema: Notes on Some Brechtian Theses', *Screen*, vol. 15, no. 2, 1974.
5. Ben Brewster, 'Film' in Dan Cohn-Sherbok and Michael Irwin, eds, *Exploring Reality*, London: Allen & Unwin 1987, p. 153.
6. Ibid., pp. 152–3.
7. It is worth pointing out here that the problem of improbability is common to a number of genres, including the horror film and what might be termed the fantasy-adventure film (films like *Jason of the Argonauts, Clash of the Titans* and so on). It is no accident, therefore, that these genres often overlap (as in *The Thing* itself, on the one hand, and a film like *Star Wars* on the other). What, in part at least, distinguishes these genres from one another is the degree and the type of motivation, of justification, they offer for the extraordinary events and agents they portray. Science fiction, of course, justifies its improbabilities on 'scientific' (or quasi-scientific) grounds. It is worth pointing out also, though, that such a justification is as conventional, and itself as subject to judgements of improbability, as the supernatural justifications of the gothic horror film, and that in the end, in any case, motivation is merely an alibi for the elaboration of aesthetic effects. (See Gerard Genette, 'Vraisemblance et motivation' in Genette, *Figures,* t. 11, Paris: Seuil 1969.)
8. Christian Metz, 'The Imaginary Signifier', trans. Ben Brewster in Metz, *Psychoanalysis and Cinema*, London: Macmillan 1982.
9. Ibid., p. 43.
10. Ibid.
11. Ibid., pp. 44–5.
12. Ibid., p. 44.
13. Christian Metz, '*Trucage* and the Film', trans. Françoise Meltzer, *Critical Inquiry*, vol. 3, no. 4, 1977.
14. Ibid., p. 667.
15. Ibid.
16. Ibid.
17. Ibid.
18. Ibid. p. 665.
19. Metz, 'The Imaginary Signifier', pp. 69–78. I have here tended to give a Lacanian account, using the term phallus, rather than a Freudian account, using the term penis, though Metz himself tends to use Freudian terms.
20. Ibid., p. 70.

14

Cataract Surgery:
Cinema in the Year 2000*

Paul Virilio

Framed by the magnificent Cité des Sciences at la Villette, the only cinema of its kind in Europe, the Géode – with its thousand-metre-square hemispheric screen – challenges all received ideas about cinematic representation. In forty minutes, today's spectator is projected in time – back to the fairground origins of cinema, and forward into the technological future lying ahead of us.

With age the cornea darkens and clouds over, calling for an operation with a splendid name: cataract surgery. Can this be happening today in the darkened chambers of an art form which recently celebrated its ninetieth birthday? As Japan develops the 'Jumbotron' with its high-definition image and open-air screen, and a Frenchman invents the reverse process – darkening the sky with smoke to make daytime firework displays possible, how can we not imagine the Géode? With its hemispheric auditorium, the Géode, as a cinematic occasion, is not just about the architecture of film theatres, not just about low audience figures in traditional cinemas (25 per cent on average, as against the Géode's 85 per cent), but also – and above all – about *filmic space*.

When screen becomes auditorium, a luminous space with no apparent points of orientation, the very scene of cinema is in the auditorium. The auditorium becomes a space whose proportions are determined no longer by architectural volume, but by the editing of the film, so that the time/space of the sequences infinitely extends the volume of the auditorium – into filmic space. No longer is it a question of 'depth' (as it might have been with CinemaScope, say); for it is no longer the film

*Translated by Annie Fatet and Annette Kuhn

being projected into the space of the theatre, but the very auditorium projecting itself into time, into the concave curvature of filmic time/space. Nor is it a question of creating an illusion – depth of field – but of staking more or less all on duration, on the *depth of time* of shots, and on the quality of editing. The running time of filmed sequences determines the architectonic balance or imbalance of the projection site, and thus the comfort or otherwise of spectators, those voyeurs on a voyage whose trajectory is tangential to script and storyline. Here architecture works like a new type of vehicle – foreshadowed, perhaps, by those high-tech fitness training machines that work on the simulation principle.

What we are witnessing here is more important than might appear. In the Géode, what is simulated is not so much depth of filmic space as depth of architectonic space: the Imax/Omnimax system is a 'ground simulator', a cinema simulator. The site of film projection suddenly becomes less important than what is shown there. Or more precisely, what is being projected determines the degree of stability of the site of the spectacle. After the long, long development of 'dynamic' moving vehicles, we are now entering the era of the static vehicle: an audiovisual vehicle, vector of apparent motion, of that sense of inertia induced by travelling vast distances – which is a substitute for physical displacement that has become more or less redundant with the immediacy of tele-communications technologies. Hence the spontaneous generation of videodiscs, and of interactive screens simulating visits to all sorts of places – cities, stately homes, museums. Simulator of a thoroughly eccentric course, the statis of the dome at La Villette becomes a palpable metaphor for time travel, a time capsule for movement without displacement, a temporality of running on the spot.

In the sophisticated electronic world of contemporary Japan, there is a new-style swimming pool in which athletes can swim on the spot against a strong current: impeding forward movement, this body of water demands power and dynamic energy on the swimmer's part simply to stay put. As with a training bicycle or a running mat, the dynamics of fluids in motion in the Japanese pool function purely to make competition swimmers combat the dynamism of the energy they are up against: this energy replaces the length of the Olympic pool, just as the running mat replaces the track. Technology which exists in microscopic form in the 'inertia powerhouse' – an essential piece of equipment for correcting the trajectory of missiles and pilotless planes – now appears on a grand scale. As a *static audiovisual vehicle*, the Omnimax auditorium is the inertia powerhouse for its occupants' on-the-spot movement, at once constructing the film and providing a comfortable pseudo-voyage for the spectators at the Géode. This is why film makers working on Omnimax productions face such extreme difficulties: any error in framing or editing irretrievably destroys the qualities of both space and narrative, and consequently the audience's pleasure.

If we are to understand this 'geodesic cinema', we can no longer separate film from auditorium, the material from the immaterial. If filmic time/space is not quite right, the site of the spectacle is ruined, becomes valueless – like a permanently immobilized vehicle, rendered useless by loss of energy in its driving force. Hence a major risk for the producers and distributors of this exemplary form of entertainment: failure in one area leads to ruin in others. Given the huge cost of this new equipment, the word ruin is no exaggeration. In view of the innovative nature of this latest type of 'vehicle', it might be useful to reconsider the very notion of energy, or 'driving force'. Physicists commonly make a distinction between two types of energy: 'potential' energy and 'kinetic' energy (*energie cinétique*), the energy that governs movement. Ninety years after the invention of the cinematograph, it might be apt to add a third: 'cinematic' energy, the energy resulting from the effect of varying degrees of speed of movement upon ocular, optical and optico-electronic perceptions. State-of-the-art simulation industries put this third form of energy into action in the form of a new driving force, the cinematic machine.

Set at a vertiginous thirty-degree incline, a thousand-metre-square screen covers its attentive viewers from head to foot. They find themselves in the position of someone contemplating sky and drifting clouds, to the point of fear of falling, *free fall*, an inverse vertigo before a chasm of images. The Géode is ultimately a cenotaph, an empty tomb in memory of the early, Euclidean, cinema; an audiovisual monument superseding architectural monuments – picture palaces, art houses, flea-pits, all outdated now because of their strict angles, the corpselike rigidities of their screens and auditoria. In many ways similar to the famous Boullée project, which was dedicated to Newton, Adrien Fainsilber's dome, following the latest in flight simulators, heralds the dawn of a 'non-Euclidean' cinema: a topological and relativistic cinema combining mobile camera with static building, the auditorium, and subjugating the screen and the various diffusers of sound, image and light to a computer. This electronic cinema has been the beneficiary of state-of-the-art technologies. The projector, a complex machine fitted with a fifteen-kilowatt hydraulically cooled Xenon light, is based on NASA designs for floodlighting rocket launching pads. We should perhaps recall that, shortly before his death, Louis Lumière was perfecting the design of light projectors for the French navy.

The Omnimax projector horizontally unrolls a wide gauge 70mm film derived from US Air Force reconnaissance films. This hypermetropic film corrects itself optically only when the image makes contact with the concave surface of the screen – a cornea transplant for a cinema suffering premature sight loss due to a multiplication of exhibition outlets and a concomitant shrinking in screen size. This is a corrective prosthesis for followers deserting the darkened chambers, an 'extra-ocular' implant banishing the need for glasses, as we await the advent of cineholography, and what might be called depth of image-form. As to intra-ocular implants, it was a British ophthalmologist who, in 1949, conceived the idea of replacing traditional eye surgery by grafts of perspex membranes: he had noticed than an ex-RAF pilot was able to tolerate fragments of cockpit screen which had lodged in his eye after an air battle. In the same vein, flight simulators used by the Air Force will soon do away completely with the spherical screen, and images of fighting will be projected directly into the pilot's eyes, through a system derived from the oculometer.

But we would miss the point if, in the context of this non-Euclidean cinema, we failed to remind ourselves of the primacy of time over space. If from now on 'depth of time' prevails over depth of field, this will be because the temporal regime of film has undergone a mutation. This is not due to choices exercised by film makers, but has to do rather with an evolution in customs and lifestyles in combination with various technological developments. From the one-reelers, the short films of early cinema, to the multi-reel features of today, cinema has hitherto invested (technically and aesthetically) in length, eventually fixing on the more or less accepted standard of ninety minutes. Recently, however, this process seems to have moved into reverse. Some of the most recent projects aim at radical reduction in time, in the duration of projection. In Douglas Trumbull's Showscan process, we get forty-five minutes, and Graeme Ferguson's Omnimax film *The Dream is Alive* (1984) lasts only forty minutes. This reduction in running time is sometimes accompanied by an increase in projection speed: from the traditional sixteen, seventeen and twenty-four frames per second up to twenty-five, thirty and even sixty frames per second with contemporary special effects. In the Ferguson film shown at the Géode, projection speed is standard, but extends well beyond the viewer's binocular field.

In fact, as in other aspects of everyday life, we are moving from an extensive, historical, time scale towards an intensive temporality of ahistorical immediacy. This is brought about by automotive, audiovisual and information technologies, all of which are moving us in the direction of restricted duration. At this point, the construction of film narrative comes under threat, along with the architectural construction of picture houses themselves. If time is history, speed is only its hallucination, a perspectival hallucination which undoes the meaning/direction (*sens*) of narrative and action for the sake of pure sensation. 'To live fifty years in two hours is happiness, life is too slow', exclaimed Fanny Ardant when talking about the shooting of Ettore Scola's film *Le Voyage*. The cinematographic processes already described will bring about a densification, a saturation, of space and time. The present shift from extensive to intensive time disturbs, and eventually destroys, the literariness of film script and dialogue, just as it ruins the metric and geometric dimensions of traditional exhibition spaces.

Having once escaped the fairground, will cinema now go back there to stay? The space of the Imax/Omnimax system translates all this perfectly: oversaturating the visual field of the dome's spectators/passengers, whilst reducing the duration of the filmic journey. If it did not do this, the voyeur/voyager might easily 'switch off', disconnect from the appeal of the 'image-chamber'; or in other words, from the spatio-temporal hallucination. In any case, it is strictly forbidden to enter or leave the auditorium while projection is in progress: though if it is inadvisable to get on or off whilst the vehicle is in motion, it is positively recommended to lean out of the window! Here again we encounter the 'vehicular' quality of the latest audiovisual productions. Indeed, the fusion/confusion of camera, projection system and auditorium in the Imax/Omnimax process is part of a long tradition of 'mobile framing' in cinema, dating from the invention of the tracking shot in 1898 by Eugène Promio, the Lumière brothers' cameraman, and extending to the most up-to-date of dollies.

What I have written, as you might guess, is motivated less by interest in ideas and technologies than by a film experiment: *The Dream Is Alive*, shown at the Géode in memory of the crew of the space shuttle *Challenger*. Unlike *Kronos*, the Géode's inaugural presentation, Graeme Ferguson's film shows the geodesic auditorium at La Villette to its best advantage: confirming once again the fusional character of the Imax/Omnimax system, the importance of a logistics of perception which subjugates auditorium/stage and spectacle – and film maker, too – to its passengers of the moment, travellers in a cinematographic hemisphere.

The Dream Is Alive was directed by the inventor of the Omnimax system, president of Ferguson Keer Limited, in collaboration with NASA, the Lockheed Corporation and the Smithsonian Institution's National Air and Space Museum. The film allows us to see for ourselves, to verify – from the viewpoint of an orbital voyage of the shuttle – the myth of the participation of the image in the conquest of space. Like an experiment on the weightlessness actually experienced by astronauts in outer space, the filmic weightlessness of the Géode is an audiovisual simulation of another simulator, a vehicle whose real passengers contend that 'the feeling is very close to that experienced in the shuttle'.

Shot in the control cabin of the shuttle during a landing in Florida, the opening sequence of the film takes us back to base – the landing strip of the Kennedy Space Center – propelling us into a hemispheric screen before tearing us away again with the launch sequence in an immeasurable backwards tracking shot. Once in orbit, the Géode tips up, toppling like the earth and sky visible through the shuttle's portholes, the sky as blue as merging clouds and continents: convex surface of a planetary globe, projection screen for solar light, for these voyagers in outer space; concave surface of the Géode's own hemi-sphere for the attentive voyeurs we are.

To complete the comparison between audiovisual and automotive vehicles, we might note that whilst shooting was taking place aboard the shuttle, the film's production group was close to the control room at the Johnson Space Center in Houston, right next to the technicians in charge of the space mission. Inside the cabin itself, the central deck holding the shuttle crew, their working quarters, the weightless bodies confirm – despite the extremely cramped spaces where the astronauts constantly bump up against one another – the topological quality of this cinema. Back on earth, meanwhile, in ground control, a vast angular space, distortions of perspective limit sensation, bringing a definite unease to spectators' comfort. All of which is proof, if proof were needed, of the difficulties already touched on concerning framing and editing in this type of production. The film's soundtrack follows the action, the unfolding of sequences, the movements of objects and characters, from a multitude of speakers placed behind the screen: the sound itself becomes a stereophonic vector, a vehicle in the time-space of this trip around the Earth.

A theatre of impressive cinematic energy, the Géode is not exactly a cinema, more a boarding and landing strip – a 'cineport' for a trip minus the travelling, a journey on the spot: a time capsule like those of the comic-strip heroes of our childhood.

A word of advice: despite the huge crowds, don't book your seat in advance, don't go to La Villette. Don't worry: the Géode will come to you – tomorrow, the day after. Unlike you, it has all the time in the world.

PART V

Intertexts

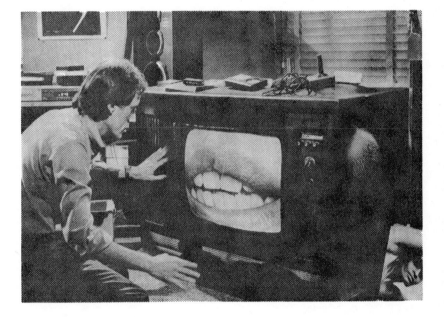

Any consideration of science fiction cinema's cultural instrumentality calls by definition for an awareness that films exist not in isolation, but in an active network of relations and practices. To understand what films. do, culturally, the question of intertextuality must necessarily be addressed. Colin McArthur's definition of intertextuality as 'the idea of works of art and discourses feeding off and dissolving into each other'[1] suggests that intertextuality works not just within and between cultural productions or texts ('works of art'), but also at the broader and perhaps more diffuse level of 'discourses'. The tendency for genre films to refer to each other as much as, or indeed more than, to the 'real world' has already been noted; in this sense, genres depend upon intertextuality. Science fiction films refer to other science fiction films simply by repeating and reworking the conventions of the genre. But increasingly in recent years, another kind of intertextuality has emerged, in the form of quotations from earlier science fiction films, quotations which purposefully draw attention to themselves, appealing overtly to the audience's 'cultural capital' of prior knowledge of the history of cinema. For example, in an explicit reference to Fritz Lang's *Metropolis* (1926), the science fiction sex comedy *Android* (1982) includes a scene in which a beautiful female robot is brought to life by a mad scientist.

Science fiction films also refer across to other film genres, either by deploying conventions commonly associated with these other genres; or by 'knowing' quotations from them. The former variant of intertextuality structures a very common generic hybrid, of which *Alien* (1979) is a prime example – the science fiction horror film; while the latter is clearly at work in a film like *Blade Runner* (1982), with its characteristically

film noir elements of world-weary detective hero, femme fatale, investigative narrative and *mise-en-scène* of mean city streets and shadowy
interiors. The quotation, the pastiche of codes, and the parody all
indicate that a postmodern sensibility is at work in certain forms of
intertextuality.

Films are also caught up, though, in discourses which operate beyond
the boundaries of text and genre. For one thing, film texts and genres are
part of that whole array of technologies, practices and pleasures that
comprises the 'machine' of cinema. The cinematic apparatus in turn
figures in a series of relations of commodification and exchange. As a
component of the cinematic apparatus, science fiction cinema is actively
– and in its own particular ways – involved in these relations. For
instance, as was noted in Part IV, science fiction cinema proposes
specific sorts of spectatorial relations, and is involved in particular
discourses of technology and relations of exchange.

Intertextuality challenges the distinction between representation and
the real which grounds certain strands of critical theory and informs a
good deal of critical work on science fiction cinema: most of the essays
in Parts I and II of this book, for example, premise their arguments in
one way or another on a representation-real distinction. Intertextuality
assumes, to the contrary, that every social practice is governed by
processes of signification – and so may be 'read' like a text. This view
undercuts the notion of the self-contained text: not by subordinating
representation to the real, but by 'textualizing' all aspects of the social. In
the same move, the distinction between representation and reality disappears, and the social formation becomes a system of interconnected
meanings. Such a view of the world is one of the defining features of the
postmodern condition, widely hailed as the 'cultural logic' of our age.[2]

Thus, for example, underlying Jean Baudrillard's notion of the insistence of simulacra as characteristic of the postmodern condition is an
evacuation of the real. Representations do not record, reflect or copy a
real world; all is simulacrum; and simulacra are copies without originals.[3] The world of simulacra is one of image, surface, an endless circuit
of intertextuality with no originating text, no basic reference point, no
escape to the real. While this might seem a nightmarish vision, some
critics have attributed to the postmodern condition a sense of excitement
– of delirium, if not exactly of liberation.

Contemporary science fiction cinema has been hailed as a privileged
cultural site for enactments of the postmodern condition – usually in its
more nightmarish aspects. Postmodernism is a slippery concept, and in
the 1980s has become a buzzword applied to a wide range of cultural
phenomena, from architecture, to urban life, to media technologies and
cultural productions, as well as to what Raymond Williams called – in an

entirely different register – 'structures of feeling'. It has even been
suggested that, as mass culture becomes ever more postmodern, distinctions between science fiction and other forms actually break down.[4] It
follows from this that writings on science fiction cinema which appeal,
implicitly or explicitly, to notions of postmodernity have constituted
their object in a whole variety of ways. One important line of division
between different approaches follows the useful distinction between
texts *about* postmodernism and texts *of* postmodernism. In the former,
postmodernism – variously understood – informs the thematics, the
enounced, of the text; while in the latter it structures its very enunciation and relations of reading.

Giuliana Bruno's essay below offers a reading of *Blade Runner* which
proposes in effect that, in the specific qualities of its *mise-en-scène* and
narrative, the film is actually about postmodernism. It *signifies* the postmodern condition especially in its organization of the world of the fiction
– the city, a Los Angeles of the not-too-distant future; and in its narrative enactment of simulation. The film's story is about the hunting
down of a group of outlaw humanoids called replicants, 'the perfect
simulacra', who – as characters – embody the peculiarly postmodern
state of schizophrenia. A number of critics have noted the recurrence in
recent science fiction cinema of stories hingeing on 'human artifice',
including instances in which the integrity of the human 'original' is called
into question, as it is in *Blade Runner*.[5] Does the postmodern quality of
this film go any further than such thematics, however? In its relentless
references to the history of cinema and quotations from classical film
genres, *Blade Runner* is certainly, as Bruno points out, marked by that
quality of pastiche – 'an aesthetic of quotations pushed to the limit' –
which is regarded as one of the defining features of postmodernism. In
the degree to which it addresses spectators as knowledgeable about
cinema, pastiche can be a mode of enunciation as well as a feature of
textual organization: but pastiche as enunciation proposes for the spectator a position of stability and mastery – over a text which in this case,
paradoxically enough, offers itself as a metaphor for the postmodern
condition, with all its uncertainties.

A text of postmodernism, as against a text about postmodernism,
would actually produce, rather than signify, the postmodern condition –
through an enunciation proposing an absence of reference points in the
real, or even performing the schizophrenia held to be characteristic of
the postmodern condition. Scott Bukatman suggests in his essay 'Who
Programs You? The Science Fiction of the Spectacle' that the film
Videodrome (1982) – a 'stunning hypostatization of the concerns of
postmodern culture' – does precisely these things. In its enunciation, this
science fiction horror film provides no stable viewpoint from which to

judge what is 'really' happening in the story, and the image itself
constantly proves unreliable: the spectator is not 'told' what is the hero's
hallucination and what is 'reality'. Indeed, the very distinction between
hallucination and reality breaks down: discourse itself is placed in
question through the estrangement of cinematic language. In this reading
of *Videodrome*, the film is not analysed as it were in isolation, but as part
of an entire system of meanings and practices in the 'society of the
spectacle' where life dissolves into media (and vice versa), and new
forms of subjectivity are produced.

The postmodern condition, in this view, extends intertextuality into
our very identities. The self loses the coherence of the humanist 'I',
becomes split, fragmented, schizophrenic. Alice Jardine has proposed
that this fragmented subjectivity has always existed in the interstices of
Western thought – but as a gap or space coded 'feminine'. Modernity –
the postmodern condition – valorizes, perhaps universalizes, this state,
for which Jardine has coined the term *gynesis*: a 'putting into discourse
of "woman" as that *process* ... intrinsic to the condition of modernity'.[6]
Barbara Creed, taking up Jardine's feminist intervention in the postmodernism debate, and following up her own discussion (in Part III) of
the monstrous-feminine in science fiction cinema, here discusses the
figuration of gynesis in the science fiction horror film.[7]

Creed contends that gynesis is at work in films which, through narrative theme and/or enunciation, put into crisis the subject, the body and
the unconscious, constituting them as at risk from dangerous and unpredictable technologies. The female body, for example, 'through the
process of gynesis, has come to signify the spaces of the unknown, the
terrifying, the monstrous'. Science fiction films whose narratives hinge
on 'becoming a woman' play on this terror, argues Creed. Among a
number of other films, Creed looks at *Videodrome*, concurring with
Bukatman that this film banishes boundaries and distinctions (hallucin-
ation/reality, self/other, and so on) in truly postmodern fashion. She
adds, though, that this may be assimilated to processes of gynesis, for the
film narrativizes the hero's assumption of qualities of femininity, whilst
constructing femininity as 'the ultimate scenario of powerlessness, the
ultimate violation of the body'.

If all this seems rather gloomy, it is indeed the case that most critical
commentary on the postmodern condition has embraced a pessimistic
view: one in fact which seems to have a natural affinity with the
apocalyptic tone of a great deal of science fiction film criticism – of the
reflectionist, as much as of the postmodern, sort. At the same time,
however, the fragmentation and unfixity of the postmodern condition
might propose, exactly in the anxiety over lost certainties, a kind of
delirium, a *jouissance*. Is there any progressive or liberatory potential in

this aspect of postmodernity? And if there is, how might it be expressed in critical theory – or indeed in film practice?

In Donna Haraway's 'Manifesto for Cyborgs', the *jouissance* of the postmodern condition infuses a text which both describes and celebrates the fragmentation of subjectivities and dissolution of boundaries which mark that condition. Using the image of the cyborg – cybernetic organism, fusion of human and machine – as emblematic of a fiction mapping our social and bodily reality, Haraway's text looks forward to a breakthrough to new socialist-feminist understandings of a world in which technology may offer the possibility of 'transgressed boundaries, potent fusions and dangerous possibilities'.[8] The manifesto also describes, and enacts, the very intertextuality inherent in such a vision. The world of cyborgs is an 'integrated circuit' of technologies, images, simulacra and social relations, in which all fixed notions of subjectivity and difference are banished.

If film and the cinematic apparatus occupy a place in the network of Haraway's integrated circuit, how might they be conceptualized, how put to use, there? Haraway does not discuss cinema in her manifesto, but she does look at writings which explore 'what it means to be embodied in high-tech worlds'. Among these are feminist science fictions which question 'the statuses of man or woman, human, artifact, member of a race, individual identity, or body'.[9] In theme and enunciation, this science fiction writing is far indeed from the high-tech dystopias and fears of otherness which, according to so many critics, mark contemporary science fiction cinema. It celebrates the gaps and spaces of gynesis in a utopian postmodern play of boundaries and identities, looking forward to an altogether new political language.

In this context, a number of critics have suggested that postmodernism does have a degree of oppositional potential, in that minority and marginal social groups (the working class, ethnic minorities, homosexuals, women) have seized on the junked meanings of the very culture that marginalizes them – not endlessly to recycle these meanings in an inward-looking aesthetic of pastiche, but to make a lively and vibrant critique of them.[10] Much feminist science fiction writing – which with justification might be counted amongst such marginal cultural practices – produces texts of postmodernism, writerly texts in which fragmentation and estrangement are translated from schizophrenia to utopia. Assuming that critique and *jouissance* can indeed together inhabit postmodernism, how might such a sensibility and such a politics inflect a feminist practice of science fiction *cinema*?

If feminist science fiction cinema does not yet exist, the moment of its invention might well be at hand – signalling transformations in both women's cinema and science fiction cinema. In discussing such possibilities. Anne Cranny-Francis, in 'Feminist Futures', refers back to some of the generic conventions of science fiction writing touched on in the introduction to this volume. Her concern, principally, is with feminist science fiction writing's distinctive conventions – including, perhaps, its utopian variants of estrangement; and she suggests that these conventions will be – or certainly ought to be – active amongst the various intertexts of feminist science fiction cinema.

Such a cinema should speak the new political language predicted in Donna Haraway's manifesto, embodying the political form of post-modernism called for by Fredric Jameson.[11] In doing so, this radically new political art, postmodern in its appropriateness to the moment of late capitalism, will engage with – struggle with – the positionalities held out to us by the society of the spectacle; not in order to reinstate the coherence of bourgeois humanist subjectivity, but to celebrate and empower the multiplicity of the marginalized, the colonized, subject.

Notes

1. In Len Masterman, ed., *Television Mythologies: Stars, Shows and Signs*, London: Comedia 1985, p. 64.
2. See, for example, Fredric Jameson, 'Postmodernism, or the Cultural Logic of Late Capitalism', *New Left Review*, no. 146, 1984.
3. Jean Baudrillard, 'The Precession of Simulacra' in *Simulations*, trans. Paul Foss and others, New York: Semiotext(e) 1983.
4. Andrew Gordon, 'Science-fiction Film Criticism: The Postmodern Always Rings Twice', *Science Fiction Studies*, vol. 14, no. 3, 1987.
5. See, for example, J.P. Telotte, 'Human Artifice and the Science Fiction Film', *Film Quarterly*, vol. 36, no. 3, 1983; and Telotte's essay in this volume, 'The Doubles of Fantasy and the Space of Desire'.
6. Alice Jardine, *Gynesis: Configurations of Woman and Modernity*, Ithaca, NY: Cornell University Press 1985, p. 25.
7. Creed's essay here is extracted from a much longer article, 'From Here to Modernity: Feminism and Postmodernism', *Screen*, vol. 28, no. 2, 1987. On feminism and postmodernism, see the introduction and bibliography in Meaghan Morris, *The Pirate's Fiancée: Feminism Reading Postmodernism*, London: Verso 1988.
8. Donna Haraway, 'A Manifesto for Cyborgs: Science, Technology and Socialist-feminism in the 1980s', *Socialist Review*, no. 80, 1985, p. 71. See also Anne Balsamo, 'Reading Cyborgs Writing Feminism', *Communication*, vol. 10, nos 3–4, 1988.
9. Haraway, pp. 92, 97. On feminist science fiction writing, see also Jean Pfaelzer, 'The Changing of the Avant-garde: the Feminist Utopia', *Science Fiction Studies*, vol. 15, no. 3, 1988.
10. See, for example, Angela McRobbie, 'Postmodernism and Popular Culture' in Lisa Appignanesi, ed., *Postmodernism: ICA Documents*, London: Free Association Books 1989.
11. Jameson, 'Postmodernism, or the Cultural Logic of Late Capitalism', p. 92. See also Vivian Sobchack, *The Limits of Infinity: the American Science Fiction Film*, New York: Ungar 1987, p. 304.

15

Ramble City: Postmodernism and *Blade Runner*

Giuliana Bruno

> History is hysterical: it is constituted only if we consider it, only if we look at it – and in order to look at it we must be excluded from it ... That is what the time when my mother was alive *before me* is – History. No anamnesis could ever make me glimpse this time starting from myself – whereas, contemplating a photograph in which she is hugging me, a child, against her, I can waken in myself the rumpled softness of her crepe de Chine and the perfume of her rice powder.[1]

That is history for Roland Barthes and history for the replicants of *Blade Runner* (1982). The replicants are perfect 'skin jobs', they look like humans, they talk like them, they even have feelings and emotions (in science fiction the ultimate sign of the human). What they lack is a history. For that they have to be killed. Seeking a history, fighting for it, they search for their origins, for that time before themselves. Rachael succeeds. She has a document – as we know, the foundation of history. Her document is a photograph, a photograph of her mother, hugging her, a child, against her, wakening in her the rumpled softness of, most probably, a hamburger. History is hysterical; it is constituted only if we *look* at it, excluded from it. That is, my mother before me – history. History/Mother/My mother. 'My mother? I'll tell you about my mother . . .'.[2]

The debate on postmodernism has by now produced a vast literature. Roughly, we might distinguish three positions: one elaborated with reference to the human sciences and literature, by Jean-François Lyotard and Umberto Eco, among others; one concerning the visual arts, recently developed in particular in the US; and one related to the discourse of and on architecture.[3] It is the latter which, for the most part, constitutes the theoretical groundwork for this paper, in which *Blade Runner* will be discussed as a metaphor of the postmodern condition. I wish to analyse, in particular, the representation of narrative space and temporality in *Blade Runner*. For this I will use two terms, pastiche and schizophrenia, in order to define and explore the two areas of investigation. The terms are borrowed and developed from Fredric Jameson's discussion of postmodernism. In this essay 'Postmodernism and Consumer Society'[4] and in the later, expanded version, 'Postmodernism, or the Cultural Logic of Late Capitalism',[5] Jameson suggests that the postmodern condition is characterized by a schizophrenic temporality and a spatial pastiche. The notion of schizophrenia which Jameson employs is that elaborated by Jacques Lacan. According to Jameson's reading of Lacan, schizophrenia is basically a breakdown of the relationship between signifiers, linked to the failure of access to the Symbolic. With pastiche there is an effacement of key boundaries and separations, a process of erosion of distinctions. Pastiche is intended as an aesthetic of quotations pushed to the limit; it is an incorporation of forms, an imitation of dead styles deprived of any satirical impulse. Jameson's suggestion has proved a viable working reference and a guideline in analysing the deployment of space and time in the film. Pastiche and schizophrenia will thus act, in the economy of my argument, as what Umberto Eco calls umbrella terms, operational linguistic covers of vast and even diverse areas of concern. My discussion of postmodernism and *Blade Runner* will involve a consideration of questions of identity and history, of the role of simulacra and simulation, and of the relationship between postmodernism, architecture, and postindustrialism.

It is useful to note that Jameson has derived his view of postmodernism from the field of architecture: 'It is in the realm of architecture ... that modifications in aesthetic productions are most dramatically visible, and that their theoretical problems have been most centrally raised and articulated; it was indeed from architectural debates that my own conception of postmodernism began to emerge'.[6] It is in the architectural layout of *Blade Runner* that pastiche is most dramatically visible and where the connection of postmodernism to postindustrialism is evident.

The film does not take place in a spaceship or space station, but in a city, Los Angeles, in the year 2019, a step away from the development of contemporary society. The link between postmodernism and late capitalism is highlighted in the film's representation of postindustrial decay. The future does not realize an idealized, aseptic technological order, but is seen simply as the development of the present state of the city and of the social order of late capitalism. The city of *Blade Runner* is not the ultramodern, but the postmodern city. It is not an orderly layout of skyscrapers and ultracomfortable, hypermechanized interiors. Rather, it creates an aesthetic of decay, exposing the dark side of technology, the process of disintegration.

Next to the high-tech, its waste. It is into garbage that the characters constantly step, by garbage that Pris awaits J.F. Sebastian. A deserted neighbourhood in decay is where Deckard goes to find the peace he needs in order to work. There he finds the usual gang of metropolitan punks exploring the ruins for unexpected marvels. In an abandoned, deteriorating building, J.F. Sebastian lives surrounded by nothing but his mechanical toys. It is a building of once great majesty, now an empty shell left to disintegrate. The rain completes the ambiance. It falls persistently, veiling the landscape of the city, further obscuring the neobaroque lighting. It is a corrosive rain which wears things away.

The postindustrial decay is an effect of the acceleration of the internal time of process proper to postindustrialism. The system works only if waste is produced. The continuous expulsion of waste is an indexical sign of the well-functioning apparatus: waste represents its production, movement, and development at increasing speed. Postindustrialism recycles; therefore it needs its waste.[7] A postmodern position exposes such logic, producing an aesthetic of recycling. The artistic form exhibits the return of the waste. Consumerism, waste, and recycling meet in fashion, the 'wearable art' of late capitalism, a sign of postmodernism. Costumes in *Blade Runner* are designed according to this logic. The 'look' of the replicants Pris and Zhora and of some of the women in the background in the bar and in the street scenes reinforces this aesthetic. Pris, the 'basic pleasure model', is the model of the postindustrial fashion, the height of exhibition and recycling.

The postmodern aesthetic of *Blade Runner* is thus the result of recycling, fusion of levels, discontinuous signifiers, explosion of boundaries, and erosion. The disconnected temporality of the replicants and the pastiche city are all an effect of a postmodern, postindustrial condition: wearing out, waste. There is even a character in the film who is nothing but a literalization of this condition. J.F. Sebastian is twenty-five years old, but his skin is wrinkled and decrepit. His internal process and time are accelerated, and he is wearing out. 'Accelerated decrepitude' is how the replicant Pris describes his condition, noting that he and the replicants have something in common. What Pris does not say is that the city suffers from it as well. The psychopathology of J.F. Sebastian, the replicants, and the city is the psychopathology of the everyday postindustrial condition. The increased speed of development and process produces the diminishing of distances, of the space in between, of distinction. Time and tempo are reduced to climax, after which there is retirement. Things cease to function and life is over even if it has not ended. The postindustrial city is a city in ruins.

In *Blade Runner*, the visions of postindustrial decay are set in an inclusive, hybrid architectural design. The city is called Los Angeles, but it is an LA that looks very much like New York, Hong Kong, or Tokyo. We are not presented with a real geography, but an imaginary one: a synthesis of mental architectures, of *topoi*. Quoting from different real cities, postcards, advertising, movies, the text makes a point about the city of postindustrialism. It is a polyvalent, interchangeable structure, the product of geographical displacements and condensations. *Blade Runner*'s space of narration bears, superimposed, different and previous orders of time and space. It incorporates them, exhibiting their trans-formations and deterioration. It is a place of vast immigration, from countries of overpopulation and poverty. While immigrants crowd the city, the indigenous petit bourgeoisie moves to the suburbs or to the 'off-world' as the case may be. Abandoned buildings and neighbourhoods in decay adjoin highly populated, crowded old areas, themselves set next to new, high-tech business districts. The film is populated by eclectic crowds of faceless people. Oriental merchants, punks, Hare Krishnas. Even the language is pastiche: 'city speech' is a 'mish-mash of Japanese, Spanish, German, what have you'. The city is a large market; an intrigue of underground networks pervades all relations. The explosive Orient dominates, the Orient of yesterday incorporating the Orient of today. Overlooking the city is the 'Japanese simulacrum', the huge advertise-ment which alternates a seductive Japanese face and a Coca Cola sign. In the postindustrial city the explosion of urbanization, melting the futuristic high-tech look into an intercultural scenario, recreates the Third World inside the first. One travels almost without moving, for the Orient occupies the next block. The Los Angeles of *Blade Runner* is China(in)town.

The pertinence and uniqueness of architecture to specific places, cultures, and times has been lost in postmodernism. The metropolis of *Blade Runner* quotes not only from different spatial structures but from temporal ones as well. The syntactic rules are broken down in post-modernism and replaced by a parataxis, a regulated aesthetic of lists. The connections are not made at random, but ruled by a different logic. It is the logic of pastiche, which allows and promotes quotations of a synchronic and diachronic order.

The resultant hybrid balances and reconciles opposed meanings. . . . This inclu-sive architecture absorbs conflicting codes in an attempt to create (what

Robert Venturi calls) 'the difficult whole'. . . . It can include ugliness, decay, banality, austerity. . . . In general terms it can be described as radical eclecticism or adhocism. Various parts, styles or sub-systems are used to create a new synthesis.[8]

In *Blade Runner* recollections and quotations from the past are subcodes of a new synthesis.[9] Roman and Greek columns provide a retro *mise-en-scène* for the city. Signs of classical Oriental mythology recur. Chinese dragons are revisited in neon lighting. A strong Egyptian element pervades the decor. The Tyrell corporation overlooks what resemble the Egyptian pyramids in a full sunset. The interior of the office is not high-tech, but rather a pop Egyptian extravaganza, to which the choreography of movement and makeup of Zhora adds exoticism. Elevators might have video screens, but they are made of stone. The walls of Deckard's apartment are reminiscent of an ancient Mayan palace. Pastiche, as an aesthetic of quotation, incorporates dead styles; it attempts a recollection of the past, of memory, and of history.

The result of this architectural pastiche is an excess of scenography. Every relation in the narrative space produces an exhibitionism rather than an aesthetics of the visual. The excess of violence is such an exhibitionism. The iconography of death as well is scenographic. The 'scene' of death becomes a sort of 'obscenity', the site of total, transparent visibility. The fight and death of Pris are rendered as a performance. Zhora dies breaking through a window in slow motion. The decor, the choreography of movement and editing, the neobaroque cinematography emphasize visual virtuosity. It has been said that scenography is the domain of postmodern architecture. Paolo Portoghesi claims that

> Postmodern in architecture can be generally read as the re-emerging of the archetypes and the reintegrations of the architectural conventions and thus as the premise for the creation of an architecture of communication, an architecture of the visual, for a culture of the visual.[10]

Pastiche and the exhibitionism of the visual celebrate the dominance of representation and the effacement of the referent in the era of postindustrialism. The postindustrial society is the 'society of the spectacle', living in the 'ecstasy of communication'. Addressing this aspect of postmodernism, Jean Baudrillard speaks of a twist in the relationship between the real and its reproduction. The process of reproducibility is pushed to the limit. As a result, 'the real is not what can be reproduced, but that which is always already reproduced ... the hyperreal ... which is entirely in simulation'.[11] The narrative space of *Blade Runner* participates in this logic: 'All of Los Angeles ... is of the order of hyperreal and simulation.'[12] There, the machinery of imitations, reproductions, and seriality, in other words, 'replicants', affirms the fiction of the real.

The narrative 'invention' of the replicants is almost a literalization of Baudrillard's theory of postmodernism as the age of simulacra and simulation. Replicants are the perfect simulacra – a convergence of genetics and linguistics, the generic miniaturization enacting the dimension of simulation. Baudrillard describes the simulacrum as 'an operational double, a metastable, programmatic, perfect descriptive machine which provides all the signs of the real and short-circuits all its vicissitudes'.[13] It would be difficult to find a better definition of the nature and functions of the replicants and their capacity of simulation in the narrative motivation of *Blade Runner*. In LA, year 2019, simulation is completely dominant as the effect of the existence and operations of the replicant/simulacrum. 'The unreal is no longer that of dream or of fantasy or a beyond or a within, it is that of *hallucinatory resemblance of the real with itself*.'[14] The replicant performs such hallucinatory resemblance. 'It' looks and acts like a he or a she. Perfect simulation is thus its goal, and Rachael manages to reach it. To simulate, in fact, is a more complex act than to imitate or to feign. To simulate implies actually producing in oneself some of the characteristics of what one wants to simulate. It is a matter of internalizing the signs or the symptoms to the point where there is no difference between 'false' and 'true', 'real' and 'imaginary'. With Rachael the system has reached perfection. She is the most perfect replicant because she does not know whether she is one or not. To say that she simulates her symptoms, her sexuality, her memory, is to say that she realizes, experiences them.

The fascination with the simulacrum has, of course, generated narratives before *Blade Runner*. We find in *Der Sandmann*, for example, one of the most influential fictional descriptions of simulacra. It is this tale, in fact, which inspired Freud's reflections on the uncanny. *Der Sandmann* concerns the android Olympia, who is such a perfect 'skin job' that she is mistaken for a real girl, the daughter of her inventor. The protagonist of the tale, Nathaniel, falls in love with her, but reality triumphs: the android is unmasked and destroyed. In Hoffmann's time, replication is still a question of imitation, for the real still bears a meaning. The replicants of *Blade Runner* are, on the contrary, as the name itself indicates, serial terms. No original is thus invoked as point of comparison, and no distinction between real and copy remains.

It is, indeed, in simulation that the power of the replicants resides. Since the simulacrum is the negation of both original and copy, it is ultimately the celebration of the false as power and the power of the false.[15] The replicants turn this power against their makers to assert the autonomy of the simulacrum.

But these replicants, 'simulacra' of humans, in some ways superior to them, have a problem: a fragmented temporality. 'Schizophrenic vertigo of these serial signs ... immanent in their repetition – who could say what the reality is that these signs simulate?'[16] The replicant affirms a new form of temporality, that of schizophrenic vertigo. This is the temporality of postmodernism's new age of the machine. The industrial machine was one of production, the postindustrial machine, one of reproduction. A major shift occurs: the alienation of the subject is replaced by the fragmentation of the subject, its dispersal in representation. The 'integrity' of the subject is more deeply put into question. Baudrillard describes the postindustrial age thus:

> We are now in a new form of schizophrenia. No more hysteria, no more projective paranoia, but this state of terror proper to the schizophrenic.... The schizophrenic can no longer produce the limits of its own being.... He is only a pure screen.[17]

A replicant.

Blade Runner presents a manifestation of the schizophrenic condition – in the sense that Lacan gives this term. For Lacan, temporality, past, present, future, memory are of a linguistic order: that is to say, the experience of temporality and its representation are an effect of language. It is the very structure of language that allows us to know temporality as we do and to represent it as a linear development from past to present and future. The experience of historical continuity is therefore dependent upon language acquisition, upon access to the realm of speech. It is dependent upon the acceptance of the Name-of-the-Father, paternal authority conceived as a linguistic function.

Schizophrenia, on the other hand, results from a failure to enter the Symbolic order; it is thus essentially a breakdown of language, which contributes to a breakdown of the temporal order. The schizophrenic condition is characterized by the inability to experience the persistence of the 'I' over time. There is neither past nor future at the two poles of that which thus becomes a perpetual present. Jameson writes, 'The schizophrenic does not have our experience of temporal continuity but is condemned to live a perpetual present with which the various moments of his or her past have little connection and for which there is no conceivable future on the horizon'.[18] Replicants are condemned to a life composed only of a present tense; they have neither past nor memory. There is for them no conceivable future. They are denied a personal identity, since they cannot name their 'I' as an existence over time. Yet this life, lived only in the present, is for the replicants an extremely intense experience, since it is not perceived as part of a larger set of experiences. Replicants represent themselves as a candle that burns faster but brighter and claim to have seen more things with their eyes in that limited time than anybody else would even be able to imagine. This kind of relationship to the present is typical of schizophrenia. Jameson notes, in fact, that 'as temporal continuity breaks down, the experience of the present becomes powerfully, overwhelmingly vivid and "material". The world comes before the schizophrenic with heightened intensity'.[19]

The schizophrenic temporality of the replicants is a resistance to enter the social order, to function according to its modes.[20] As outsiders to the order of language, replicants have to be eliminated. Theirs is a dangerous malfunction, calling for a normalization, an affirmation of the order of language and law. Their killing constitutes a state murder. It is called 'retirement', a word which connotes exclusion from the productive and active social order.

If the replicants are to survive, the signifiers of their existence have to be put in order. Some semblance of a symbolic dimension has to be put together to release them from the trap of the present. Their assurance of a future relies on the possibility of acquiring a past. In their attempt at establishing a temporally persistent identity, the replicants search for their origins. They want to know who 'conceived' them, and they investigate their identity and the link to their makers. The itinerary is that of an Oedipal journey. To survive for a time, the android has to accept the fact of sexual difference, the sexual identity which the entry into language requires.

Of all the replicants, only one, Rachael, succeeds in making the journey. She assumes a sexual identity, becomes a woman, and loves a man: Deckard, the blade runner. Rachael accepts the paternal figure and follows the path to a 'normal', adult, female, sexuality: she identifies her sex by first acknowledging the power of the other, the father, a man. But the leader of the replicants, Roy Batty, refuses the symbolic castration which is necessary to enter the symbolic order; he refuses, that is, to be smaller, less powerful, than the father. Roy commits the Oedipal crime. He kills his father; and the Oedipal topos of blindness recurs, reversed. Roy thus seals his (lack of) destiny, denying himself resolution and salvation.

In this tension between pre-Oedipal and Oedipal, Imaginary and Symbolic, the figure of the the mother becomes a breaking point in the text. Replicants can be unmasked by a psychological test which reveals their emotional responses as dissimilar to those of humans.[21] *Blade Runner* begins with such a test as it is being administered to Leon, a replicant who is trying to hide his identity. Leon succeeds up to a certain point, but there arises a question which he cannot handle. Asked to name all the good things that come to his mind thinking about his mother, Leon explodes, 'My mother, I'll tell you about my mother', and kills the inquirer. The mother is necessary to the claiming of a history, to the affirmation of an identity over time. Unmasked by the same test, Rachael goes to her inquirer, Deckard, to convince him, or herself rather, that she is not a replicant. Her argument is a photograph, a photograph of a mother and daughter. 'Look, this is me, with my mother.' That photograph represents the trace of an origin and thus a personal identity, the proof of having existed and therefore of having the right to exist.

A theoretical link is established in *Blade Runner* between photography, mother, and history. It is a connection that we also find in Barthes's writings on photography. In *Camera Lucida*, reflections on photography are centred on the figure of the mother as she relates to the question of history. Photography and the mother are the missing link between past, present, and future. The terms of the configuration photography/mother/history are knotted together in dialectics of totality and division, presence and absence, continuity and discontinuity.

The name of Photography's noeme will therefore be 'that-has-been,' or again the Intractable. In Latin, this would doubtless be said: *interfuit*: what I see has been there, and yet immediately separated; it has been absolutely, irrefutably present, and yet already deferred.[22]

As a document of 'that-has-been', photography constitutes a document of history, of its deferred existence. A history conceived as hysterical is established only in an act of exclusion, in a look that separates subject and object. History is that time when my mother was alive before me. It is the trace of the dream of unity, of its impossibility. The all-nourishing mother is there, yet as that which has been given up. The Imaginary exists as a loss.

Photographs are documents of existence in a history to be transformed into memories, monuments of the past. Such is the very challenge of history, as Michel Foucault has pointed out. 'History is that which transforms documents into monuments.'[23] The document is for Foucault a central question of history; for *Blade Runner* it is the essential element for the establishment of a temporality, of perceiving past and future. Foucault defines history as 'one way in which a society recognizes and develops a mass of documentation with which it is inextricably linked'.[24] Photographs can be such documentation for the replicants. Not only does Rachael exhibit her document-photograph of that past moment with her mother, but she is fascinated by photographs generally. In a second visit to Deckard, she produces her memories in response to his photographs. She attempts to look like the woman in his old photograph, and plays the piano to recapture a memory, an atmosphere. Leon's preciously kept pictures serve no apparent purpose other than the documentation of the replicant's existence in history. Deckard understands this motivation when he finds the photos. 'I don't know why replicants would collect photos. Maybe they were like Rachael, they needed memories.'

The desire of photography in *Blade Runner* is essentially a phenomenological seduction: 'In photography I can never deny that "the thing has been there". There is a superimposition here of reality and of the past.'[25] Photography is perceived as the medium in which the signifier and the referent are collapsed onto each other. Photographs assert the referent, its reality, in that they assert its existence at that (past) moment when the person, the thing, was there in front of the camera. If a replicant is in a photograph, he or she is thus real.

The function of photography in film's temporal construction is further grasped in Barthes's observation that

> the photograph's immobility is the result of perverse confusion between two concepts: the Real and the Live. By attesting that the object has been real, the photograph surreptitiously induces belief that it is alive. . . . Photography, moreover, began historically as an art of the Person: of civil status, of what we might call, in all senses of the term, the body's formality.[26]

Replicants rely on photography for its perverse confusion, as it induces the surreptitious belief and hope of being alive.

Investigating the other side of the body's formality and the civil status of the replicants, blade runners also make use of photography. Once Deckard finds the photographs/documents in Leon's apartment, he proceeds by questioning them. History as a process of investigation is involved in a questioning of the document.

> History now organizes the document, divides it up, distributes it, orders it, arranges it in levels, establishes series, distinguishes between what is relevant and what is not, discovers elements, defines unities, describes relations.[27]

Foucault's description of the historical process exactly describes the way in which Deckard interrogates the documents/photographs producing history. Deckard puts a photograph in a video machine to analyse it. The photograph is decomposed and restructured visually through the creation of new relations, shifting the direction of the gaze, zooming in and out, selecting and rearranging elements, creating closeups of what is relevant. The dissected and reorganized signifiers of photography result in a narrative. At work is the same process of investigation and detection

that we find in *Blow-up*: the serialization of the still image, the photograph, produces a new meaning, a story, a filmic text. The revelation of
the secret is an effect of the sequentialization, and thus narrativization,
of the still image. This is how and why the murder is discovered in *Blow-
up* and the replicant Zhora is discovered in *Blade Runner*. Searching the
document/photograph, Deckard unveils the investigative and narrative
process of history. *Blow-up* stops at the level of the signifier of photography; *Blade Runner* wants to believe in its referent: Zhora has-been-
there; therefore she is (to be captured) real and alive. Not far off is
Barthes's comment, 'I went to the photographer's show as to a police
investigation'.[28]

Blade Runner posits questions of identity, identification, and history in
postmodernism. The text's insistence on photography, on the eye, is
suggestive of the problematics of the 'I' over time. Photography, 'the
impossible science of the unique being', is the suppressed trace of
history, the lost dream of continuity. Photography is memory. The status
of memory has changed. In a postmodern age, memories are no longer
Proustian madeleines, but photographs. The past has become a collection of photographic, filmic, or televisual images. We, like the replicants,
are put in the position of reclaiming a history by means of its reproduction. Photography is thus assigned the grand task of reasserting the
referent, of reappropriating the Real and historical continuity. The
historical referent is displaced by a photographic referent. In a world of
fragmented temporality the research of history finds its image, its photographic simulacrum, while history itself remains out of reach. Schizophrenia and the logic of the simulacrum have had an effect on historical
time. The meaning of history is changed, and changed too is the representation in which history, forever unattainable, merely exists.[29]

The loss of history enacts a desire for historicity, an (impossible)
return to it. Postmodernism, particularly in art and architecture,
proclaims such a return to history as one of its goals. It is, however, the
instantiation of a new form of historicity. It is an eclectic one, a historical
pastiche. Pastiche is ultimately a redemption of history, which implies
the transformation and reinterpretation in tension between loss and
desire. It retraces history, deconstructing its order, uniqueness, specificity, and diachrony. Again, as with the photographic reconstitution, with
the logic of pastiche, a simulacrum of history is established.

A tension is expressed in *Blade Runner* between the radical loss of
durée and the attempt of reappropriation. This very tension, which seeks
in the photographic signifier the fiction of history and which rewrites
history by means of architectural pastiched recycling, underlies as well
the psychoanalytic itinerary: an itinerary suspended between schizo-

phrenia, a fragmented temporality, and the acceptance of the Name-of-the-Father, standing for temporal continuity and access to the order of signifiers.

Notes

1. Roland Barthes, *Camera Lucida*, trans. Richard Howard, New York: Hill and Wang 1981, p. 65.

2. Thus answers the replicant Leon when asked about his mother. He then kills his questioner.

3. The literature is by now extensive, if not particularly distinguished. See, for example, Robert Venturi, Denise Scott Brown and Steven Izenour, *Learning from Las Vegas*, Cambridge, MA: MIT Press 1977; Charles Jencks, *The Language of Postmodern Architecture*, New York: Rizzoli 1977; Paolo Portoghesi, *Postmodern l'Architettura nella societa postindustriale*, Milan: Electa 1982.

4. Fredric Jameson, 'Postmodernism and Consumer Society' in Hal Foster, ed., *The Anti-Aesthetic*, Port Townsend: Bay Press 1983, pp. 111–25.

5. Fredric Jameson, 'Postmodernism, or the Cultural Logic of Late Capitalism', *New Left Review*, no. 146, 1984.

6. Ibid., p. 54.

7. On the history of waste, see Dominique Laporte, *Histoire de la merde*, Paris: Christian Bourgeois 1978. Laporte traces the history of waste as a cyclic process of repression and return.

8. Jencks, p. 90.

9. Among other elements, the city of *Blade Runner* includes a set called 'New York Street', built in 1929 and used in a number of Humphrey Bogart and James Cagney movies; and the Ennis-Brown house designed by Frank Lloyd Wright.

10 Portoghesi, p. 11.

11. Jean Baudrillard, *Simulations*, trans. Paul Foss, Paul Patton and Philip Beitchman, New York: Semiotext(e) 1983, p. 146.

12. Ibid., p. 25.

13. Ibid., p. 4.

14. Ibid., p. 142. See also Guy Debord, *The Society of the Spectacle*, Detroit: Black and Red Press 1983.

15. For this aspect of the theoretical discussion of the simulacrum, see Gilles Deleuze, 'Plato and the Simulacrum', trans. Rosalind Krauss, *October*, no. 27, 1983.

16. Baudrillard, p. 152.

17. Jean Baudrillard, 'The Ecstasy of Communication', trans. John Johnston, in *The Anti-Aesthetic*, p. 132.

18. Jameson, 'Postmodernism and Consumer Society', p. 119.

19. Ibid., p. 120.

20. Jameson states that 'schizophrenia emerges from the failure of the infant to accede fully into the realm of speech and language' (ibid., p. 118).

21. A further observation on schizophrenia is made in regard to the test. In the novel from which *Blade Runner* was adapted (Philip K. Dick, *Do Androids Dream of Electric Sheep?*, New York: Ballantine Books 1982), a moral question arises from the possibility that humans might be 'retired' by mistake. It is proved, in fact, that a certain 'type' of human responds to the test in the same way as replicants. This type is the schizophrenic. Thus replicants and schizophrenics are 'scientifically' proved to be the same.

22. Barthes, p. 77.

23. Michel Foucault, *The Archaeology of Knowledge*, trans. A.M. Sheridan Smith, New York: Pantheon 1982, p. 7.

24. Ibid.

25. Barthes, p. 76.

26. Ibid., p. 79.

27. Foucault, p. 6.

28. Barthes, p. 85.

29. The debate on questions of memory and history in postmodernism is well represented in the special issue on 'Modernity and Post-Modernity' of *New German Critique*, no. 33, 1984.

16

Who Programs You? The Science Fiction of the Spectacle

Scott Bukatman

We are living in the era of the blip, what Alvin Toffler has labelled *blip culture*.[1] Toffler has written of our bombardment by these 'short, modular blips of information',[2] but for others the blip is more pervasive and more crucial in its implications. Into the 1990s, the human subject has become a blip: ephemeral, electronically processed, unreal.[3] Numerous writers have noted this implosion, the passage of experiential reality into the grids, matrices and pulses of the electronic information age. Exploration outward has been superseded by the inward spiral of orbital circulation – in cybernetic terms, the feedback loop. The world has been reconstituted as a simulation within the mega-computer banks of the Information Society, and terminal identity exists as the mode of engagement with the imploded culture.

Jean Baudrillard writes of orbital circulation as the matrix of the implosive process,[4] which implies a constant *turning-in,* and Arthur Kroker adds the valuable metaphor of 'black hole', that massive gravitational anomaly which draws all into it, from which no information can reliably emerge. Below the event horizon lie only abstraction and hypothesis; direct experience is, by definition, impossible. Acknowledging the strength of McLuhan's axiom, 'the medium is the message' ('the key formula of the age of simulation')[5], Baudrillard notes that it is not only this implosion of the message in the medium which is at stake, but also the concurrent '*implosion of the medium and the real* in a sort of nebulous hyperreality ...'.[6]

Television, still the axiomatic form of electronic simulation, due to its mass penetration and continually functioning national and global networks, is therefore not to be seen as presenting an image or mirror of reality (neutral or otherwise), but rather as a constituent portion of a new reality. Society, the arena of supposed 'real' existence, increasingly becomes 'the mirror of television'.[7] 'The result of this image bombard-ment', Toffler wrote in *Future Shock*, 'is the accelerated decay of old images, a faster intellectual through-put, and a new, profound sense of the impermanence of knowledge itself'.[8] In the science fiction horror film *Videodrome* (David Cronenberg, 1982), media prophet Brian O'Blivion informs us that 'Television is reality, and reality is less than television'. Soon, 'everyone will have special names ... names designed to cause the cathode-ray tube to resonate'. A new subject is being constituted, one which begins its process of being through the act of viewership. 'The TV self is the electronic individual *par excellence* who gets everything there is to get from the simulacrum of the media', write Kroker and Cook.[9]

The technologies of the mass media have thus been crucial to the maintenance of instrumental reason as a form of rational (and hence natural, invisible and neutral) domination. 'Domination has its own aesthetics', wrote Marcuse, 'and democratic domination has its demo-cratic aesthetics'.[10] The plurality of channel selections serves as a kind of guarantee of the freedom of the subject to choose, to position one's *self* within the culture, while the constant flow of images, sounds and narra-tives seemingly demonstrates a cultural abundance and promise. Yet the choice is illusory: to view is to surrender. Early on, Baudrillard wrote: 'It is useless to fantasize about state projection of police control through TV.... TV, by virtue of its mere presence, is a social control in itself....'[11]

Guy Debord's 1967 manifesto, *Society of the Spectacle*, begins by acknowledging the passage into a new mode of phenomenological and commercial existence. 'In societies where modern conditions of produc-tion prevail, all of life presents itself as an immense accumulation of *spectacles*. Everything that was directly lived has moved away into a representation.'[12] The citizen/viewer, no longer engaged in the act of producing reality, exists now in a state of pervasive separation – cut off from the producers of the surrounding media culture by a unilateral communication and detached from the mass of fellow citizen/viewers as the new community of television families and workplaces arise invisibly to take their place.

The spectacle controls by atomizing the population and reducing their capacity to function as an aggregate force, but also by displaying a surfeit of spectacular goods and lifestyles among which the viewer may electronically wander and experience a simulation of satisfaction. Within the conditions of late capitalism, 'the satisfaction of primary human needs is replaced by *an uninterrupted fabrication of pseudo-needs* which are reduced to the single pseudo-need of maintaining the reign of the autonomous economy.' (thesis 51, my emphasis) 'The real consumer becomes a consumer of illusions.' (thesis 47) Kroker and Cook describe the 1980s self as 'a blip with a lifestyle'.[13]

Science fiction (from the 1950s), like critical theory (from much earlier), has frequently portrayed the mass media as a pacifying force; an opiate. In Ray Bradbury's *Fahrenheit 451* (1953), for example, the wife of the book-burning fireman is addicted to both tranquillizers and television. This juncture of technology, control and addiction evokes the writings of William S. Burroughs, whose incantatory prose reveals a world – a galaxy – completely given over to the pervasiveness and vulnerability of addiction. Addiction is pervasive in that it transcends the use of narcotics: one can be addicted to money or to dope; there are orgasm addicts, control addicts and image addicts. Vulnerability exists because when the desperation of addiction is brought into being, the potential for manipulation escalates. 'The pusher always gets it all back. The addict needs more and more junk to maintain a human form ... buy off the Monkey. Junk is the mold of monopoly and possession.' Burroughs then analogizes addiction and capitalist control: 'Junk is the ideal product ... the ultimate merchandise. No sales talk necessary. The client will crawl through a sewer and beg to buy ... the junk merchant does not sell his product to the consumer, he sells the consumer to his product.'[14]

The nexus commodity/addiction/control is replicated in Debord's post-Frankfurt School analysis. The spectacle is the ultimate commodity in that it makes all others possible: advertisements generate the conditions for consumption, and thus for production as well. The spectacle stimulates the desire to consume (the one permissible participation in the social process), a desire which is continually displaced onto the next product, and the next. It is infinitely self-generating. Ultimately, the spectacle takes on the totalizing function of any addictive substance; it differs from dope only in that its addictive properties remain hidden within the rational economic structures of capitalist society. Contrast the metaphors of Burroughs to these of Debord: 'The spectacle is the moment when the commodity has attained the *total occupation* of social life.' (thesis 42) 'The spectacle is a permanent opium war which aims to make people identify goods with commodities and satisfaction with survival . . .'. (thesis 44) '[T]he spectacle is the *main production* of present-day society.' (thesis 15) 'The spectacle subjugates living men to the extent that the economy has totally subjugated them.' (thesis 16)

The spectacle-addict recurs in science fiction, and the more sophisticated works begin with the premise of voluntarism. The addiction to the video-narcotic means that the control apparatus is already emplaced and

invisibly operating to secure the false consciousness of cohesion, democratic order and freedom. Works such as *Fahrenheit 451* or Orwell's
1984 ignore the crucial postulate of Marcuse's democratic domination:
an effective ideological state apparatus replaces the need for the overt
exercise of power. As Burroughs observed, 'A *functioning* police state
needs no police'.[15]

According to Marshall McLuhan, our (post)modern technological
capabilities function as 'the extensions of man'.[16] 'During the mechanical
ages we had extended our bodies in space', while today, 'we have
extended our central nervous system in a global embrace, abolishing
both time and space as far as our planet is concerned'.[17] The metaphor
reassures by fostering an acceptance of media culture as a natural evolutionary state. To extend the nervous system outside the body further
empowers the brain and further centralizes the individual.

Other theorists are less sanguine. Debord clearly posits unilateral
forms of communication as an intrusive force: 'Lived reality is materially
invaded by the contemplation of the spectacle.' (thesis 8) Technologies
might hold the possibility of revolutionizing society but, since 'freedom
of the press is guaranteed only to those who own one',[18] the possibility
also exists that it will serve to consolidate rather than disseminate power.
Power is the operative lack in McLuhan's discourse, rendering his vision
compelling but incomplete. Baudrillard's writings share McLuhan's
fascination with technological change, but always accompanied by a
massive awareness of power's reification. He differs from Debord in
several ways which distance him from a traditional Marxist position.
First, technology replaces economics as the structuring force of the
discourse on power. Second, there is Baudrillard's rejection of 'use-
value' in favour of a position which guarantees no rigid site of
meaning.[19] Finally, he argues that power has been subsumed by technological forces to such a degree that it is no longer the province of the
state, much less the citizen.[20] In Baudrillard's imploded universe, human
power has itself become a simulation.[21] Power now resides in a technology which holds humanity in its thrall. The media are invading; there
will be no survivors.

This shift accounts for the changing style of Baudrillard's prose from
a rationally argued Debordian resentment at the reifying deployment of
spectacular power, to a hyper-technologized, jargon-ridden language
which refuses the possibility of a critical position. Baudrillard's text
aspires to the condition of science fiction, and ultimately becomes
performative of the process he once merely described.

The usurpation of power by the new technologies of information
control leads Baudrillard to reject the neural metaphors of McLuhan. In
its place, another biological trope is employed. What exists now is 'a

viral, endemic, chronic, alarming presence of the medium ... dissolution of TV into life, the dissolution of life into TV'.[22] The media are no longer the extensions of man, man instead extends the media in becoming a 'terminal of multiple networks'.[23]

Burroughs has frequently deployed virus as a metaphor for all the infiltrating forces of control to which people are subject. *Junky, Naked Lunch* and *Cities of the Red Night* all incorporate viral figures, but it is in the Nova trilogy,[24] and especially in *Nova Express*, that the control virus appears as an *image*: a media-form controlled by invading alien forces. Biology and the media are linked through the node of the image. Images are tangible and material, neither ephemeral nor temporary. A death-dwarf is a literal image-addict ('images – millions of images – That's what I eat . . .' [*Nova Express (NE)*, p. 68]).

As Burroughs demonstrates, science fiction becomes the discourse best equipped to contend with this new state of things. Samuel Delany and Teresa de Lauretis both argue that the genre is defined by rhetorical heightening and a continual linguistic play resistant to any totalization of meaning.[25] Something further is added in what we may term the science fiction of the spectacle, a subgenre which includes works by Burroughs; J.G. Ballard; James Tiptree, Jr (Alice Sheldon); Philip Dick; David Cronenberg; Norman Spinrad and others. Representation and textuality become the explicit subjects of the text; discourse will comprise the content as well as determine textual form. The inherent rhetoricity of the genre is extended as the text turns in upon its own production and status. The science fiction of the spectacle often demands the recognition of its own imbrication in the implosion of the real. These discursive strategies are dominant in contemporary critical writing as well: Baudrillard's essays, for example, bear rhetorical resemblances to the fictions of Dick and William Gibson, resemblances which are hardly coincidental.

Burroughs has generated his mythology for the space age around the nexus of junk, virus, addiction, control and surrender: 'Hell consists of falling into enemy hands, into the hands of the virus power, and heaven consists of freeing oneself from the power, of achieving inner freedom, freedom from conditioning.'[26] In the Nova trilogy, 'image *is* virus', and 'junk is concentrated image'. Baudrillard nearly quotes Burroughs when he writes about 'this viral contamination of things by images'.[27] The Nova Police reports: 'This virus released upon the world would infect the entire population and turn them into our replicas' (*NE*, p. 48).

The virus is a powerful metaphor for the power of the media, and Burroughs's hyperbolic Manicheism does not completely disguise the accuracy of his analysis. Whether the viral form is an actual living protocell or simply a carrier of genetic information, it clearly possesses an exponentially increasing power to take over and control its host organism. The injection of information leads to control, mutation, and passive replication: the host cell 'believes' that it is following its own biologically determined imperative; it mistakes the new genetic material for its own. The image/virus is posited as invasive and irresistible; a parasite with only self-replication as its function.

Compare this to Debord's economic analysis, where the pervasiveness of the spectacle serves the similar function of creating a deceptive cohesion for the purpose of infinite self-regeneration. The hegemony of the subject is illusory; indeed, imagistic; while control over these images is elusive; in fact impossible. The recurrent image of the virus (the virus of the image), biologizes the rise of spectacle and the consequent waning of autonomous reason. The subject becomes a 'carrier' of spectacle, of image, of pseudo-reality. This is what Eric Mottram has called 'the virus transformation into undifferentiated man, the terminal image of man as patient-victim'.[28] Earth's fate is all too clear: 'The entire planet is being developed into *terminal identity* and complete surrender'. (*NE*, 19) Terminal identity: an unmistakably doubled articulation in which we find both the end of the subject and a new subjectivity constructed at the computer station or television screen. Again the human is configured as a 'terminal of multiple networks'.

McLuhan wrote that *Nova Express* takes place 'in a universe which seems to be someone else's insides',[29] recognizing that Burroughs's work represents an inversion of his own. He further notes that: 'The human nervous system can be reprogrammed biologically as readily as any radio station can alter its fare.' In this statement, which anticipates *Videodrome*, there is an acknowledgement of political and social control which is rare in McLuhan, and which allows a perception of the unasked question which lurks behind a reading of his works: whose nervous system is this, anyway?

The similarities between Burroughs and film maker David Cronenberg are certainly extensive. The invasion and mutation of the body, the loss of control, and the transformation of the self into Other are as obsessively deployed in the works of the latter as in those of the former. Christopher Sharritt has written that the pervasive concern for both is 'the rise of the addictive personality cultivated by dominant culture and the changing structures of power.... [Neither] finds a solution in organized revolt since the new technological environment absorbs and dilutes ideological principles and abstract values'.[30] Similarly, Baudrillard has written that

All the movements which bet only on liberation, emancipation, the resurrection of the subject of history, of the group, of speech as a raising of consciousness ... do not see that they are acting in accordance with the system, whose imperative today is the overproduction and regeneration of meaning and speech.[31]

Language is, in multiple senses, the definition and controller of the self, the site of identity; and Baudrillard's pessimism and rhetorical surrender are commensurate with Burroughs's tactics. Like Baudrillard, Burroughs assimilates the linguistic excess of science fiction, but goes further than Baudrillard towards the demolition of communication. The appropriation of other authors and other texts wrecks the hegemony of both writer and novel, while the technique of the cut-up, in its explicit evocation of surgical procedure which links textual and corporeal bodies, obliterates the linear coherence which generally defines the identity of the text. Relations among signifiers are lost, each now exists in glittering isolation: the rational *telos* of the narrator is replaced by a rhetorical intensification which foregrounds and reveals the random bombardments of the spectacular society. Mutation becomes an act of sabotage, and the cut-up becomes a crucial *immunization* against the invasive forces of the media-virus.

Cronenberg replaces this emphasis on the physicality of language with an attention to the image of the body. While he constructs an elaborate semiotics of the body in all his work, it is only in *Videodrome*, to date, that he fully addresses the construction of *the body of the text*: the cinematic signifier. In Cronenberg's films, the eruptive and incisive mutations which the body undergoes rival Burroughs's cut-ups for their violence, randomness, and capacity to produce chaos. The penile organ emerging from Marilyn Chambers's armpit in *Rabid* (1976), the extruded 'children' of *The Brood* (1979), and the genetic cut-up represented by the human/fly melange in *The Fly* (1986) all enact the breakdown of human hegemony through the deployment of new technologies. Burroughs wrote: 'The realization that something as familiar to you as the movement of your intestines the sound of your breathing the beating of your heart is also alien and hostile does make one feel a bit insecure at first.'[32]

These transformations cannot be completely subsumed within the mind/body dualism of Cartesianism, as one critic proposes to do.[33] Such a humanistic balance fails to account for the evident and pervasive antihumanism of Cronenberg's production, as demonstrated by the recurrent fears of human contact, sexuality, or physicality in any form. David Cronenberg is the film maker of *panic sex* (Kroker's pungent phrase) with the body as the overdetermined site for the expression of profound social anxiety.[34] The subject of the Cronenberg film is hardly human action: it is instead, as Sharritt states, the structures of external power and control to which the individual (in body *and* soul) is subjected. The dissolution of identity into new forms is connected to the rise of new technologies, and this has become evident in three of his more recent films, *Scanners* (1980), *Videodrome* and *The Fly*, in which the apparent mind/body dichotomy is superseded by the *tri*chotomy of mind/body/machine. Carrie Rickey is closer to the mark when she writes that Cronenberg is: 'a visionary architect of a chaotic biological tract where mind and body, ever fighting a Cartesian battle for integration, are so vulnerable as to be *easily annexed by technology*.'[35] The mind/body struggle is a blind for the larger Burroughsian issues of addiction, technological control, and the malleability of reality and identity.

Videodrome presents a destabilized reality in which image, reality, hallucination and psychosis become indissolubly melded: the most estranging portrayal of image addiction and viral invasion since Burroughs. 'Videodrome', a TV programme, itself broadcasts brutal torture and sadism in a grotesque display which exerts a strong influence upon its viewers. Cable-station operator Max Wren desires 'Videodrome': as a businessman he needs it to rescue his foundering station; as an individual he finds himself drawn irresistibly to its horrors. Connected to Wren's quest for the source of 'Videodrome' is a profoundly ontological passage beyond spectacle to the ultimate dissolution of the boundaries which might serve to separate and guarantee definitions of 'spectacle', 'subject' and 'reality' itself.

At times *Videodrome* seems to be a film which hypostatizes Baudrillard's own polemic. Here, with remarkable syntactic similarity, Baudrillard and a character from Cronenberg's film are both intent upon the usurpation of the real by its own representation; upon the imbrication of the real, the technologized and the simulated. The language is hypertechnologized but anti-rational; moebius-like in its evocation of a dissolute, spectacular reality:

Jean Baudrillard: 'We are here at the controls of a micro-satellite, in orbit, living no longer as an actor or dramaturge but as a terminal of multiple networks. Television is still the most direct prefiguration of this. But today it is the very space of habitation that is conceived as both receiver and distributor, as the space of both reception and operations, the control screen and terminal which as such may be endowed with telematic power . . .'.[36]

Professor O'Blivion: 'The battle for the mind of North America will be fought in the video arena – the Videodrome. The television screen is the retina of the mind's eye. Therefore the television screen is part of the physical structure of the brain. Therefore whatever appears on the television screen emerges as raw experience for those who watch it. Therefore television is reality and reality is less than television.'

Both, in fact, seem to be following Debord's programme that 'When *analyzing* the spectacle one speaks, to some extent, the language of the spectacular itself in the sense that one moves through the methodological terrain of the very society which expresses itself in spectacle' (thesis 11) – precisely why science fiction has obtained such a lately privileged position. Baudrillard embraces a high-tech, alienating and alienated science fictional rhetoric to explore the very paradigm of high-tech alienation, while Cronenberg's horror films about the failure of interpersonal communications are an integral part of an industry which privileges the spectacular over the intimate, and pseudo-satisfaction over genuine comprehension. Both construct discourses of anti-rationalism to expose and ridicule any process or history of enlightenment occurring through the exercise of a 'pure' reason.

Television pervades *Videodrome*. O'Blivion is the founder of the Cathode Ray Mission, a kind of TV soup kitchen for the city's derelicts: 'Watching TV will patch them back into the world's mixing board.' Television is often a medium of direct address. Wren is awakened by a videotaped message. O'Blivion refuses to appear on television 'except *on* television', his image appears on a monitor placed beside the programme's host (in a gesture reminiscent of Debord's own pre-recorded lectures).[37] As Wren awaits his own talk show appearance, he chats with Nicki Brand, but an interposed monitor blocks our view. The image on the monitor is coextensive with its own background, however – Magritte-like – and consequently, the conversation is between a live Wren and a video Brand. Such examples offer a preliminary blurring of the distinction between real and televisual experiences.

This parody of McLuhan's global TV village serves as backdrop to the enigma of 'Videodrome', which is finally revealed to be a government project. The explanation for 'Videodrome' is at least as coherent as any from Burroughs: Spectacular Optical, a firm which specializes in defence contracts, has developed a signal which induces a tumour in the viewer. This tumour causes hallucinations which can be recorded, then revised, then fed back to the viewer: in effect, the individual is reprogrammed to serve the controller's ends. Burroughs offered a similar vision: 'you are a programmed tape recorder set to record and play back/who programs you/who decides what tapes play back in present time.'[38]

But as Barry Convex of Spectacular Optical asks Wren, 'Why would anyone watch a scum show like "Videodrome"?' 'Business reasons', is Wren's fast response, but his interest transcends the commercial. Coincident with his exposure to the 'Videodrome' signal is his attraction to Nicki Brand, an outspoken, alluring personality for C-RAM radio.[39] Transgression thus enters Wren's life in at least three ways: socially, via his soft-porn, hard-violence cable TV station; sexually, through his forays into sadomasochism with Brand; and the political and sexual transgressions of 'Videodrome' itself. The three levels are linked in a spiralling escalation which culminates in Wren's own hallucinated appearance on 'Videodrome', whipping, first Brand, then her image on a television monitor. Brand is the guide who leads Wren on towards his final destiny; after her death, her image remains to spur him on. Her masochism might indicate a quest for sensation: this media figure admits that: 'We live in overstimulated times. We crave stimulation for its own sake.' Brand wants to 'audition' for 'Videodrome': 'I was *made* for that show', she brags, but it might be more accurate to say that she was made *by* that show. Wren is told that 'They used her image to seduce you'.

The 'Videodrome' programme is explicitly linked by both Wren and Convex to male sexual response (something 'tough' rather than 'soft') and penetration (something that will 'break through'). Wren takes on the 'tough' sadistic role with Brand, and yet there is no doubt that it is she who controls the relationship, she who dominates.[40] Similarly, the power granted to the 'Videodrome' viewer to observe and relish its brutality masks the programme's actual function: to increase social control and establish a new means of dominance over the population. Wren is superficially the master of Brand and 'Videodrome', but ultimately master becomes slave. In a Baudrillardian revision of the Frankenstein myth, even Brian O'Blivion is condemned: the creator of 'Videodrome' is its first victim.

The Third World flavour of the *mise-en-scène* of the 'Videodrome' programme, found in its low-tech electrified clay walls and the neo-stormtrooper guise of the torturers, exists in distinct contrast to the 'Videodrome' technology, which is electronic and invisible, disseminated 'painlessly' through the mass media. 'In Central America', Wren tells Brand, 'making underground videos is a subversive act'. In North America too, it would seem, as the 'Videodrome' signal is subversive of experience, reality, and the very existence of the subject.

It is the voluntarism of the television experience which permits the incursion of controlling forces. A strictly political-economic reading of *Videodrome* would find little difficulty in situating the work within Debord's model, but *Videodrome* moves beyond the classically political through its relentless physicality. Following his exposure to the 'Video-drome' signal, Wren begins a series of hallucinations. Wren assaults Bridey, his assistant, and in a series of shot/reverse shot pairings, Bridey becomes Brand, then Bridey again. Disoriented, Max apologizes for hitting her. Bridey answers, 'Max . . . you didn't hit me'. As O'Blivion tells him: 'Your reality is already half-video hallucination.'

A videotaped message from O'Blivion suddenly becomes more interactive. 'Max', he says, all trace of electronic filtering gone, 'I'm so happy you came to me'. O'Blivion explains the history of the 'Videodrome' phenomenon while being readied for execution: the executioner is Nicki Brand. 'I want *you*, Max', she breathes. 'Come to me. Come to Nicki.' Her lips fill the screen, and the set begins to pulsate, to breathe. Veins ripple the hardwood cabinet; a videogame joystick waggles obscenely. All boundaries are removed as the diegetic frame of the TV screen vanishes from view: the lips now fill the movie screen in a vast closeup. Wren approaches the set as the screen bulges outward to meet his touch, literalizing the notion of the screen as breast. His face sinks in, his hands fondle the panels and knobs of the set as the lips continue their panting invitation.

Later, Wren's body literally opens up – his stomach develops a massive, vaginal slit – to accommodate a new videocassette 'programme'. Image addiction and image virus reduce the subject to the status of a videotape player/recorder; the human body mutates to become a part of the massive system of reproductive technology ('you are a programmed tape recorder'). The sexual implications of the imagery are thus significant and not at all gratuitous: video becomes visceral.[41]

Cronenberg moves the viewer in and out of Wren's hallucinations, creating a deep ambiguity regarding the status of the image. It is easy to accept his attack as real, although the transmigration of identities clearly marks Wren's demented subjectivity. Yet the attack was entirely hallucinated: the 'real' cinematic image is unreliable. In the extended hallucination of the eroticized, visceral television, the film maker gracefully dissolves the bonds which contain the spectacle. The TV screen is contained by its own frame, but Cronenberg's closeup permits the image to burst its boundaries and expand to the non-diegetic limits of the cinema screen. In a later hallucination, a video-Brand circles Wren with whip in hand, proffering it for him to wield. The image moves from video hallucination to cinematic reality within a single shot; the shift in visual register marks the spectacle's passage from visual phenomenon to new reality. Wren accepts the whip, but Brand is now no longer present in corporeal form; she only exists, shackled, on a TV screen. Wren attacks the bound(ed) image in another moment which recalls the visual punning of Margritte.

Cronenberg, then, does not reify the cinematic signifier as 'real', but continually mutates the real into the image, and the image into the hallucination. There is no difference in the cinematic techniques employed, no 'rational' textual system, which might distinguish reality from hallucination for the film viewer. Each moment is presented as 'real': that is, as corresponding to the conventions of realist film making. These unbounded hallucinations jeopardize the very status of the image: we must believe everything or nothing. Through these textual mutations, these estrangements of cinematic language, the science fiction of the spectacle destabilizes the field of representation by constructing a set of indefinite semantic constructs.[42]

Wren hallucinates his appearance on 'Videodrome', but is 'Videodrome' a programme composed entirely of recorded hallucinations? If so, then there is a progression from hallucination, through image, to reality: the scene is real because it is televised, it is televised because it is recorded, it is recorded because it is hallucinated. In its themes and structure, the film serves as a graphic example of Baudrillard's viral immixture of TV and life (which echoes Burroughs's injunction that 'image *is* virus'). Baudrillard adds that the media is a virus which 'controls the mutation of the real into the hyperreal'. The viral metaphor is strikingly apt when applied to *Videodrome* – the literalized invasion of the body by the image, and the production of tumours which produce images. Image is virus; virus virulently replicates itself; the subject is finished. We remain trapped within a universe which seems to be someone else's insides.

Body and image become one: a dissolution of real and representation, certainly, but also of the boundaries between internal and external, as the interiorized hallucination becomes the public spectacle of the 'Videodrome' programme. In the post-spectacle society all such boundaries dissolve: 'We will have to suffer this new state of things, this forced extroversion of all interiority, this forced injection of all exteriority ... we are now in a new form of schizophrenia.' Our response changes: 'No more hysteria, no more projective paranoia, properly speaking, but this state of terror proper to the schizophrenic: too great a proximity of everything, the unclean promiscuity of everything which touches, invests and penetrates without resistance.'[43] The subject has 'no halo of private protection, *not even his own body*, to protect him anymore'.[44]

The slippage of reality which marks the textual operations of *Videodrome* can certainly be associated with the commensurate process in the writings of the saboteur Burroughs, who repeatedly declared that we must 'Storm the Reality Studio and retake the universe'.[45] Burroughs's cinematic metaphor reaches a kind of apotheosis in *Videodrome*, as the images flicker and fall, their authority ultimately denied, but there is no glimpse of a Reality Studio behind the levels of reality-production.

Reality-slippage, with its echoes from Plato's cave, is also the province of science fiction author Philip K. Dick, another obvious influence on Cronenberg. Dick's paranoid sensibility explores the alienation which results from seeing *through* the spectacle. The central characteristic of his protagonists involves their crises of subjectivity which begin when the real violently dissolves around them. Such a metaphysical dilemma does not represent a failure to map oneself onto the world, but is interwoven with ontological change and primarily with the rise of spectacle and the expansion of the technologies of reproduction.

Dick challenges the instrumental rationalism of spectacular society through estranging rhetorical structures which construct a maze of decentred ambivalence in which multiple characters interact in a futile quest to fix reality, and therefore themselves, in place. The reader is plunged into the neologistic excess which characterizes the science fiction text. These terms cannot be read through, for the unfamiliarity they engender is precisely their purpose. The discursive ambiguities of *Videodrome* surely derive from Dick's, and Burroughs's, spectacular/ structural deformations.

Dick's novel *UBIK* (1969) is dominated by telepaths and half-lifers, dead people who retain some residual brain function and exist in a cryogenic partial existence. Joe Chip (a blip culture name if ever there was one) is subjected to reality erosion, as temporality itself seems to reverse its valence. Only UBIK, a product packaged in historically appropriate forms (aerosol, ointment, elixir), can briefly restore the familiarity of the present day, and so the narrative propels its characters on a quest for answers and for UBIK. *UBIK* first seems to stand as a Platonic meditation on the rift between appearance and reality. Objects are shadows of an ideal form. Chip's refrigerator devolves from computerized servant to freon-based cooling system to icebox: a reversed succession of manifestations of the Idea of a Refrigerator. Appearance, image and spectacle are homologous terms when placed in dichotomous opposition to 'the real'. If *UBIK* simply remained with this Platonic analysis, it would only be notable for its ultimate reification of a reality which underlies shifting levels of appearance. But *UBIK* undermines such idealism. A character's ability to alter the past implies the existence of myriad presents, none more real, finally, than any other.

The depressing truth is that Chip is trapped in half-life, his 'reality' subject to the whims of a deranged, but stronger, psyche. He might be privileged to look upon the final level, the Reality Studio where reality is staged: but reality is nothing more than the fantasies of a madman. A final shift moves the reader out from Chip's half-life experience to his employer's position in the 'real world'. The living human finds currency adorned with the image of Joe Chip, just as Chip had earlier found money bearing his employer's image. 'This was just the beginning.' Final reality is itself only a shadow; the reification of the real is replaced by a recursive structure of infinite regression. *UBIK* presents, not a dichotomy of appearance and reality, but an unresolved dialectic.

Further, *UBIK* gains its force and originality by examining the central importance of the *idea* of reality, while resisting its existence. UBIK is in demand because it fixes reality (in both senses of the word: it repairs the real and locks it in place). Appearance is not simply negated as a deception, but is posited as a necessary condition of existence.

Five years after *UBIK*'s publication, Dick reworked it as a screenplay for Jean-Pierre Gorin. In a manoeuvre recalling the cinematic mutations of Burroughs's screenplay-novel, *The Last Words of Dutch Schultz* (1975),[46] Dick wanted his work to end by regressing to black and white stock, silent footage, flickering effects, and by finally bubbling and burning to a halt. The screenplay retains some of this: a drive through a simulated landscape features the repeating backgrounds of inexpensive television cartoons; a character speaks with defective sound synchronization; another scene is 'very dim, as if "bulb" is weak in "projector"'.[47] Film becomes a physical substance which bears traces of reality, but which remains pure appearance. Dick's manipulations, like Cronenberg's, deny cinema's status as transparent conduit of truth.

UBIK performs an effective deconstruction through its very structures, but it is in that commodity of commodities, UBIK, that the work rejoins the analysis of the spectacle performed by Debord, Baudrillard, Burroughs and Cronenberg. UBIK is the product which permits the maintenance of appearance and, in the novel, each chapter begins with an advertisement for this mysterious and ubiquitous balm. In becoming a consumer, the subject overcomes perceived lack, fixes appearance, becomes an image. The commodity defined reification for Marx; labour's abstraction is contained in its inertia.[48] Commodities and spectacles reassure and threaten by confirming a relation to the world through a temporary pseudo-satisfaction lasting only until the can is empty or a new commercial is on. UBIK stands as the ultimate example: the ur-commodity. *UBIK* becomes *the* work of commodity fetishism, featuring a product whose function is *only* to sustain the illusion of coherence. 'I came to UBIK after trying weak, out-of-date reality supports', beams a happy and secure(d) housewife.

In the screenplay these commercials interrupt the action, but also serve as a superimposition, a layering of images which blocks appearance. 'We understand that despite [the image's] fidelity to graphic representationalism, it is incomplete.' (p. 31) The spectacle is displayed in spectacular fashion, faithful to reality but, through its apparent incompletion, not interchangeable with it. 'Something has come between us and what we have been watching, something in a sense more real or anyhow real in a visibly different sense.' Diegetic reality shatters in a gesture which reflects on the experience of the real through the experience of the cinematic, as in *Videodrome*.

Reprogrammed by Bianca O'Blivion in *Videodrome*, Max Wren prepares to take the next step. 'You've become the video word made flesh', she tells him. 'Death to "Videodrome" – long live the new flesh.' The terror must be overcome, the attachment to the body surrendered. Wren makes his way to a rusted hulk – a 'condemned vessel' – in the harbour. The decaying walls match the colour of his jacket. Wren is another 'condemned vessel', trapped within the confines of the old flesh, an outmoded conception of the body and the self. Aboard the vessel, Max fires at his own temple and there the film concludes; ambiguously, unsatisfyingly. What is the new flesh?

One postulation might hold that Max has attained the paradoxical status of pure image – an image which no longer retains any connection with the 'real'. *Videodrome* comes strikingly close to moving through the four successive phases of the image characteristic of the era of simulation as described by Baudrillard.[49] First, the image functions as 'the reflection as a basic reality'. Clearly, until the hallucinations begin, the viewer trusts the cinematic image as the sign of truth. Doubts may be raised concerning the enigmatic image of the 'Videodrome' programme, its ostensible Third World aesthetic belied by its Pittsburgh transmission point. Here the image 'masks and perverts a basic reality'. In the third phase, the image 'masks the *absence* of a basic reality', which has, in fact, been the argument behind the works explored here. The film propels its audience along this trajectory, possibly achieving the status of Baudrillard's fourth phase, in which image 'bears no relation to any reality whatever: it is its own pure simulacrum'. Beyond representation itself, such an image could not be represented, and thus the film ends. *Videodrome*, then, enacts the death of the subject and the death of representation simultaneously, each the consequence of the other.

Videodrome presents a destabilized reality in which image, reality, hallucination and psychosis become indissolubly melded, and it is on this level that the film becomes a work *of* postmodernism, rather than simply a work *about* it. The subversion of conventional structures of filmic discourse here corresponds to the 'progressive' use of language in science fiction where a neologistic excess and literalization of language foreground the reading process in a discursive play which resists the totalization of meaning. The viewer of the film is analogous to the viewer of the TV show: trapped in a web of representations which infect and transform reality. Cronenberg evidences an extensive concern with this dissolution of boundaries in all of his films. Plague viruses and parasites demonstrate the vulnerability of the body to invasion from without; telepathy and physical projection break down the dichotomy between public and private; subjectivity and temporality collapse; man merges with machine; a teleporter is proclaimed to end all concepts of borders. A particular yearning cuts across Cronenberg's body of work (work of the body); a desire for dissolution which is always accompanied by a fear of the void.

The final stage of Baudrillard's four phases of the image, wherein the image no longer bears a relation to an unmediated reality, is the hallmark of the age of postmodernism. The potential trauma which might be expected to accompany this realization is frequently elided by a regression to simple nostalgia, as both Jean Baudrillard and Fredric Jameson have noted.[50] Arthur Kroker has further written that 'The postmodern scene is a panic site, just for the fun of it'; an era of crises for their own sake, where the injunction of crisis now ironically serves to cover over the abyss of non-meaning.[51] Conversely, the insistent figurations of Baudrillard, Burroughs, Cronenberg and Dick represent a stunning hypostatization of the concerns of postmodern culture, and constitute a discursive field which retains the power to unsettle, disorient and initiate the crucial action of questioning the status of the sign in sign culture: a spectacular immunization against the invasive powers of the image virus.

Notes

1. Alvin Toffler, *The Third Wave.* New York: Bantam Books 1981, p. 165.
2. Ibid., p. 166.
3. Arthur Kroker and David Cook, *The Postmodern Scene: Excremental Culture and Hyper-Aesthetics,* New York: St Martin's Press 1986, p. 279.
4. Jean Baudrillard, *In the Shadow of the Silent Majorities,* trans. Paul Foss, New York: Semiotext(e) 1983, p. 21.
5. Ibid., p. 101.
6. Ibid.
7. This variation on Oscar Wilde is to be found in Kroker and Cook, p. 268.
8. Alvin Toffler, *Future Shock,* New York: Bantam Books 1971, p. 161.
9. Kroker and Cook, p. 274.
10. Herbert Marcuse, *One-Dimensional Man,* Boston: Beacon Press 1964, p. 65.
11. Jean Baudrillard, 'Requiem for the Media', in *For a Critique of the Political Economy of the Sign,* trans. Charles Levin, St Louis: Telos Press 1981, p. 172.
12. Guy Debord, *Society of the Spectacle,* Detroit: Black & Red 1983, thesis 1. Henceforth, thesis numbers follow quotations in the body of the text.
13. Kroker and Cook, p. 279.
14. William S. Burroughs, *Naked Lunch,* New York: Grove Press 1959, pp. xxxviii and xxxix.
15. Ibid., p. 36.
16. Marshall McLuhan, *Understanding Media,* New York: New American Library 1964.
17. Ibid., p. 19.
18. A.J. Liebling, *The Press,* second revised edn, New York: Ballantine Books 1975, p. 32.

19. Jean Baudrillard, *The Mirror of Production*, trans. Mark Poster, St Louis: Telos Press 1975.

20. Jean Baudrillard, *Forget Foucault*, trans. Nicole Dufresne, New York: Semiotext(e) 1987, p. 11.

21. Ibid.

22. Jean Baudrillard, 'The Precession of Simulacra', in *Simulations*, trans. Paul Foss, Paul Patton and Philip Beitchman, New York: Semiotext(e) 1983, pp. 54–5.

23. Jean Baudrillard, 'The Ecstasy of Communication', in Hal Foster, ed., *The Anti-Aesthetic: Essays in Postmodern Culture*, Port Townsend, WA: Bay Press 1983, p. 128.

24. The trilogy includes *The Soft Machine* revised edn (1966), *The Ticket that Exploded* revised edn (1967) and *Nova Express* (1964). All titles published by Grove Press, New York.

25. See Samuel R. Delany, 'About 5,750 Words', in *The Jewel-Hinged Jaw: Notes on the Language of Science Fiction*, Elizabethtown, NY: Dragon Press 1977· or Teresa de Lauretis, 'Signs of W[a/o]nder', in Teresa de Lauretis, Andreas Huyssen and Kathleen Woodward, eds, *The Technological Imagination: Theories and Fictions*, Madison, WI: Coda Press 1980.

26. Cited in Eric Mottram, *William Burroughs: The Algebra of Need*, London: Marion Boyars 1977, p. 40.

27. Jean Baudrillard, 'Rituals of Transparency', in Sylvere Lotringer, ed., *The Ecstasy of Communication*, trans. Bernard and Caroline Schutze, New York: Semiotext(e) 1988, p. 36.

28. Mottram, p. 56.

29. Marshall McLuhan, 'Notes on Burroughs', *The Nation*, 28 December 1964, pp. 517–19.

30. Christopher Sharritt, 'Myth and Ritual in the Post-Industrial Landscape: The Horror Films of David Cronenberg', *Persistence of Vision* nos. 3/4, 1986, p. 113.

31. Jean Baudrillard, 'The Implosion of Meaning in the Media', in *In the Shadow of the Silent Majorities*, p. 109.

32. *The Ticket that Exploded*, p. 50.

33. William Beard, 'The Visceral Mind: The Films of David Cronenberg', in Piers Handling, ed., *The Shape of Rage: The Films of David Cronenberg*, New York: New York Zoetrope 1983.

34. See the articles in the disturbing and entertaining Arthur and Marilouise Kroker, eds, *Body Invaders: Panic Sex in America*, New York: St Martin's Press 1988.

35. Carrie Rickey, 'Make Mine Cronenberg', *The Village Voice*, 1 February 1983, p. 64.

36. 'The Ecstasy of Communication', p. 128.

37. One of these 'Perspectives for Conscious Alterations in Everyday Life' is reprinted in *Situationist International Anthology*, ed. and trans. Ken Knabb, Berkeley: Bureau of Public Secrets 1981, pp. 68–75.

38. Burroughs, 'The Invisible Generation', in *The Ticket that Exploded*, p. 213.

39. Perhaps it should be noted that the RAM acronym is one familiar to computer users, and stands for Random Access Memory.

40. This exploration of sexuality is granted considerably more weight in Cronenberg's recent *Dead Ringers* (1988).

41. For an important feminist analysis of the figuration of the body, see Tania Modleski, 'The Terror of Pleasure: The Contemporary Horror Film and Postmodern Theory', in Tania Modleski, ed., *Studies in Entertainment: Critical Approaches to Mass Culture*, Bloomington: Indiana University Press 1986.

42. The phrase is borrowed from de Lauretis, p. 160.

43. 'The Ecstasy of Communication', p. 132.

44. Ibid. Emphasis mine.

45. *The Soft Machine*, p. 155.

46. William Burroughs, *The Last Words of Dutch Schultz*, New York: Seaver Books 1975.

47. Philip K. Dick, *Ubik: The Screenplay*, Minneapolis: Corroboree Press 1985, p. 120.

48. Karl Marx, *Capital* Volume 1, trans. Ben Fowkes, New York: Vintage Books 1977, pp. 163–77.

49. Ibid., pp. 11–12.

50. See Baudrillard, 'The Precession of Simulacra', p. 12; and Jameson, 'Postmodernism, or the Cultural Logic of Late Capitalism', *New Left Review*, no. 146, 1984, pp. 66–8.

51. *The Postmodern Scene*, p. 27.

17

Gynesis, Postmodernism and the Science Fiction Horror Film

Barbara Creed

In *Gynesis: Configurations of Woman and Modernity*, Alice Jardine maintains that within gynesis the 'feminine' signifies, not woman herself, but those 'spaces which could be said to conceptualize the master narrative's own 'non-knowledge', that area over which the narrative has lost control.[1] This is the unknown, the terrifying, the monstrous – everything which is not held in place by concepts such as Man, Truth, Meaning. Interestingly, she does not claim that this situation is new; in fact, she stresses the importance of remembering

> that all of the words used to designate this space (now unbound) – nature, Other, matter, unconscious, madness, hylé, force – have throughout the tenure of Western philosophy carried feminine connotations (whatever their grammatical gender).... Those connotations go back, at the very least, to Plato's *chora*. Julia Kristeva has pointed out that space in general has always connoted the female: 'Father's Time, mother's species,' as Joyce put it; and, indeed, when evoking the name and destiny of woman, one thinks more of the *space* generating and forming the human species than of *time*, becoming, or history.[2]

The science fiction horror film's current interest in the maternal body and processes of birth point to changes taking place on several fronts.[3] Among the most important of these are the developments taking place in reproductive technology which have put into crisis questions of the subject, the body and the unconscious. Jean-François Lyotard draws attention to this. In a discussion on architecture and the postmodern, he speaks of the fact that the mother's body, the infant's first home, is under threat; given the possibility of birth taking place in an artificial womb, we may well in our lifetimes witness the 'disappearance of that first dwelling'.

My question is the following: the body is to my mind an essential site of resistance, because with the body there is love, a certain presence of the past, a capacity to reflect, *singularity* – if this body is attacked, by techno-science, then that site of resistance can be attacked. What is the unconscious of a child engendered *in vitro*? What is its relationship with the mother and with the father?[4]

The science fiction horror film, I would argue, is using the body of woman not only to explore these possibilities in a literal sense, but also as a metaphor for the uncertainty of the future – the new, unknown, potentially creative and potentially destructive future. The threat offered by the 'alien' creature, particularly the alien that impregnates woman, is also one of an uncertain future. The theme of birth and the possibility of new modes of conception and procreation is, of course, not new to science fiction. Over the decades the SF horror film has dealt with scientific alternatives to human conception (the Frankenstein films); other modes of sexual reproduction (*Invasion of the Body Snatchers*); parthenogenetic modes of conception (*The Thing*); cloning (*The Boys From Brazil*); the transformation of robots into human beings (*D.A.R.Y.L.*); and the impregnation of women by aliens (*I Married a Monster From Outer Space, Village of the Damned, Xtro, Inseminoid*). There is even a soft-porn film based on the latter – a deliberate parody of *Xtro* called *Wham Bang! Thank You Mr Spaceman.*

In more recent years, as experiments with reproductive technology have begun to make enormous headway, the SF horror film has become increasingly preoccupied with alternative forms of the conception-gestation-birth process. One of the most interesting and significant developments in the genre has been a concentration on imagery connected with the female reproductive cycle. The latter is most thoroughly explored in films such as *Xtro, Dune, Blue Velvet, Inseminoid,* the John Carpenter remake of *The Thing, Alien* and *Aliens.* A study of these films, particularly the last three, reveals a fascination with the maternal body – its inner and outer appearance, its functions, its awesome powers. In many of these texts, it is not the body of the human/earth woman which is being explored but rather the 'bodies' of female alien creatures whose reproductive systems both resemble the human and are coded as a source of abject horror and overpowering awe. In the final scenes of *Aliens* we confront the mother alien – a monstrous, deadly procreative machine, prepared to protect her young at all costs – primitive, amoral, female. In the two *Alien* films, this coding is taken to extremes – virtually all aspects of the *mise-en-scène* are designed to signify the female: womb-like interiors, fallopian-tube corridors, small claustrophobic spaces.

Xtro pushes the birth-potential of woman's body to extremes: woman is impregnated by an alien, and a short time later gives birth to a fully grown man. Here, the body becomes a site of the 'unknown' – physically capable of mating with the 'other', able to expand like a balloon, without physical limits. In *Inseminoid*, woman is impregnated by an alien, later giving birth to two monstrous half-human twins who, it is indicated, will eventually return to Earth and wreak havoc on the planet. In the remake of *The Fly*, the heroine wakes up from a nightmare in which she sees herself giving birth to a giant maggot. In *The Brood*, woman gives birth to a monstrous brood of dwarf children in a symbolic materialization of her inner rage. Her womb is a large sac attached to the side of her stomach. In the final scenes, when her husband secretly watches a birth, he is repelled and disgusted, particularly when she bites through the umbilical cord and looks up at him, her face smeared with blood. In *Aliens* human bodies become nests for alien embryos; when the alien infant is ready to hatch it gnaws its way through the stomach. The human body, both male and female, has become a cocoon for a hostile life form. Why this preoccupation with the maternal body, process of birth, monstrous offspring, the alien nature of woman, her maternal powers – and most recently the representation of the male body as 'womb'? I would argue it is because the body, particularly the woman's body, through the process of gynesis, has come to signify the spaces of the unknown, the terrifying, the monstrous. This would register Lyotard's concern about the body losing its capacity to function as 'an essential site of resistance' – clearly a postmodern anxiety.

I think we can also see this process of gynesis at work in cinema's increasing preoccupation with the theme of 'becoming woman' – literally. If a collapse of the symbolic function gives rise to what Jardine describes as 'an inability of words to give form to the world', then this may well lead to a struggle to control that which has discredited the paternal function – the 'space which has begun to threaten all forms of authorship (paternity)'. The new theoretical discourses (feminism? post-modernism?) which have begun to take the place of the master discourses, seeing themselves as no longer in 'a system of loans and debts to former master truths' have, according to Jardine, begun to conceptualize a new space, that of woman.[5]

The theme of 'becoming woman' is explored symbolically in the horror film (*Psycho, Dressed To Kill*) and literally in those science fiction films in which man either gives birth to 'another' (*Alien* and *Aliens*) or in which he gives birth to himself (*Altered States, The Terminator*) or to himself as another life form (*The Thing, The Fly*). I am not suggesting that this is a new theme; it is dealt with in all the mad-scientist films in which man attempts to create his own life forms in the laboratory – the scientist as Mother/God. However, in the contemporary text, there has been an intensification in the exploration of 'becoming woman'. Most critical articles written on crossdressing in the cinema rarely consider the possibility that man, at an unconscious level, may well desire to 'become woman' (*Tootsie, Some Like It Hot*). In France this possibility is treated with seriousness – a male poet must become a woman in order to write. Deleuze and Guattari, of course, have written at length about the whole world 'becoming woman', although this again has little to do with actual women.

In her article on postmodern theory, 'The Terror of Pleasure',[6] Tania Modleski analyses David Cronenberg's *Videodrome* in these terms: the hero having been subjected to 'massive doses of a video signal' not only discovers he can no longer distinguish reality from fantasy but also that his body, completely unable to resist attack, has become a video terminal. Modleski draws attention to the fact that the wound which opens up in his stomach, into which the videocassette is inserted, is 'gaping' and 'vagina-like'. He has become – to cite Baudrillard – 'a pure screen, a switching centre for all the networks of influence'.[7]

Modleski – and Pete Boss in the 'Body Horror' issue of *Screen*[8] – see films such as these, in which there is a breakdown in distinctions between subject and object, as postmodern. The individual is a prey to everything, unable to produce the limits of his own body or being. In defining the postmodern, Boss argues that the 'categories of Otherness which traditionally functioned in the horror film are no longer adequate', a distinction which I think – in the light of Jardine's work – needs further qualification.[9] Traditional concepts of Otherness may currently be rejected (or embraced?), yet they may well emerge in a new form. It is relevant to note that the male protagonist of *Videodrome* also inserts his gun into the vagina-like wound in his stomach – his gun as symbolic phallus, like the cassette, signifies a different narrative, one in which he is man violating himself-as-woman. Significantly, his desire to experiment with 'Videodrome' was aroused by the masochistic desires of his female lover. He eventually takes her desires as his own. Clearly, one way of analysing the process in which man becomes woman is to regard it, from a male perspective, as the ultimate scenario of powerlessness, the ultimate violation of the body. In *Alien* the scenes in which man 'conceives' and gives birth through his stomach are represented as major scenarios of horror: the oral 'impregnation' of the man, the details of the birth scene, his pain, the savage tearing apart of his stomach, the horrified faces of the crew – all of these are shown in graphic detail.

In Cronenberg's more recent film, *The Fly*, a witty pastiche of the horror genre, 'becoming woman' is represented as a true metamorphosis comparable to the one in Kafka's novel. When a woman appears on the scene, the male scientist suddenly realizes why his experiments are not working – he is ignorant of the flesh, the body. Woman signifies carnal pleasure: man is intellectual, remote from the body. She awakens his libido, he is able to progress with his research. Not until he begins the metamorphosis does he experience bodily pleasures to the full. Through the metaphor of the body, the film draws parallels between the woman and the fly – reinforced by the nightmare in which she gives birth to a gigantic maggot. The film plays continually with audience expectations of 'bad taste' and always manages to go one step further. In the final scene the connections are developed through the *mise-en-scène*. The metamorphosis is complete and the giant insect advances menacingly towards the 'castrated' male victim (he has lost several limbs), recalling a similar scene from *The Incredible Shrinking Man* in which the hero falls victim to a giant black spider – compared through crosscutting with his wife. Through the early stages of the metamorphosis, the fly is referred to as the 'Brundle-fly' – it is a cross between man and fly. Not until the metamorphosis is complete does man fully signify the female – a monstrous fetishized insect. Interestingly, Jardine in her discussion of the process of becoming woman in the texts of French male writers, particularly Deleuze and Guattari, also refers to a metamorphosis:

> For what is involved here is *le devenir femme de tout le monde*, the becoming woman of everyone, everything, the whole world. With D & G, 'to become woman' is less a metaphor for describing a certain social or textual process than a true metamorphosis – one thinks of Kafka's Gregor Samsa waking up as a bug.[10]

Notes

1. Alice Jardine, *Gynesis: Configurations of Woman and Modernity*, Ithaca, NY: Cornell University Press 1985.
2. Ibid., pp. 88–9.
3. For further discussion of this question, see Barbara Creed, '*Alien* and the Monstrous-Feminine' in this volume.
4. Jean-François Lyotard, 'A Response to Kenneth Frampton' in *Postmodernism*, London: ICA 1986.
5. Jardine, p. 100.
6. Tania Modleski, 'The Terror of Pleasure: the Contemporary Horror Film' in Tania Modleski, ed., *Studies in Entertainment: Critical Approaches to Mass Culture*, Bloomington: Indiana University Press 1986.
7. Jean Baudrillard, 'The Ecstasy of Communication' in Hal Foster, ed., *The Anti-Aesthetic*, Port Townsend: Bay Press 1983, p. 133.
8. Pete Boss, 'Vile Bodies and Bad Medicine', *Screen*, vol. 27, no. 1, 1986. See also Scott Bukatman, 'Who Programs You?', in this volume.
9. Boss, p. 24.
10. Jardine, pp. 214–15.

18

Feminist Futures: A Generic Study

Anne Cranny-Francis

The intertexts of a contemporary practice of feminist science fiction cinema would include: science fiction writing and its generic conventions; feminist cultural practice; and cinema itself – particularly science fiction film and feminist film – as a set of discursive and signifying practices.

Science fiction writing offers the politically committed author a number of possibilities via the conventions which constitute it as a genre. Like all fictional (sub)genres, science fiction is a composite of conventions negotiated by writers and readers with varying degrees of orthodoxy. In other words, a writer (and a reader) may engage with the contemporary articulation of generic conventions in a literal, non-transgressive, way, so constructing a text which is orthodox – generically, and therefore discursively. And since the discursive practice of most generic forms is essentially conservative, the text which is thus unproblematically inflected will usually be politically conservative as well.

Or writers may challenge the conventions, thereby problematizing the text and its reading. Generic conventions are themselves, of course, sites of/for ideological contestation; so that when writers engage with the conventions, they also necessarily engage in an ideological textual practice. For example, a particular convention may be deployed slightly differently from the way it is traditionally or ordinarily used, with a number of possible consequences. Firstly, such a practice may *denaturalize* that convention, making visible its discursive operation. Secondly, it may *confront* readers with their own expectations, revealing these as discursively constructed and motivated. Thirdly, as a negotiation of signifying practices and meanings, it may produce wholly *new meanings*, new knowledge. Readers may thereby be positioned discursively in a new space, realigned in relation to their former discursive position – a realignment which readers must then renegotiate in their own terms. This almost inevitably entails a shift of subject position.

Recent feminist science fiction writing offers precisely this kind of challenge to the genre. Feminist writers rework or redeploy generic conventions in ways which foreground their normative operation, whilst also enacting a different, feminist, discourse. The reader is discursively repositioned, and so implicated in a renegotiation of her/his own subject positioning (subjectivity) – which in the final instance may or may not align with the discourse (feminist) enacted in the text.

The conventions of science fiction writing were themselves originally a renegotiation of those of another genre, literary gothic. When Mary Shelley wrote her novel of scientific experimentation and horror, *Frankenstein*, and science – rather than magic or devilry – resulted in the automatization of the first man-made man, the genre of science fiction was also born. One of *Frankenstein*'s strategies which was to become a convention of the genre was the narrative use of, or reference to, science and/or technology. In *Frankenstein*, scientific experimentation devoid of social responsibility leads to the making of a monster. In other words, Shelley's narrative use of science and technology is also an interrogation of scientific discourse, made explicit through an investigation of its alignment with gender discourse. Victor Frankenstein's Promethean act is the appropriation of a power which resides not with the gods, but with women. *Frankenstein* enacts the appropriation of maternity by patriarchy, and here maternity's circumscription by patriarchal ideology results in monstrous neglect and in pathologization of women themselves. Science and technology, in *Frankenstein*, are patriarchal constructs.

Science fiction writers after Shelley were not always so politically radical. H.G. Wells, a Fabian socialist, did use scientific achievements – like the time machine – to construct a fictional explanation of bourgeois attitudes of his time. On the other hand, Jules Verne used science simply as a prop for conventional stories of adventure and heroism, stories which enact a conservative discursive formation. The Wells-Verne split represents a major bifurcation in the discursive operation of science fiction. From Verne comes the high-tech science fiction of the first part of this century, enamoured of the power of whizz-bang technology and devoid of any concern with its social implications. This (symptomatically named) 'hard' science fiction writing unproblematically enacts the dominant discursive formation. In these texts scientific discourse is essentially a patriarchal, bourgeois and white imperialist way of knowing and manipulating the world. In the 'soft', or sociological, science fiction of Wells and his followers, however, scientific discourse may be inflected in the cause of social criticism. That is, science may operate as a means of displacement from the tyranny of the everyday, from common sense, and thus may de/reconstruct hegemonic ways of knowing and manipulating the world. If high-tech 'hard' science fiction is the fiction of the nuclear age, sociological science fiction belongs to the postnuclear, postmodern, age.

Feminist writers have worked principally with soft science fiction. 'Toys for the boys' science fiction is patently patriarchal and almost invariably conservative on all fronts. Only one feminist writer has worked successfully with hard science fiction – and she, significantly, published under a male pseudonym, James Tiptree Jr (Alice Sheldon). Sheldon's texts enact patriarchal discourses of various kinds, but then deconstruct them.[1] The majority of feminist science fiction writers use science and technology as narrative elements which facilitate a social critique removed from the constraints of the everyday, from the dominant discursive formation. As Pamela Sargent writes:

> Only SF and fantasy literature can show us women in entirely new or strange surroundings. It can explore what we might become if and when the present restrictions on our lives vanish, or show us new problems and restrictions that might arise. It can show us the remarkable woman as normal where past literature shows her as the exception. Will we become more like men, ultimately indistinguishable from them with all their faults and virtues, or will we bring new concerns and values to society, perhaps changing men in the process? How will biological advances, and the greater control they will bring us over our bodies, affect us?[2]

For many writers – and indeed film makers – science is a strategy which produces this effect of estrangement. In films as diverse as *The Day the Earth Stood Still* (1951), *2001: A Space Odyssey* (1968), *Silent Running* (1971) and *Star Wars* (1976), high technology produces a fictional setting very different in appearance from the spectator's own world. Not that such estrangement is necessarily politically radical: it may simply give a futuristic gloss to a dominant discursive formation. But as Sargent notes, it can still have a liberating effect.

This connects with another of Mary Shelley's textual strategies which have entered into the conventions of the science fiction genre: displacement in time and/or space. Shelley's narrative is set in the writer's past, the eighteenth century, in a series of exotic locations – continental Europe, the Orkneys, an ice-becalmed ship near the Arctic. These displacements function to locate Frankenstein's terrible experiments ambiguously, preventing realist readings in which the narrative's premises could be dismissed as impossible or implausible. This kind of displacement was already familiar in the gothic tradition, in which all sorts of terrible (and often salacious) events took place in the previous century, in another place (often, for an English readership, continental Europe).

In the work of Wells and Verne, however, this displacement is inflected in distinct ways, again with ideological implications. Verne, not surprisingly, tended towards realism; whilst Wells would project his narrative thousands of years into the future or onto other planets, thereby representing his own society with its ideological operations revealed rather than concealed, naturalized, in 'commonsense' discourses. Feminist science fiction writers have adopted Wellsian strategies to good effect: displacing narratives into other times and/or places can strip the patriarchal practices of contemporary society of their naturalizing discourses. In Ursula LeGuin's *The Left Hand of Darkness*, for example, a patriarchal male character is placed in a non-patriarchal environment, in such a way that patriarchal discourse is exposed in operation. In Marge Piercy's *Woman On the Edge of Time*, the time traveller is a poor non-white woman who takes with her on her travels to another possible Earth the patriarchal (and racist) discourses by which she is described in her own time.

In *The Left Hand of Darkness*, LeGuin shows the operation of patriarchal discourse through a patriarchal male character; in *Woman On the Edge of Time*, Piercy does the same with the feminine subject of patriarchy. In a reversal of this strategy, a non-patriarchal character may be translated to a patriarchal environment, as in Joanna Russ's *The Female Man*. Russ uses narrative displacement to bring into the contemporary environment a character whose subjectivity is not formed within patriarchy – a non-patriarchal female subject. This character's responses to patriarchal subjects (male and female) denaturalize the patriarchal ideology which the latter take for granted: here, a non-patriarchal character demonstrates the formation and operation of the patriarchal subject.

The concept of the alien is also central to science fiction. As soon as science fiction narratives moved off-world (or even under-world), it was inevitable that characters from other worlds would appear; though there had in fact been an alien even before science fiction moved from the skin of the earth: it appeared first in *Frankenstein*. Dr Frankenstein's monstrous creation is the first science fiction alien, a creature totally new to this world, the great-great-great-grandfather of *Blade Runner*'s replicants and the cyborgs of the postmodern age. It is highly significant that these aliens – cyborgs, replicants, androids, and their patchwork ancestors – are man-made; for as such they expose the ideology of their makers – which is usually patriarchal, bourgeois, white supremacist. But their other function is to 'see' the society of the writer and the reader through different eyes, alien eyes; not with the eyes, from the perspective, the subject position, of the dominant discursive formation. Thus, for example, Frankenstein's creature analyses the class structure of the society in which he finds himself, offering a kind of proto-Marxian deconstruction of the appropriation of labour.[3] A century and a half later, the replicant Roy Batty in *Blade Runner* says to Chew, maker of eyes for Nexus-6 replicants, 'If only you could see what I've seen with your eyes'.

Because the alien is not formed within the ideology of its found world, it (she/he) is able to re-vision that world for the reader. The reader is invited to see, through alien eyes, a society's discursive practices in operation: through alien eyes, these practices no longer appear 'natural'. This, at least, is the possibility represented by the alien. The alien can in fact be conservative: its eyes might see with those of the dominant discursive formation, reinforcing the elision of contradictions within hegemonic ideology. In the film *Star Wars*, for example, the characters Luke Skywalker, Han Solo and Princess Leia enact a patriarchal, bourgeois (liberal humanist), white supremacist narrative in a setting uncannily similar to today's USA.

In feminist writing, however, the alien usually exposes patriarchal ideology in operation. The alien's deconstruction of contemporary patriarchy in *The Female Man* is one such instance; and in Ursula LeGuin's *The Dispossessed* an anarchist character travels to a patriarchal society on a neigbouring planet, where his non-sexist behaviour and his society in general are objects of curiosity and contempt. In Sonya Dorman's story 'When I Was Miss Dow' and in Carol Emshwiller's 'Sex and/or Mr Morrison', an alien's responses to patriarchal behaviour and constructions of gender reposition the reader as a feminist subject, inviting her to see patriarchal ideology in practice. In 'When I Was Miss Dow', an alien takes on the body of a woman and experiences her/its construction/representation by her patriarchal male employer. Initially, she/it observes this from the outside, and the man's attitudes seem pathetic and childish. But then the alien begins to adopt this representation as her/its own, and her self-image becomes dependent upon the employer's attention. Here the trajectory of the (metamorphic) alien character represents the construction of the (female) subject in patriarchal ideology.[4] Emshwiller's story is comparatively (and deceptively) simple: a naked man is merely described through alien eyes, demystifying the representation of the penis and its status as all-powerful signifier in patriarchal narratives.[5]

Woman as alien, the non-patriarchal alien in a patriarchal society, the patriarchal alien in a non-patriarchal society, the non-patriarchal alien experiencing the stress of positioning as a patriarchal subject – all are strategies used by feminist science fiction writers to deconstruct patriarchal ideology and its practice. Another characteristic strategy of recent feminist science fiction writing is a selfconscious use of narrative: this, too, can be traced back to *Frankenstein*, where multiple narratives enhance the novel's critiques of patriarchal and bourgeois discourses, and of contemporary scientific discourses. The creature's story deconstructs bourgeois discourse; Frankenstein's, by implication, that of science; in combination they offer a complex critique of patriarchy. The framing narrative of Walton constructs a further analysis of bourgeois ideology, relating it back to patriarchal assumptions encoded in scientific discourse.

Some recent feminist writings also develop their critiques of patriarchy in complex narrational strategies. *The Female Man*, for example, is a composite of four narratives, in whose interaction are foregrounded the formation of the subject in patriarchal ideology, her/his revisioning of that ideology, and the subsequent negotiation of a subjectivity which involves active resistance to, and intervention in, contemporary patriarchal discourse. A similar tactic is used in *Woman On the Edge of Time* to highlight the positioning of the individual as patriarchal subject and to motivate a renegotiation of this positioning.

Science fiction, then, embodies a number of generic conventions which may be drawn upon in the construction of a feminist text: a text, that is, which makes sense only when read from a feminist perspective, which positions the reader as feminist. Perhaps this is not surprising if it is recalled that the genre was itself invented by a woman who was a feminist, a feminist constructing a text about patriarchal exploitation. The conventions pioneered by Mary Shelley and still available to the contemporary feminist writer include: engagement with – and critique of – current scientific and technological discourses; narrative displacement in space and/or time; the character and viewpoint of the alien; and narrative structure complicated by intersecting or framing narratives.

These literary conventions suggest a range of possible directions for a feminist science fiction cinema – a genre which, save for isolated examples in the culturally marginal spheres of avant-garde and independent film, does not yet exist.[6] And yet a feminist practice of science fiction film could draw on a whole range of intertexts, including – but by no means confined to – the conventions of contemporary feminist science fiction writing, to transform both feminist cinema and science fiction cinema. One film which points the way towards such a practice is *Born In Flames* (1983), a feature written and directed by US film maker Lizzie Borden.

Born In Flames is set in a hypothetical near-future New York City, ten years after the world's first successful social democratic revolution. The narrative is activated by a marked deterioration in the status and opportunities of women as the new regime enters its second decade, and the formation of a Women's Army to fight these injustices. The film has 'the look of a documentary (after Chris Marker) and the feel of contemporary science fiction (the post-new wave science fiction of Samuel Delany, Joanna Russ, Alice Sheldon or Thomas Disch)'.[7] It has no central character in the classical sense, though the formation of an anti-government coalition between diverse groups of women (black, white, lesbian, straight, young, old, activist, intellectual) is precipitated by the death in custody of a leader of the Women's Army.

But there is much more to *Born In Flames* than a different sort of story in a different sort of a setting: it is, after all, cinema. Teresa de Lauretis argues that

> A social technology, a textual machine of representation – cinema, for example – is the semiotic apparatus in which the encounter [of subject, codes and social formation] takes place and the individual is addressed as subject; cinema is at once a material apparatus and a 'signifying practice' in which the subject is implicated, constructed, but not exhausted.[8]

Its deployment of cinematic codes, of film language, lends *Born In Flames* a 'writerly' quality which challenges the conventions of both science fiction cinema and women's cinema, proposing entirely new modes of subjectivity, an 'aesthetic of reception' rather than of textuality.[9] The signifying practices of cinema are deployed as an element of a de/re/construction not only of genre film, but also of its spectators. The text subverts the apparatus of cinema and establishes a viewing position from which the film makes sense (narratively, technologically) only in feminist terms.

The narrative of *Born In Flames* is multiple, complex, heterogeneous: the spectator is engaged neither by a classical cause-effect narrative logic nor by identification with characters, but by the film's very discursive multiplicity. The complex narrative, in combination with its setting in a 'parallel universe', constitutes a comment upon, an analysis of, not merely patriarchy but also the politics of the women's movement, women's cinema, even of science fiction cinema itself.

> This is a new mode of representation for the SF film: one that does not regress to the past, does not nostalgize, and does not complacently accept the present as the only place to live. It does indeed imagine a future – but one contiguous with the present, and in temporal and spatial relation to it. It is political and

empowering and has a momentum not 'transfixed' by excess scenography or caught up in an overwhelming and paralyzing material heterogeneity.[10]

The aesthetic of reception is not confined to this one film, nor indeed to women's cinema in general, but is fundamental to postmodernist cultural practice. The vigorous play with genres which characterizes postmodernist (film and other) texts is a concomitant of the collapse of modernist divisions between high and low culture, and of the breakdown of commodity fetishism (there is no need to fetishize what you can replace) in postindustrial capitalism.

A certain postmodern attitude reaches its populist zenith in the Hollywood science fiction film *Blade Runner* (1982). Structured entirely by its intertexts, this film is the late monopoly capitalist heir to Shelley's *Frankenstein. Blade Runner* tells the story of a band of renegade replicants, man-made beings, who return to their place of manufacture – a desperately polluted, dying, Earth – to find a way to prevent their own deaths: Nexus-6 replicants have built-in obsolescence, a four-year lifespan. The disposition of the replicant bodies, their representation as commodities (Combat Model, Pleasure Model, and so on), is a critique of the commodity system which has produced the decaying world they find on Earth. Replicant 'subjectivity' is a mirror of that world – replicants are given photographs and memories to convince them of their own, 'real' history. Finally, the central question of *Blade Runner* becomes: who is not a replicant?

In 'A Manifesto for Cyborgs', Donna Haraway writes about this collapse of the categories human and machine as the point at which the cyborg first appears, where boundaries are transgressed – where replicants are made. If the categories collapse, so too does the appropriation of one category by another – which may lead to 'the final imposition of a grid of control on the planet ... the final abstraction embodied in a Star Wars apocalypse waged in the name of defense ... the final appropriation of women's bodies in a masculinist orgy of war'. Alternatively, though, such a collapse of categories might produce a utopian world 'in which people are not afraid of their joint kinship with animals and machines, not afraid of permanent partial identities and contradictory standpoints'.[11] This cyborg consciousness, says Haraway, could extend to feminist practice – where there is also a necessity to live without fear of partial identities and contradictory standpoints, a need to avoid reproducing the dehistoricized, essentialist, category: Woman.

Haraway's conceptualization of the cyborg body is extended, in her manifesto, to a postmodern conceptualization of pleasure – located in an interplay of surfaces, intertexts and generic dialogisms. The subjectivity proposed by this interplay is decentred and unstable, but also infinitely accessible: it cannot be phallogocentric, for there is no centre. This aesthetic of intertextuality, which involves an interactive practice of recognition and transformation, is also an aesthetic of reception. The text proposes no integrative, integrated, seamless narrative; but a fragmented and diverse positionality whose political counterpart is, in Haraway's terms, affinity, not identity. Such an aesthetic, Teresa de Lauretis has suggested, is essential to an accommodation of differences between women, the recognition of which must be the next step in the development of a feminist cultural practice which is neither Anglocentric nor bourgeois.

Feminist science fiction cinema will therefore engage with contemporary science fiction writing, with feminist theories, with film as technology and signifying practice, and with postmodernist textual (and intertextual) practices. All of these offer possibilities for inscription, invision, in a film practice which would be characterized by a play across a matrix of surfaces: pleasures and politics as interplay, the flip-flop of the integrated circuit constituting the transgressive communication of a diverse – and yet inclusive – feminist positioning.

Notes

1. See, for example, James Tiptree Jr, 'The Women Men Don't See', in Robert Silverberg, ed., *Warm Worlds and Otherwise*, New York: Ballantine 1975.
2. Pamela Sargent, ed., *Women of Wonder: Science Fiction Stories by Women About Women*, Harmondsworth: Penguin 1978, p. 48.
3. Mary Shelley, *Frankenstein* (1818), London: Dent 1963, chapter XIII.
4. Sonya Dorman, 'When I Was Miss Dow' in Pamela Sargent, ed., *Women of Wonder*.
5. Carol Emshwiller, 'Sex and/or Mr Morrison', ibid.
6. Apart from Lizzie Borden's *Born In Flames*, which is discussed in this essay, possible examples include Valie Export's *Invisible Adversaries* (1976); Sandra Lahire's *Terminals* (1986) and *Uranium Hex* (1987); and Lis Rhodes's *The Cold Draught* (1989).
7. Teresa de Lauretis, 'Aesthetic and Feminist Theory: Rethinking Women's Cinema', in E. Deidre Pribram, ed., *Female Spectators: Looking at Film and Television*, London: Verso 1988, pp. 183–4.
8. Teresa de Lauretis, 'Through the Looking-glass' in Teresa de Lauretis and Stephen Heath, eds, *The Cinematic Apparatus*, New York: St Martin's Press 1980, pp. 187–8.
9. Teresa de Lauretis, *Technologies of Gender: Essays on Theory, Film and Fiction*, Bloomington: Indiana University Press 1987, pp. 141.
10. Vivian Sobchack, *Screening Space: The American Science Fiction Film*, New York: Ungar 1987, p. 305.
11. Donna Haraway, 'A Manifesto for Cyborgs: Science, Technology and Socialist-Feminism in the 1980s', *Socialist Review*, no. 80, 1985, p. 72.

Further Reading

Alliez, Eric and Feher, Michel, 'Notes on the Sophisticated City', *Zone*, nos 1/2, [n.d.], pp. 41–55.

Amelio, Ralph, J., *Hal in the Classroom: Science Fiction Films*, Dayton, OH: Pflaum Publishing 1974.

Annas, Pamela, 'Science Fiction Film Criticism in the US', *Science Fiction Studies*, vol. 7, no. 3, 1980, pp. 323–9.

Anobile, Richard, J., ed., *Alien*, London: Futura Publications 1979.

Balsamo, Anne, 'Reading Cyborgs Writing Feminism', *Communication*, vol. 10, nos. 3/4, 1988, pp. 331–44.

Bergstrom, Janet, 'Androids and Androgyny', *Camera Obscura*, no. 15, 1986, pp. 37–64.

Best, Steven, 'In the Ditritus [sic] of Hi-technology', *Jump Cut*, no. 34, 1989, pp. 19–26.

Brain, Bonnie, 'Saviors and Scientists: Extraterrestrials in Recent Science Fiction Films', *Et Cetera: A Review of General Semantics*, vol. 40, no. 2, 1983, pp. 218–29.

Broderick, Mick, *Nuclear Movies: A Filmography*, Northcote, Vic: Post-Modern 1988.

Bundtzen, Lynda K., 'Monstrous Mothers: Medusa, Grendel And Now Alien', *Film Quarterly*, vol. 40, no. 3, 1987, pp. 11–17.

Chevrier, Yves, '*Blade Runner*: Or, The Sociology of Anticipation', *Science Fiction Studies*: vol. 11, no. 1, 1984, pp. 50–60.

Codell, Julie F., 'Murphy's Law, Robocop's Body, and Capitalism's Work', *Jump Cut*, no. 34, 1989, pp. 12–19.

Creed, Barbara, 'From Here to Modernity: Feminism and Postmodernism', *Screen*, vol. 28, no. 2, 1987, pp. 47–67.

Creed, Barbara, 'Horror and the Monstrous-Feminine: An Imaginary Abjection', *Screen*, vol. 27, no. 1, 1986, pp. 44–70.

Davis-Genelli, Tom and Davis-Genelli, Lyn, '*Alien*: A Myth of Survival', *Film/Psychology Review*, vol. 4, no. 2, 1980, pp. 235–40.

Dean, Joan, F., 'Between *2001* and *Star Wars*', *Journal of Popular Film and Television*, vol. 7, no. 1, 1978, pp. 32–41.

Dempsey, Michael, '*Blade Runner*', *Film Quarterly*, vol. 36, no. 2, 1982–3, pp. 33–8.

Dervin, Daniel, 'Primal Conditions and Conventions: The Genres of Comedy and Science Fiction', *Film/Psychology Review*, vol. 4, no. 1, 1980, pp. 115–47.

Desser, David, '*Blade Runner*: Science Fiction and Transcendence', *Literature/Film Quarterly*, vol. 13, no. 3, 1985, pp. 172–9.

Doll, Susan and Faller, Greg, '*Blade Runner* and Genre: Film Noir and Science Fiction', *Literature/Film Quarterly*, vol. 14, no. 2, 1986, pp. 89–100.

Ellington, Jane Elizabeth and Critelli, Joseph W., 'Analysis of a Modern Myth: the "Star Trek" Series', *Extrapolation*, vol. 24, no. 3, 1983, pp. 241–50.

Elkins, Charles, ed., 'Symposium on *Alien*', *Science Fiction Studies*, vol. 7, no. 3, 1980, pp. 278–304.

Entman, Robert and Seymour, Francie, 'Close Encounters with the Third Reich', *Jump Cut*, no. 18, 1978, pp. 3–6.

Fitting, Peter, 'Futurecop: the Neutralization of Revolt in *Blade Runner*', *Science Fiction Studies*, vol. 14, no. 3, 1987, pp. 340–54.

Franklin, H. Bruce, 'Future Imperfect', *American Film*, vol. 8, no. 5, 1983, pp. 47–9, 75–6.

Glass, Fred, 'The "New Bad Future": *Robocop* and 1980s' Sci-Fi Films', *Science as Culture*, no. 5, 1989, pp. 7–49.

Gordon, Andrew, '*Back to the Future*: Oedipus as Time Traveller', *Science Fiction Studies*, vol. 14, no. 3, 1987, pp. 372–85.

Gordon, Andrew, '*The Empire Strikes Back*: Monsters from the Id', *Science Fiction Studies*, vol. 7, no. 3, 1980, pp. 313–18.

Gordon, Andrew, '*E.T.* as Fairy Tale', *Science Fiction Studies*, vol. 10, no. 3, 1983, pp. 298–305.

Gordon, Andrew, 'Science Fiction Film Criticism: The Postmodern Always Rings Twice', *Science Fiction Studies*, vol. 14, no. 3, 1987, pp. 386–91.

Goscilo, Margaret, 'Deconstructing *The Terminator*', *Film Criticism*, vol. 12, no. 2, 1987–8, pp. 37–52.

Greenberg, Harvey R., 'Fembo: *Aliens*' Intentions', *Journal of Popular Film and TV*, vol. 15, no. 4, 1988, pp. 165–71.

Greenberg, Harvey R., 'The Fractures of Desire: Psychoanalytic Notes on *Alien* and the Contemporary "Cruel" Horror Film', *The Psychoanalytic Review*, vol. 70, no. 2, 1983, pp. 241–67.

Greenberg, Harvey R., 'In Search of Spock: A Psychoanalytic Inquiry', *Journal of Popular Film and Television*, vol. 12, no. 2, 1984, pp. 52–65.

Greenberg, Harvey R., 'Reimagining the Gargoyle: Psychoanalytic Notes on *Alien*', *Camera Obscura*, no. 15, 1986, pp. 87–108.

Hark, Ina Rae, '"Star Trek" and Television's Moral Universe', *Extrapolation*, vol. 20, no. 1, 1979, pp. 20–37.

Heung, Marina, 'Why E.T. Must Go Home: The New Family in American Cinema', *Journal of Popular Film and Television*, vol. 11, no. 2, 1983, pp. 79–84.

Higashi, Sumiko, '*Invasion of the Body Snatchers*: Pods Then and Now', *Jump Cut*, nos. 24/25, 1981, pp. 3–4.

Jameson, Fredric, 'SF Novels/SF Film', *Science Fiction Studies*, vol. 7, no. 3, 1980, pp. 319–22.

Kellner, Douglas, Leibowitz, Flo, and Ryan, Michael, '*Blade Runner*: a Diagnostic Critique', *Jump Cut*, no. 29, 1984, pp. 6–8.

LaValley, Albert J., 'Traditions of Trickery: the Role of Special Effects in the Science Fiction Film' in Slusser and Rabkin, eds. pp. 141–58.

Lehman, Peter and Dasso, Don, 'Special Effects in *Star Wars*', *Wide Angle*, vol. 1, no. 1, 1979, pp. 72–7.

Markey, Constance, 'Birth and Rebirth in Current Fantasy Films', *Film Criticism*, vol. 7, no. 1, 1982, pp. 14–25.

Mead, Gerald and Appelbaum, Sam, '*Westworld*: Fantasy and Exploitation', *Jump Cut*, no. 7, 1975, pp. 12–13.

Nagl, Manfred, 'The Science Fiction Film in Historical Perspective', *Science Fiction Studies*, vol. 10, no. 3, 1983, pp. 262–77.

Naureckas, Jim, '*Aliens*: Mother and the Teeming Hordes', *Jump Cut*, no. 32, 1987, pp. 1, 4.

Necakou, Lillian, '*The Terminator*: Beyond Classical Hollywood Narrative', *Cineaction*, no. 8, 1987, pp. 84–6.

Niogret, Hubert, 'Un peu de magie par nécessité et par plaisir', *Positif*, no. 273, 1983, pp. 22–8.

Pielke, Robert G., '*Star Wars* vs *2001*: A Question of Identity', *Extrapolation*, vol. 24, no. 2, 1983, pp. 143–55.

Roth, Lane, 'Death and Rebirth in *Star Trek II: The Wrath of Khan*', *Extrapolation*, vol. 28, no. 2, 1987, pp. 155–66.

Roth, Lane, '*Vraisemblance* and the Western Setting in Contemporary Science Fiction Film', *Literature/Film Quarterly*, vol. 13, no. 3, 1985, pp. 180–6.

Rushing, Janice Hocker, '*E.T.* as Rhetorical Transcendence', *Quarterly Journal of Speech*, vol. 71, no. 2, 1985, pp. 188–203.

Sammons, Todd H., '*Return of the Jedi*: Epic Graffiti', *Science Fiction Studies*, vol. 14, no. 3, 1987, pp. 355–71.

Scigaj, Leonard M., 'Bettelheim, Castaneda and Zen: the Powers Behind the Force in *Star Wars*', *Extrapolation*, vol. 22, no. 3, 1981, pp. 213–36.

Shelton, Robert, 'Rendezvous with HAL: *2001/2010*', *Extrapolation*, vol. 28, no. 3, 1987, pp. 255–68.

Slusser, George E. and Rabkin, Eric S., eds, *Shadows of the Magic Lamp: Fantasy and Science Fiction Film*, Carbondale: Southern Illinois University Press 1985.

Sobchack, Vivian, 'Child/Alien/Father: Patriarchal Crisis and Generic Exchange', *Camera Obscura*, no. 15, 1986, pp. 7–34.

Sobchack, Vivian, 'Cities on the Edge of Time: The Urban Science Fiction Film', *East-West Film Journal*, vol. 3, no. 1 (1988), pp. 4–19.

Sobchack, Vivian, *Screening Space: The American Science Fiction Film*, New York: Ungar 1987.

Sofia, Zoe, 'Exterminating Fetuses: Abortion, Disarmament, and the Sexo-Semiotics of Extraterrestrialism', *Diacritics*, vol. 14, no. 2, 1984, pp. 47–59.

Strick, Philip, 'The Age of the Replicant', *Sight and Sound*, vol. 51, no. 3, 1982, pp. 168–72.

Strick, Philip, 'Future States', *Monthly Film Bulletin*, no. 661, 1989, pp. 37–41.

Tarratt, Margaret, 'Monsters from the Id' in Barry K. Grant, ed., *Film Genre*, Metuchen, NJ: Scarecrow Press 1977, pp. 161–81.

Telotte, J.P., 'The Dark Side of the Force: *Star Wars* and the Science Fiction Tradition', *Extrapolation*, vol. 24, no. 3, 1983, pp. 216–26.

Telotte, J.P., 'Human Artifice and the Science Fiction Film, *Film Quarterly*, vol. 36, no. 3, 1983, pp. 44–51.

Williams, Tony, 'Close Encounters of the Authoritarian Kind', *Wide Angle*, vol. 5, no. 4, 1983, pp. 22–9.